Gerard McBurney

May 97

D1615131

RUSSIAN
MUSIC

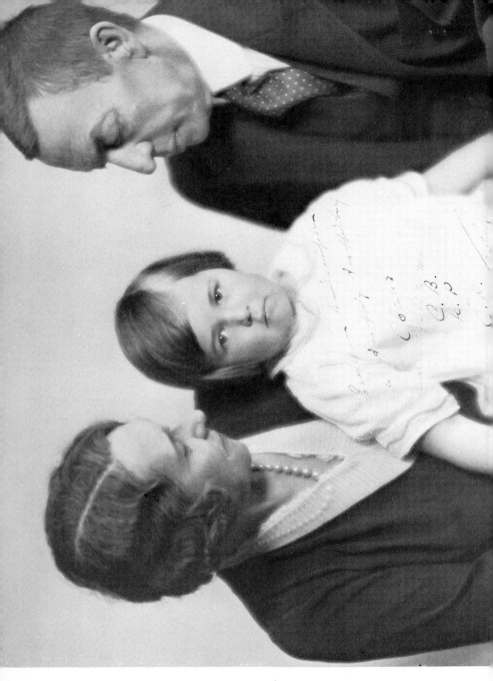

Rachmaninov with his wife and grand-daughter. Inscribed to Katherine V. and Alfred A. Swan, April 1931.

RUSSIAN MUSIC

AND ITS SOURCES IN CHANT AND FOLK-SONG

ALFRED J. SWAN

4, 5 & 6 SOHO SQUARE LONDON

© 1973 ALFRED J. SWAN

Published in 1973 by
JOHN BAKER (PUBLISHERS) LTD
4, 5 & 6 Soho Square
London W1V 6AD

ISBN 0 212 98421 7

Printed in Great Britain by
T. AND A. CONSTABLE LTD
Hopetoun Street, Edinburgh

Contents

Illustrations   7

Acknowledgements   10

Foreword   11

Preface   15

1 The sources   19
    Folk-songs   19
    Liturgical chants   29

2 The makers of folk-songs and liturgical
    melodies   39
    The makers of the Znamenny *Chant*   39
    Russian polyphony in the liturgical books   45

3 The eighteenth century   48
    The forces of the new music   48
    The eighteenth century   51

4 Glinka   60

5 The Balakirev Circle   73
    Russia in 1855   73
    The formation of the Balakirev Circle   76

6 Moussorgsky and Rimsky-Korsakov,
    1868-81   91

7 Tchaikovsky and Borodin   105
    Tchaikovsky (to 1881)   105
    Borodin (1833-87)   110

8 Church music and the Imperial Chapel   115

9 Secular music in the eighties—the Belaieff
    Circle   121

Contents

10 Return to the sources   135
     Precursors   135
     The main sweep   139

11 Scriabin and Rachmaninov, 1886-1903   147

12 The Third Renaissance, 1903-15   155
     St Petersburg   156
     Moscow   166

13 Beginnings of modernism   181
     Karatygin and the evenings of contemporary
     music   181
     Prokofiev (to 1920)   183

14 War and revolution   188
     The war years (1914-17)   188
     After 1917   191

15 The eclipse of modernism   196

16 Conclusion   203

Appendices

I Russian folk-song collections from the beginning of the collection era   206

II Stages of clarification and readability of the old (Kriuk) notations   207

III The wedding rite of the village Gorodishche, Pskov province   210

     Bibliography   217

     Index   221

Illustrations

PLATES

Rachmaninov with his wife and grand-daughter *frontispiece*

Between pages 64-5
1. Manuscript without cinnabar marks
2. Group of women singers of Pechory (Maria Spies is kneeling at the right, Liza Ukatova sits in the centre)
3. Russian peasant women singers of Pskov
4. Piatnitzky choir recording, 1911
5. Eugenie Lineva
6. Nicholas Findeisen
7. Ivan Gardner, 1970
8. Maxim Brajnikov
9. Nicholas Lvov
10. Ivan Rupini (real name Rupin, Italianized for Moscow)
11. Prince Vladimir Odoyevsky, 1844
12. Mili Balakirev

Between pages 80-1
13. César Cui in the mid 1870s
14. Modest Moussorgsky
15. The Rubinsteins: Anton, the elder; Nicholas, the younger
16. Nicholas Rimsky-Korsakov
17. Alexander Borodin
18. Ludmilla Shestakova

Between pages 144-5
19. Tchaikovsky in the 1870s
20. Steven Smolensky

21. Tertius Filippov, Folk-song collector
22. Herman Laroche
23. Alexander Glazunov, a portrait by A. M. Lubinov, 1928
24. George Dyutch, Anatole Liadov, Nicholas Lavrov
25. Maxim Gorky, Vladimir Stassov, Ilya Repin, Mrs Repina, 1904
26. Boris Assafiev (pseudonym, Igor Glebov)

Between pages 160-1
27. Ivan Lapshin, philosopher and art critic, 1935
28. Anton Preobrajensky
29. The first page of Rachmaninov's *Concert Spiritual*
30. Glinka
31. Stravinsky at the Hôtel du Chatellard, 1913
32. Musical gathering at the Lamm's, 1923
33. Nicolas Medtner with wife Anna and Alfred Swan, 1948

EXAMPLES IN THE TEXT

1. Kniga Golubinaya, The Dove Book, Riazan province   23
2. *Vaizay s prilejaniem (Gaze with attention).* Two variants of the same song from different parts of Russia   23
3. *Tausen (The God of the Fields)*, Riazan province   24
4. *Sneshki belye, pushisty (White fluffy snow)*, Archangel province   25
5. *Po seyan, seniushkam (On the porch, the little porch)*, from an old Cossack wedding rite   27
6. *Da svaty moi (So, my marriage brokers).* Listopadov   27
7. *Da u Lebedia*   28
8. *Troparion*, eighth echos, *znamenny* chant, from *The Triodion*, 1899   37
9. Four trichords of *znamenny* chant   37
10. *Gospel Sticheron* by Feodor the Christian, echos I (beginning)   43
11. *Cherubim Song*, from MS of the late seventeenth century   47
12. Melody ascribed to Empress Elizabeth, harmonized by Prach, 1790   57
13. Variations on a folk-song, by Ivan Khandoshkin   59
14. *Loochina (The Spill)*, from the Kashin Collection, 1833   61

15. (*a*) Mozart; (*b*) Glinka, *Life for the Czar* — 65
16. *Russlan*, prologue, Bayan's song, Glinka — 68
17. *Roundelay*, Balakirev folk-song collection of 1866 — 83
18. *Prayer*, Moussorgsky, 1865 — 85
19. Russian folk-song from the Prokunin, 1872-3 — 108
20. (*a*) Nineteenth century court chant from the Bakhmetev Ordinarium 1869. (*b*) *Znamenny* chant of the seventeenth century from the synodal square note notation Obikhod — 117
21. *Russian soldier's song* from Balakirev album, 1866, by Rimsky-Korsakov — 125
22. *Fifty Songs of the Russian People*, 1902, Liadov — 143
23. *Ten Arrangements from the Obikhod*, Liadov — 144
24. *Christmas Kontakion*, Kastalsky, *znamenny* chant harmonized in 1902 — 145
25. *Sadko*, Tableau One, Rimsky-Korsakov — 157
26. *Symphony*, *No. 1*, Scherzo, 1898, Balakirev — 160
27. *Vision*, 1903-4, Balakirev, words by Khomiakov — 161
28. *Vespers*, opus 37, No. VII, Rachmaninov — 175
29. *Winter Night*, 1903, Medtner — 180
30. *Why, O Willow, are you bending?* 1912, Medtner — 180

Acknowledgements

But for the help received from my Russian friends and colleagues, the writing of this book would have been a far more difficult task. I am particularly indebted to IVAN B. SEMENOV, a noted collector of musical antiquities and owner of a museum in Leningrad, for supplying me with numerous books, music, and pictures, for checking references and showing a constant interest in the progress of my work; to MAXIM V. BRAJNIKOV, mention of whose invaluable research has frequently been made in the ensuing pages, for a transcription of a Cherubim Song from Codex 182 of the collection of the State Historical Museum in Moscow (end of the seventeenth century); to IVAN A. GARDNER for a memoir of S. Smolensky from the archives of Munich University; to KATHERINE N. ALEXEYEVNA for a photostat of Rachmaninov's 'Concert Spiritual' from the Central Museum of Musical Culture in Moscow, and to IZALY J. ZEMTZOVSKY to whose books on folklore I have had to have frequent recourse.

To Haverford College I owe special thanks for the help I have received with the copying of the various versions of the manuscript and other technical assistance.

ALFRED J. SWAN

With the death of my husband on 2 October 1970, I was left with the task of completing this manuscript for publication. In my work, I am greatly indebted to Professor FRANKLIN ZIMMERMAN for his many hours spent in editing, and SERGE JENOUK for advice and translations; any mistakes that may have crept in are, I am positive, my own. I should like to dedicate this book to my son Alexis, as my husband wished, knowing that they share the same spiritual values.

JANE BALLARD SWAN
Haverford, June 1971

Foreword

I find it difficult to know from which angle I should write this foreword to my uncle's book. Shall I look up at him, as I did at the age of fourteen, when he courteously listened to my very intermediate piano playing and advised my father about my future career? Then Uncle Alia appeared an awe-inspiring, somewhat austere figure—I was glad he left the room as I did my feeble rag-time improvizations. Shall I recall him as I grew up to know him as a violinist, prolific composer and pianist, when the austerity had vanished and I began to understand the scholar in him? Shall I recall the year when I discovered that he and I shared a parallel interest in folk music and religious music—that his discovery, that the *znamenny* chant in the Russian villages underlay Russian church music, was as exciting to him as was my discovery that Pete Seeger and Sydney Carter were to underlay the new hymns of tomorrow? Or shall I recall him (with Jane) as my gay, humorous, light-hearted host in Haverford College, at work on his latest composition, or his newest book, ready to go anywhere to hear a new piece by one of his students, totally empathizing with their deepest instincts? These pictures flash in my memory, but clearly, they are all side-angles—today I have to welcome him as author of this absorbing book, *Russian Music*. I never dreamed I should be doing so after his death, as he grew visibly younger, more contemporary and forward-looking with every passing year.

Russian music, as my uncle writes on every page of this book, was part of his bloodstream—irrelevant that his ancestors were British. His whole approach to life was formulated by his student years in St Petersburg, imbibing every aspect of Russian musical life. The way he refers to

' the commotion at one of the Siloti occasions on the night when Rasputin was shot. It so happened that in the box next to me . . .'

is enough to show how close music was to his heart. The mad
monk may have toppled an empire, but it did not upset my
uncle's judgment of that concert. But am I right to say my
uncle's British ancestors were irrelevant? From the Russian
soil, he appeared for an intensive musical three years in Oxford,
where the story goes that he decided on Exeter as opposed to
Balliol because it was easier to get the piano through the door.
After some literally fabulous experiences during the war and
revolution—when he evacuated nearly a thousand St Petersburg children to a quieter place on the Volga, was pushed back
to Vladivostok, finally taking the children home, two years
later, via Yokohama and the USA—my uncle settled in the
Quaker corridor of Pennsylvania, in Swarthmore and later
Haverford Colleges. Is this not an international Russian writing
here, the sort of person who can consider Russian music both
from within and from without?

I find his *znamenny* explorations fascinating and eagerly
await more research on this subject if it ever falls into my hands.
I'd like my uncle's pen to be the broom that cleans up Russian
church music. All his life he fought the weak acceptance of
nineteenth-century harmonic clichés; and if, as I hope, this
book will be translated into different languages (especially
Russian) this purging can continue. It is scarcely credible that
when my uncle arranged the traditional Russian chants in a
more personal chromatic idiom, he encountered, from the
old-fashioned choir masters, the sort of reaction Stravinsky
received in 1913, with *The Rite of Spring*. Just before writing
these lines, I listened to a record of Russian church music by
various composers, including Kastalsky, Rimsky-Korsakov,
Rachmaninov and two small pieces by Alfred Swan. Accuse
me of nepotism in reverse, my uncle's 'new arrangements' are
the only ones I can bear to listen to a second time. He was
moving ahead, you see, and music *has* to do that.

What about the content of this book itself? I find the personal
reminiscences enthralling (I can't think how he restrained
himself from saying that he once slept in Rachmaninov's night
shirt); I like to re-live, with him, my own admiration for Glinka,
Moussorgsky, Borodin and Balakirev; I enjoy the evocative
illustrations and certain touches amuse me exceedingly—like
learning there was a singer called Loggin-the-Cow and that

César Cui was an expert in fortification; I like my uncle's stand for his friend, Medtner, because Medtner has yet to find his proper recognition; and I've read with fascination how the 'Beatle' Scriabin magnetized my uncle and his friends. It matters not a whit to me that the author's intuitions stop just short of the new generation of Russian composers. Sufficient is the unexpected insight into the older generation, and through them right into the heart of the Middle Ages.

I hope this book will range far beyond the critic who wants to use it to check the 'Russian music' entry in *Grove's Dictionary*, or the student who wants to look up Liadov's dates. It took my uncle seventy-nine years of life in three continents to see his way clearly, and it took my aunt's total devotion to his work to see this book into print after his death. I thank them both.

DONALD SWANN

Preface

In one of his diaries, dated 27 June 1888, Tchaikovsky, speaking of Glinka, voiced his utter amazement at the way in which this 'composer of dilettante music' produced a first opera that might be placed alongside those of Mozart and Beethoven. He was also impressed by Glinka's symphonic poem *Kamarinskaya* in which every bar was the product of the highest creative power:

Nearly fifty years have passed since it was written. Many Russian symphonic works have appeared; we can almost say that there is a real Russian symphonic school. And what do we see? It is all contained in the *Kamarinskaya*, just as the whole oak is contained in the acorn. And for long, Russian composers will draw from this rich source, as much time and strength is needed to exhaust all its riches.

In pursuing this point we ask, 'Wherein lies the source of the *Kamarinskaya* and where are all its riches hidden?' There is only one answer: in the Russian folk-song and the old liturgical chant.

The histories of Russian music that have been written fall into several categories. In the first are the works of those who concerned themselves primarily with the nineteenth century. It was assumed that before Glinka, Russian musical culture was a vast desert over which only foreign musicians and composers travelled haphazardly. By this reasoning the appearance of Glinka was nothing short of a miracle, similar to the coming of Pushkin in Russian literature.

The next group of historians set up the cry 'back to the sources' and published original letters, documents, and references from the chronicles. The most outstanding work in this group was N. Findeisen's *Sketches for the history of music in Russia*

(Moscow and Leningrad, 1928), translated into English by W. S. Pring but, strangely, never published in translation. It was followed, almost immediately, by Assafiev's[1] *Russian Music from the beginning of the nineteenth century* (Moscow-Leningrad, 1930), which was published in English by J. W. Edwards, Ann Arbor, Michigan, in my translation, in 1953. While Findeisen is chiefly a musicologist, Glebov is a critic, and for sheer depth of critical insight his work remains unsurpassed to the present day.

The third group is formed by more recent Soviet historians in which the authors go back to the beginnings of pagan Russia, but then rather hastily skip to much later periods. Along these lines run also the non-Russian accounts by German and English writers. General interest in these sources has not abated; indeed it has led to some penetrating studies of the folk-songs. But one big sector has been left untouched: the development of the liturgical chants. As the latter is, in fact, the only accurately recorded aspect of the music in the Russian Middle Ages and Renaissance, the gap caused by its omission can well be imagined. Folk-songs tell us a great deal, for to them we can trace the bulk of Russian music. But without their counterpart, or natural complement—the ancient chant—the picture is incomplete.

In recent years there has been massive publication of folk-song collections. The quality of the collected material is on the wane, as may be expected with the penetration into the villages of urban ways and manners; but, contrary to what has often been predicted, the folk-song is anything but dead, and if we rummage in the hundreds, even thousands, of new melodies brought to light, we continually find new gems of popular creation. Problems attendant upon study of chant have been much more complicated for two reasons: (*a*) the unreadable or only partly readable notations used for the writing down of church music (eleventh to seventeenth centuries); (*b*) the severe ban on all matters connected with the Church since the Bolshevik revolution in 1917: we know that, as the ikon-painters of Palekh had to turn to secular subjects, so the few remaining liturgical musicologists and composers dealt with

---

[1] Boris Vladimirovich Assafiev (1884-1949) made his début as a critic under the pseudonym of Igor Glebov and stuck to this name until, around 1930, he reverted to his own name.

matters of little concern to them. But the path towards the numberless undeciphered manuscripts of church music, though grown over, has not been allowed to disappear.

Since the death of Stalin, scholarly communication with the USSR has been established, though with difficulty in a few areas. However, normal transmission of the results of research is still a long way off, and it is with the greatest caution that Soviet scholars allow westerners to examine their work. Through old ties, incessant correspondence, and repeated journeys to the Russian capitals, I have obtained various glimpses of it upon which I have reported from time to time in magazines and newspapers. It is time now to present a comprehensive view of some of the discoveries being made in Russia, especially in the neglected domain of church music. It is here that in the last fifteen years considerable and rather startling progress has been made. It is imperative for the historian of 1970 to supplement the history of Russian music with these findings and to fill in lacunae.

My long preoccupation with the church music of the Eastern Churches, as well as my still longer delight in Russian folk-music and my efforts to preserve it, have convinced me that all subsequent developments are, in a sense, the projection and supplementation of song and chant as original cultural sources, and that all Russian composers, even those who have shown little interest in them and gone on an alien, westernized way, are in some form indebted to these. The narrative of the subsequent pages is conducted in this light.

I

The sources

FOLK-SONGS

Organized efforts to collect and publish folk-songs began in Russia nearly two hundred years ago, since which time there has been no abatement of the zeal with which subsequent collectors have gone about their business. Neither wars, nor twentieth-century revolutions, nor prolonged famine have had much effect on the ceaseless flow of folk-material from the villages into the hands and now on to the tapes of the collectors and, finally, into published volumes.[1] In Appendix I are listed the best-known collections, to which frequent reference is made in the subsequent pages.

Early collections were often made indiscriminately and without plan, collectors noting mostly what hovered in the minds of townspeople, i.e. urban versions of village intonations. However, greater care to record faithfully was manifested in the nineteenth century. The first journeys were undertaken by Stakhovich around 1850, and from then on it was taken for granted that folk-songs would be collected on the spot, direct from the performers. In quite a few volumes we find very illuminating accounts of how this task was accomplished and of the difficulties that had to be overcome. Here is what Istomin said in 1886:

Upon arrival we inquired about the village administration and invited a responsible official to our room. In simple words I tried to explain to him the purpose of our coming and asked him to

---

[1] The collections of Eugenie Lineva represent the one important loss. The publication of these was planned for the catastrophic years 1919-20. The sad story of her terrible difficulties, illness, and death has been recounted by Mr Charles Crane (see Ch. 14, pp. 192-3).

assemble the singers. Not infrequently I had to resort to the Czar's name and to the funds that he had granted to the expedition. This always produced the necessary impression and hastened the preparations. After some time the man returned to say that the singers were there, but were too shy to come forward. Then *we* would go out to them, finding them at the opposite end of the village all dressed up in festal attire and surrounded by the village folk. We gradually lured them to our quarters and motioned them to sit down. But even then they made excuses, pleading the poor quality of the songs. Meanwhile the hut was filled with people who stood in a dense crowd keeping a respectful distance from us. The silence was profound. At last an irresolute sound would emerge from some girl in a kerchief. A second and third voice followed and soon the whole chorus was intoning the song.[2]

In 1936, fifty years after Istomin, I embarked on my expedition. My original purpose was to study some sixteenth-century books with liturgical melodies in the ancient Pechory (Pskov) monastery. By the provisions of the Versailles Treaty this famous Russian site found itself on the territory of the independent Republic of Estonia and thereby within the reach of the traveller. Walking in the streets of Pechory I was one day stopped by a young woman. Neither her features nor her speech betrayed peasant origins, yet she was dressed as one and walked barefoot. She wondered if I might be the musician who had arrived in search of the musical treasures of the district. 'I think I have a great treat in store for you,' she suddenly said. 'If you would care to come to a village about seventeen versts (twelve miles) from here you will hear something you may not easily forget.'

So the day was set—a Sunday—and we were driven there in a four-wheeled cart without springs, over the usual unpaved roads all covered with dust. The village was near the lake of Pskov on the banks of a deliciously cool and rapidly flowing river. As we were resting there the sounds of a women's chorus reached us. The voices fell hard and strong, never too agreeable in their deep chest quality, but true, with the instinct of nature itself.

The sight of the approaching singers was amazing. They

[2] *Songs of the Russian People* collected in the Archangel and Olonezk provinces in 1886 by Th. Istomin and G. Dyutch (published in 1894), p. xi.

were dressed in the old peasant costumes (compare with Istomin's 'festal attire'): brocaded skirts, gilded headgear, and heavy silver chains in several rows around their necks. They were marching in file, as if on parade, followed by other women and a few older men.[3] As I listened, it dawned on me that it was not for liturgical matters that I had travelled a thousand miles, but to hear the still living fount of music, interpreted by the very same people and possibly in the same way as it was done ages ago.

I had no recording equipment with me. Pencil and paper were utterly useless for catching the elusive polyphony of the Russian folk-song. So I had to appeal to my friend who had brought me there to induce the singers to go to the nearest town, where some sort of recordings could be made. After weeks of negotiations and a considerable drain on my purse we got eleven of them to submit to this rather painful ordeal. We went to the old university town Tartu (the former Dorpat), and there I gathered the material for my small collection.

My friend Maria Spies, a Moscow woman of German descent, was the sort of dedicated person who would sacrifice her life for an ideal. Hers was to preserve peasant art. She was not a musician, so she collected texts only and, before my arrival, had published a booklet with the entire Gorodishche Wedding Rite (Gorodishche was the village where we were assembled on that June day). But its melodies, though always sung together with the text, were still unrecorded anywhere. Not content with including some excerpts of the rite in the group of folk-songs, I continued my annotations by hand.

GROUPING OF THE FOLK-SONGS

In Appendix III I have inserted, at the appropriate places, those precious bits of music. In 1939 I was on the way to Gorodishche to complete the recording of the Wedding Rite, but was held up by the outbreak of the war. Meanwhile Elsa Mahler, a collector from Basel, had come there, and in her collection we find several other Gorodishche melodies, together with excerpts from the rite of neighbouring villages. Thus

---

[3] A most vivid description of this 'parade' is to be found in Ekaterina Swan: *Stat'y, raskazy, opisaniya* (articles, stories, descriptions), New York, 1946, pp. 11-27.

collectors—half a century apart—face more or less the same problems.

As we look through all our collections we meet with approximately the same order or grouping of the various types of songs: (*a*) Spiritual Verses; (*b*) *byliny* or historical songs; (*c*) wedding songs and incantations; (*d*) roundelays and dance songs; (*e*) love songs, laments, family songs, soldiers' and prison songs.

Some collectors, e.g. Filippov, held the Spiritual Verses to be the oldest, but I am inclined to place the Wedding Rite in an even earlier period for reasons that are inherent in it: its many pagan implications, its confusion of idolatrous and Christian traits, its ties with nature and natural phenomena pertaining to the seasons. But while the Wedding Rite is still cherished in nearly every village with special pride as the oldest and most beautiful of all, the Spiritual Verse has become exceedingly rare, one might say non-existent. Yet at one time it was one of the main forces in popular literature and music, permeated by subjects taken from hagiography in the early stages of Christianity with its semi-historical, semi-legendary heroes and saints, nay even Biblical stories of Abraham, David and Elijah. For instance, how touching in its charming confusion is the account of the great Dove Book (*golubinaya kniga*) falling out of a cloud on Jerusalem, and of all the Christian princes rushing there to find out from it the story of the creation of the world. The eternal question was: which is the *oldest* city, mountain, river, tree, or beast? King David, as the ruler of the oldest city, Jerusalem, had to provide the answer (Examples 1, 2).

The imprint of early Byzantine culture on Russia was very deep. It was Russia's mission in history to preserve this ancient tradition, especially when it was crumbling under the blows of the victorious Turks; and it was Russia's tragedy that alien elements moving in from Europe eventually pushed what remained of the old tradition into the remotest corners of the land. Together with the Spiritual Verses their secular counterpart—the *bylinas*—were being pushed out. Both types survived longest in the extreme north. The main heroes of the *bylinas* are the Russian *bogatyrs* (Knights) headed by the renowned Ilya Murometz; and, after them, personages from Russian history, such as Czar Ivan the Terrible, the Pretender Grigory (the false Dimitry), the Cossack Chief Stenka Razin. Some of the newer *bylinas* glorify Peter the Great and even Alexander II. The melodies of the *bylinas* vary between chant-like recitatives and wide-range cantilenas, but as the latter take over, the historical figures of the texts begin to lose their identity.

Example 1. Kniga Golubinaya, The Dove Book, Riazan province, collected by A. Liadov, published in *Thirty-five Songs of the Russian People*, 1902.

Example 2. *Vaizay s prilejaniem (Gaze with attention).* Two variants of the same song from different parts of Russia.
  (*a*) *Latgallin*, from Zavoloko, *Spiritual Verses of Olden times*, 1933.
  (*b*) Olonetzk province, from the Istomin and Dyutch collection of 1894.

If the above categories are found chiefly in the north, central Russia abounds in the roundelays (*Khorovodnyia*) and dance-songs (*pylasovyia*); of these all our collections show a vast number. The *Khorovod* is an arrangement of the dancers either in a circle, or, more frequently, in two long lines facing each other and always advancing towards each other in the progress of the dance. They represent two opposing camps vying with each other in vigour, brave exploits, and skill, in playing some game that is recounted chorally while the dance is going on. Each season of the year stresses particular games or rites. The yearly round starts with the carols. These are found almost exclusively in the south-western regions of Russia, the Ukraine and Byelorussia. The Russian name (*kolyada*) is derived from the latin *caleo* (heat), and they begin with the Christmas festivities, when the sun turns back towards summer. Many traces of paganism can be found in the carols, e.g. the mythical person-age of Ovsen or Tausen, a dweller in the fields (Example 3).

Example 3. *Tausen (The God of the Fields)*, Riazan province, collected by Liadov from *Thirty-five Songs of the Russian People*, 1902.

At Epiphany were sung the fortune-telling songs (*podbliudnyia*) in spring—the real *khorovody* with invocations of the pastoral deities—Did Lado, Lei—from which the usual refrains of this type of dancing songs derive (*oi lushenki, luli*). The roundelays, like the *bylinas*, are quickly vanishing. In fact, they are not listed in recent collections.

But one category of folk-song is as alive now as ever—the long-drawn-out elegy (*protyajnaia*), whether in the form of a love song, or lament, or soldier's tale. It stands independent of any particular historical epoch, a strictly individual out-pouring of sentiment to all humanity. The occasional allusions to contemporary events or personages are of no account; the core of the song is complaint, or grief. Whether it is the soldier's widow, or the young bride who had to suffer from a gnarling mother-in-law, or the young lover separated from his beloved: the mournful curves of the melody are equally eloquent, and move within the familiar range and order of intervals. It is from here that springs the peculiar and mysterious touch which the Russians call (*Pesennost*), the sum-total of song-like intona-tions that characterize any idiom as Russian, as distinct from western or eastern, from German, or Italian. This is what was imperceptibly heard and intoned by Feodor the Christian in the sixteenth century, by Glinka in the nineteenth; nor can it elude any of us in the twentieth, so long as we are those who have ears to hear. The *Protyajnaia* are the most popular and widespread type of folk-song, and the study of them by folk-lorists has never ceased (Example 4).[4]

[4] Zemtzovsky, I., *Russknaya Protyajnaia Pesnya*, Leningrad, 1967.

In their singing of music they do not produce their songs in unison, as is done elsewhere, but polyphonically with a number of different melodies, so that in a crowd of singers . . . you will hear as many melodies as there are people, and a distinct variety of parts finally coming together in a simple consonance.

This thirteenth-century testimony of Giraldus Cambrensis concerning folk-singers in Wales and Northumberland, though vague, has been quoted repeatedly as proving the way in which

Example 4. *Sneshki belye, pushisty* (*White fluffy snow*), Archangel province, collected by Istomin and Dyutch, 1894.

Welsh, and possibly northern English, singers would intone their songs. It is precisely the vagueness of the description that fits to perfection the practices of Russian singers also. Starting with a solo intonation (*zapevalo*), the ensemble of singers would without any warning split into parts, each of which was also a self-sufficient melody not too divergent from the one that could conceivably be termed 'principal'. In actual fact there was *no* principal melody. Each singer could contend with justice that he was giving the basic contours of the song. The resultant tonal image converged into unison only at the very end, while the bulk of the song—always excepting the solo opening—was intoned in a kind of unfixable, yet new and baffling harmony. Musicologists have given it a specific name: *heterophony*. In contradistinction to harmony and polyphony, the laws of this popular heterophony are indeterminable. They would be one thing in Wales and another in Russia. Collectors had been aware of this occurrence of many parts in the Russian folk-song and for long did not know what to do with it. They continued to affix on paper only one line of melody, except where they could clearly hear discernible intervals (see Stakhovich, Odoyevsky in his writings on the folk-song). Then a group of collectors began to notate each variant separately (*podgoloski*). But the folk-singers, unaccustomed to sing separately, complied only with difficulty. Yet the appearance of these variants, along with what was taken for the 'principal' melody, helped to formulate the laws of heterophony (Melgunov, Prokunin, Palchikov). Not until Lineva arrived with her phonograph in 1903, however, could a more systematic study be made, and even then some of the coincidences were so elusive that the transcription from the record to the stave was fraught with difficulties.

Kastalsky trained himself to listen with infinite care, and after perusing the entire Lineva collection published his booklet *Peculiarities of the Russian Popular System*, a work of startling revelation, that must be viewed as the foundation for all future study (1923). A unified system, such as we have for Palestrinian or Bachian polyphony, can never be attained, since the folksinger obeys only such laws as are dictated by natural beauty and taste. Natural beauty (*euphony*) is a compound of consonance and dissonance, the latter occurring in a passing movement and never obscuring the former. We can observe essentially the same thing, only with differing details, in Palestrina and even Bach. The innate good taste of the folk-singer precludes any kind of abuse of the one or the other. Thus a delicate and highly musical balance is maintained, and those who have imputed to the peasant an unrestrained and chaotic use of dissonant intervals[5] will eventually be convinced of their error. On the other hand it would be vain to seek in heterophony some of the rigid and obtuse 'rules'—not laws—that have crept into so-called academic harmony and counterpoint with the passage of time. The peasant has no pedantic fear of parallels, whether they be fifths or octaves. Even parallel fourths and sevenths may occur, on very rare occasions, if they happen to suit the melodic line of the performer (Example 5). It is doubtful if any sort of system or compendium can ever be constructed here, and the folk-singer is comparable only to the great composer who, at all times, suited himself in the matter of either complying with convention or simply ignoring it.

[5] Several Soviet musicologists have concluded this from their readings of certain extant monuments of three- and four-part polyphony in church canticles.

But if its harmony gives the folk-song a delicate character of its own, even greater originality lies in the moulding of the song, its complete freedom from symmetrical (not to say square-cut) construction. This is conditioned mainly by the absence of any firm tonic. Again Palestrina and those who came

Example 5. *Po seyan, seniushkam* (*On the porch, the little porch*), from an old Cossack wedding rite collected by Listopadov, vol. V.

before him—Ockeghem, Josquin, Obrecht—can be cited as models of a fascinating instability. In fact, wherever we are confronted with the mediaeval modes or scales, the feeling of a tonic, as a magnet or gravitation, is faint. Russian folk-song has been viewed in the light of the mediaeval—or, what is

Example 6. *Da svaty moi* (*So, my marriage brokers*), collected by Listopadov.

worse, the ancient Greek—modes. True, it can sometimes be described as lying in the Dorian, Mixolydian, or Aeolian scale: more often, however, it eludes such feeble constraints. In Example 6, from the 'Don Cossack' Wedding Rite collected

by Listopadov (see Appendix I), we have a Dorian turn in bar
two, but in bar four the Aeolian of the opening is aimed at
but not established, as the last chord is Ionian (major), and
so it ends, to be re-stated in its quaint waywardness.

Equally wayward is the metrical construction of the folk-
song, which it has in common with the liturgical chant. Try
to determine where the strong accent comes! The bar-line is
more of an impediment than an aid (Example 7).[6] All this is
still far from known and far from being ingrained in our

Example 7. *Da u Lebedia,* collected by Listopadov.

musical perception. It provides an everlasting challenge to
immerse oneself in the fount of the sources and come out
invigorated and enriched.

The impact of the folk-song on Russian composers has been
enormous. Each epoch and generation heard in them what was
congenial to it, as our subsequent exposition will show. Unfortunately we have no direct records of it prior to the age
of Catherine the Great, but an indirect connection is being
gradually established for much earlier times as the works of
such sixteenth-century composers as Feodor the Christian and
Markél the Beardless come to light. Deeper research into folk-
song will undoubtedly continue to advance measurably aided
by the ever-growing energy spent in collecting what is left with

[6] Anyone interested in the infinite capriciousness of the Russian folk-
song is referred to my article in the *Musical Quarterly* for October 1943,
The Nature of the Russian Folk-Song.

modern recording equipment and by the gradual clarification of liturgical manuscripts of the sixteenth and seventeenth centuries. These latter, incidentally, reveal a surprising affinity between the two Main Russian sources, the secular and the religious. Collecting is now a less cumbersome, more effective way of study than formerly. But unfortunately the material uncovered is perhaps less pure and genuine, at least where the texts are concerned, than that which will undoubtedly shine forth from the works of the old masters when their music is at last made accessible through transcriptions and commentaries by leading musicologists.

LITURGICAL CHANTS

If with the folk-songs the main problem was collecting something that was and is alive in the hearts of the people, but scattered all over the country, with liturgical chants we arrive at a heritage already contained in written documents in the form of song-books. The *libri usuales*, which were used during religious services, had been collected and copied out by competent scribes at all times during the progress of Russian history. Hence these books go back to the end of the eleventh century, and many of them have survived. Twenty-six are known to belong to the Kievan period of the eleventh to thirteenth centuries. Then came the destructive invasions of the Tartars, and in consequence we have little material from the later thirteenth and fourteenth centuries. As the Mongol yoke was gradually cast off, the number of books rapidly increased. In the fifteenth century it reached hundreds and from that time forward copies appeared by thousands. The most creative period came in the reigns of the music-loving Czars Vassili III, Ivan IV, and Feodor. As we scrutinize the output of their century (1505-98) we can well believe that this must have been a golden age for Russian music. The seventeenth century was a time of transition from the old Russian religious culture to the innovations that flowed from the West. In church music it was a time of struggle between the old heritage and the alien intonations brought in by the Poles and Ukrainians.

Thenceforward the picture becomes clearer, since it was chiefly through the procedures of western musical theory and practice that real penetration could be made into the innumerable books with the old Russian (*Kriuk* or *neume*) notations. Though the new methods utilizing the musical stave and clefs were applied not so much to the old material as to new music pouring in from the West, a goodly bulk of the old was nevertheless picked up in the western stream and thereby preserved from oblivion. This brings us to our principal problem with the liturgical source: the entire early part of it, and in fact almost everything before the transitional seventeenth century, is obscured from our view by the largely unexplained and undeciphered musical alphabet of the old Russian masters.

Neume notations go back to early Christian times when the liturgical books showed by chironomic (i.e. hand-movement) symbols certain upward and downward movements of the conductor's hand above and below the texts in the Gospels to facilitate the expressive reading of them. From this, whole systems of notation developed both in the East and the West. But while the West moved quickly, introducing through efforts of various inventors such as the monk, Guido of Arezzo, our system of parallel lines on which the notes were written, the East clung to *neumes* and Russia followed the Byzantine system which had been introduced at the time of christianization. From this complex tradition, the Russians developed their own notation which, however, they failed to explain adequately, leaving us very much in doubt as to the meaning of a number of the signs used. In Appendix II, I have briefly described the various endeavours of theoreticians old and new to fathom those signs. But no matter how touching the efforts of Byzantine and Russian specialists, and how ingenious their findings, the bulk of the pre-seventeenth-century Russian religious music can hardly be used by singers or composers as a living source. Only the last stage of the *neume* notation, amply supplied with the red-letter[7] marks, can be read by the connoisseurs, among whom are the so-called Old Believers (*Raskolniki*), Orthodox Christians who seceded and fled from the ruling Church when some seventeenth-century western innovations were sanctioned for general usage.

By the year 1700 we enter the 'musical stave period' of

[7] The auxiliary marks invested by the Novgorod master Ivan Shaidur, or Shaidurov (see Appendix II and p. 64).

Russian church music, and only from here on can we speak of true familiarity with its profoundly important source. The great good fortune was that, along with the appearance on the stave of the alien melodies and harmonies imported by westerners, some of the old chants were likewise transcribed and eventually published (1772) by enterprising singers and typographers. It is from these transcriptions that we derive our knowledge of *Znamenny* Chant, the essential glory of Russian church music.

No one would be inclined to argue about the origin of folksongs: like rivers and forests they are an outgrowth of the Russian soil, the faithful companions of the husbandmen and herdsmen, the choice treasures of families, the adornment alike of young girls and older women. But with the chant the question is not so simple. As an attribute of a new faith imported from abroad, it naturally was received as an alien phenomenon which only time and persistent use might assimilate and render familiar. This assumption was touched off by the testimony of a document belonging to the Golden Age, which coincided with the reign of Ivan IV, a curious chronicle called the Degree Book (*Stepennaya Kniga*). It was the work of the Moscow Metropolitan Makari, a famous author of the times and also compiler of Lives of the Saints. The passage in question reads as follows:

In the year 6559 (1051) three Greek singers came to Kiev from Byzantium and brought with them the *znamenny*, tripartite, and the beautiful *demestvenny* singing, and from them it spread through the entire Russian land.

Even if it were true that the *znamenny* and *demestvenny*[8] chants had come from Byzantium, the inclusion of tripartite singing exposes the authors of the book, of which the Metropolitan Makari was only one of several, to the suspicion that they, as laymen in matters of singing, simply assumed that what was current in their time—the sixteenth century—must have existed before. For long this testimony dominated all accounts of the origin of the Russian chants, but nowadays it is not taken seriously.

[8] See p. 36 below for an explanation of this term.

Actually the entire connection of the chants with what
arrived with the Byzantine ritual in the tenth century is now
doubtful. Maxim Brajnikov, the most comprehensive of all
modern scholars of Russian church music, makes the following
statement in his latest publication:[9]

> Russian Church Music—the *Znamenny* Chant—was in the long past
> derived from Byzantium, but was no sooner on Russian soil than it
> encountered an entirely new medium—the musical perception of
> the Russian people, its whole culture and custom, and thus began
> its second Russian life.

This conclusion of Brajnikov sums up a whole series of earlier
pronouncements on the subject of the origin of the chant, the
earliest being by the anonymous author of a preface to an
anthology of sacred music of *c.* 1650 who directs his principal
blow precisely at the statement of the Degree Book:

> from whom [he exclaims] could those three singers have obtained
> the *znamenny* chant and its variants, since in all Greek lands and in
> Palestine the singing is different from ours . . . ?

The next authoritative word to emphasize the Russian origin
of the chant was from the famous theoretician Alexander Mezenetz, who headed a commission to revise and systematize the
whole body of the *znamenny* melodies and compiled the most
detailed manual of it (1668):

> . . . and this mysterious, i.e. hidden alphabet of abbreviations was
> discovered and called by its proper names by the former Slavonic-
> Russian church singers and composers, *over four hundred years ago* and
> more . . .[10]

Mezenetz's 'Alphabet' remained long forgotten since from
his time on church music went entirely on new and non-
Russian paths. Only nineteenth-century writers and scholars
turned to it anew. It had to wait until 1888 for its revised
edition. This was done by Smolensky, who was in complete

[9] *New Monuments of the Znamenny Chant*, Leningrad, 1967, p. 6.
[10] In the Russian musical alphabet every sign had its peculiar, and very
eloquent, designation. The names convince us even more of the very
Russian origin, or at least transformation, of what may have originally
hailed from Byzantium.

agreement with Mezenetz, but in his epoch had to admit that a return to the *neume* notation was impossible. Yet he encouraged and almost forced all his pupils—among whom were Rachmaninov and even Scriabin—to learn how to read music from the *neumes* (Kriuki).

The estrangement of Russian church music from its proper and legitimate source—the *znamenny* chant—which began with the introduction of the seventeenth-century innovations, forms one of the great and tragic enigmas of all Russian music. It is as if a broad current of the purest spring-water were suddenly to disappear underground and continue flowing beneath the surface. Thus anyone suspecting its hidden flow had first to shut himself off from all that he could hear in churches and even monasteries and dig deep into the soil in order to partake of the crystalline liquid. This is precisely what Mezenetz did, exhorting others to follow his example. But only very few hearkened to him, among them the patriarchal treasurer, Tikhon of Makarievsk, who is actually the last theoretician of the *znamenny* chant before its disappearance from sight. He was still alive in 1706. His main achievement was that he was able, only just in time, to transcribe onto the stave a number of *znamenny* melodies. In his '*Kliech*' (Key) his main theoretical work, he showed them side by side with a mass of imported chants, already harmonized in the western manner. This bulk of chaff makes it almost impossible to single out the isolated bits of precious grain.

The story of how in the books published by order of the Holy Synod in 1772 a large section of the *znamenny* chant was included is one of the few miracles of the Russian eighteenth century. About 1767, the head technician of the Moscow Synodal Typography, Stephen Byshkovsky, became convinced that there was no reason why the typographical printing of music should not be patterned on some extant models going back to the end of the seventeenth century, and he presented a memo to that effect to the Holy Synod, the highest ecclesiastical authority in Russia. Byshkovsky was an ardent lover of antiquity and he found among the deacons and singers of the Moscow Synodal School some who had preserved the manuscripts from the time of Alexander Mezenetz and Tikhon of Makarievsk. These he arranged in four books:

c

I. *Heirmologion*, the oldest and purest collection of *znamenny* canticles, listing over one thousand specimens of the *heirmos*, which is the model stanza for the great Kanon with its nine odes forming a vast musical panorama in the early morning service. The *heirmos* itself is a brief canticle and because of this brevity and conciseness one of the most eloquent.

II. *Octoechos*, the book in which the longer canticles (but also *heirmoi*) are listed in the form of eight (*octo*) domains that underlie the entire body of the *znamenny* chant, each domain consisting of a set of characteristic sound patterns by which the *echoe* (*Octo-echos*) are recognized. While the names *heirmologion* and *octoechos* point to a direct Byzantine derivation, the musical nature of the canticles in all these books is purely Russian.

III. *Prazdniky*, being the nine great immovable feasts of the church year: Nativity of the Virgin, Exaltation of the Cross, Presentation of the Virgin at the Temple, Christmas, Epiphany, Purification of the Virgin, Annunciation, Transfiguration, and Assumption of the Virgin. Canticles are here listed in accordance with the texts that are appropriate for all these occasions.

IV. *Obikhod* (*ordinarium*), listing the canticles in their proper succession, as they follow each other in the daily round of services, starting with the Vespers and ending with the Divine Liturgy.

While in I, II, and III nearly the entire material is composed of *znamenny* melodies, IV contains a substantial dose of post-*znamenny* canticles, i.e. the melodic material which flowed into Moscow in the second half of the seventeenth century in the wake of western innovations. All these later chants are to a greater or lesser degree simplifications of the *znamenny*, or entirely new formations (as, e.g., the so-called Greek chant) definitely designed for simple harmonizations.

All through the nineteenth century these books remained a beacon for those who longed to recapture this virtually lost heritage. The very sensitive Odoyevsky pointed them out to Glinka. The actual repertoire of the churches and cathedrals, and even of monasteries, was a direct outcome of the seventeenth-century innovations and led further away from the great liturgical source. Only in the haunts of the Old Believers, far out in the Ural mountains and western Siberia, did the *znamenny* melodies still sound from untranscribed song-books.[11]

Most of what we know of the *znamenny* chant is contained in the four books of it that appeared in 1772. Naturally those who were conversant with *neume* notation, especially during its last period when it was conjoined with the red-letter marks, were eager to add their own transcriptions to the printed material. But, by and large, no great amount of further material was added until, late in the nineteenth century, a fifth volume came out. In keeping with the unscientific way in which so much valuable material was brought out in old Russia no one had troubled to advise us how this last volume came into being; the fact remains that there are now five books in place of four and a sixth in the form of an epitome representing all five.

This fifth book is of material pertaining to Easter, the movable feast, and was probably compiled as a counterpoint to Volume III with its nine immovable feasts. Contingent on the date of Easter are the Septuagesima and Sexagesima Sundays and the whole Lenten cycle, which in turn determines the date of Pentecost. This book is called *Triodion*, 'lenten and florid', and consists of *znamenny* canticles. But it represents the last and most ornamented period of the chant, probably belonging to the late seventeenth and early eighteenth centuries. The fact that this material went back to the seventeenth century assures us that most of it derives from the *znamenny* chant with *Shaidur* marks. In the *Obikhod* some specimens of later chants such as Kiev, Greek and Bulgarian were also included.

It so happened that Byshkovsky's plan was strengthened, independently, by a similar suggestion to the Holy Synod, coming from a musical practitioner, a bass in the Imperial Chapel, Gavril Golovnia, one of those Ukrainians possessed of a luscious voice and in great favour at the time. Golovnia was

---

[11] The Old Believers were eventually repatriated after the promulgation of laws pertaining to freedom of worship. I happened to run into one of their communes in Riga in 1936. They sang from an elevated song-book in the old *neume* notation, ranged in a circle. The precentor conducted in the manner that we know from fifteenth-century engravings showing Jean Ockeghem leading his choir in the cathedral of Tours (cf. plate 120 in Heinrich Besseler, *Die Musik des Mittelalters und Der Renaissance*, Potsdam, 1931, p. 234).

probably responsible for the inclusion, especially in the book of the Great Immovable Feasts, of innumerable embellishments, vocalizes and all sorts of figures, intended for the display of a solo singer. The two projects, on reaching the Synod, were studied for all of three years and the decision was to go ahead under the supervision of Byshkovsky. The event was one of the first magnitude, and nothing better could have happened for the preservation of *znamenny* chant. The printing took two more years and was completed in 1772, a memorable date in the history of Russian church music.

Just before the cataclysmic events of 1917 there were several congresses of teachers of church singing in Novgorod (1911-13) as a result of which another—and alas final—book came out under the title *The Choir-Master's Companion* (actually the reader's fellow-traveller). It presents nothing new in material and is a medley of chants, from the *znamenny* on.

Before concluding this survey of the age-old music of the Church another chant must be mentioned; in fact it was touched on already in the spurious testimony of the Degree Book: *Demestvenny*. Though we know extremely little about it, it looks as though it may eventually stand out as a corollary to the *znamenny*, perhaps not quite as old as the latter, but essentially worthy of it. Defining it as strictly liturgical, Johann von Gardner goes on to say of *demestvenny* that in the second half of the seventeenth centuries it stood

> next to and parallel to the *znamenny*, being reserved for festal occasions, while the *znamenny* served for all purposes. . . . In the course of the eighteenth century it disappeared in the official church, but is still used by the Old Believers, in a more restricted fashion.[12]

There are a few *demestvenny* melodies listed at the end of the *Obikhod* (IV). For the rest they must be transcribed from a late stage of *neume* notation—with the red-letter mark.

NATURE OF THE 'ZNAMENNY' MELODIES

The melodies are inextricably tied to the texts. Hence the length of each phrase is determined by the corresponding

[12] Johann von Gardner: Band 25 in *Slavistische Beitrage*, Munich, 1967, p. 80.

length of the verbal phrase. Any hard and fast rhythm or
metre is out of the question. The canticle proceeds with a
stately delivery, the singer being free to make retards and actual
breaks at the termination of each sentence. From Example 8 it
can be seen that the melodies are strictly diatonic. No chromatic
steps are to be found in any of the material available in our

Example 8. *Troparion,* eighth echos, *znamenny* chant, from *The
Triodion,* 1899.

five books. They move in the middle of a range extending from
the G below the middle C to the B flat or C of the next octave.
The low notes of this range of twelve notes, as well as the high
ones, are used only as an exception. Wide leaps (such as a
fourth or a fifth) may occur, but are also the exception rather
than the rule (Example 9).

Example 9. Four trichords of *znamenny* chant.

Though every domain (*echos, glas*) of the *znamenny* chant has
its own set of patterns (*popevki*) and is recognized by their
recurrence, there are also many patterns common to several
echoi, which results in a general similarity of the sound. On the
whole, however, the attempt to describe the individual domains
as maintaining a certain predominant mood or colour (vigorous,
confident, mournful, dirge-like, etc.) has not been too successful. To be appreciated, *znamenny* chant as a whole must be
singled out as a *corpus melodiarum,* a type of music unlike anything else whether in the Middle Ages or in more modern
times, and must be placed side by side with other bodies of
music. Then it will gradually become clear that it is akin not
so much to Gregorian, Ambrosian, or other liturgical dialects,

as to the vast domain of the Russian folk-song. It is its Russian character that is the determining factor, and not its appurtenance to purposes of worship, prayer, and glorification, though the latter in their turn determine its flow and dignity, its elevated, solemn progress. It stands to reason, then, that the category of folk-song nearest to the *znamenny* chant consists of the *protyajnaia*, the love-songs, the laments, and the family songs of all types.

It is not necessary here to quote related melodic patterns from folk-song and chant, but this relationship is stressed ever more with every new stage in the readability of the old manuscripts. One of the last expeditions in quest of antiquity undertaken by the Soviet traveller, Vladimir Malyshev, in 1955 yielded, in lieu of ikons or folk-songs, a precious anthology of liturgical music. His experience was not unlike Istomin's or Lineva's. On arrival in a village he would question the older peasants about ancient books. Here are some of the answers that he got:

'Yes, we remember seeing some of those, but in those days people were ignorant and used to write on leather (parchment). Now we use paper.' 'So what did you do with the books?' 'We burnt them for fuel.'

But the anthology was his reward, and in it were contained eleven Gospel canticles marked as the work of one of the most famous masters of the Golden Age—Feodor the Christian (see next chapter). When deciphered by Maxim Brajnikov, they were found to be suffused in a folk-song idiom, leaving far behind all that we had theretofore associated with *znamenny* chant, and showing that in the earlier stages the two great bodies of Russian music—the religious and the secular—may have been united by the closest common ties.

2

The makers of folk-songs and liturgical melodies

THE MAKERS OF THE *ZNAMENNY* CHANT

The great traditions of church singing and the folk-songs grew gradually and collectively. Hence for most of the material no names of composers have been recorded. The further we go back the truer this is, but as time rolls on certain individuals begin to emerge, such as St Ambrose of Milan, or Gregory I. Byzantine music, likewise, is at one stage associated with the Master John Koukouzeles, and though our Russian chronicles are particularly disappointing on musical matters, we cannot altogether write them off. True, there are names of singers and performers, but the performer here is the actual creator.

Composing in mediaeval times did not mean inventing something new. On the contrary, the best composer was the one who could come nearest in manner and skill to his master. For *znamenny* chant a great number of thoroughly familiar patterns were set up. Often these were listed at the end of a book of canticles, and when a new work was needed for the glorification of a new saint, or any other occasion, the singer was expected to manipulate these patterns in such a way as to do justice to the new words and make his work a worthy sequel to those already in existence.

At first we hear of copyists. Thus a collection of canticles of the twelfth century from Novgorod[1] has the following inscription:

---

[1] Listed in V. M. Metallov, *Russian Liturgical Singing of the Pre-Mongol Period*, Moscow, 1908, p. 204.

This *sticherarium*[2] belongs to St Vlassy, and whoever will sing from it, may he live long and this manuscript was written by a man whose Christian name is Jacob, known in the world as Tvorimir, sexton of St Nicholas who, though but poorly skilled, has written it, saying amen, amen.

About the same time (1137) there is mention of the 'eunuch Manuel, a great expert in singing'.[3]

The Voskressensky chronicle reports a startling occurrence under the date of 22 September 1441:

The Novgorod Prince Dimitry Krasny was lying dead on a bench in the hall where the guardsmen slept. Suddenly the dead man threw off the blanket and cried aloud: 'Peter recognized that he was the Lord' and began to sing in *demestvenny* chant: 'Sing unto the Lord and glorify Him forever,' then Alleluiahs, and a verse of the canticle 'He who dwelleth on high' and other Marian hymns.

The honour of being the first Russian composer known by name belongs to no less a personage than the Czar Ivan IV. Historians now assign to him the composition of two *stichera* in the year 1547 when he was only seventeen years old.[4] His whole reign was crucial to the development of music. In 1551 he appeared at a Council of the Realm (the council of the hundred chapters—*stoglav*) making recommendations for the teaching of music in schools all over the country. From the enactments of that council we get a glimpse of the great austerity of Russian culture. A number of decrees are directed against vagabond minstrels, so like those popular in contemporary Tudor England, yet it was they who travelled from village to village, singing folk-songs, playing instruments, and carrying on the musical tradition. Ivan himself, in his less official capacities, summoned them to his court and is said to have participated in their ribald antics.[5] But, leaving aside the darker moments of Ivan's reign, we continue to admire him for his unceasing love of music. From the great Novgorod he collected the most famous singers of the time, and it was about them that the anonymous author

[2] Collection of *Stichera* (the old designation of more elaborate canticles).
[3] Metallov, op. cit., p. 197.
[4] There is still doubt whether Ivan composed the text only, or the music as well. See N. Findeisen, *Sketches*, vol. I, Moscow, 1928, p. 247.
[5] Kurbsky, his great antagonist, reproached him for 'assembling the *skomorokhi* (minstrels) with pipes and songs, hateful to God'.

of the Preface reported after having shattered the testimony of the Degree Book (see Chapter I, p. 32):

I have heard with mine own ears from various folk about the old masters, to wit Feodor, the Pope, surnamed Christian, who was famous here in the city of Moscow, the residence of the Czar, and greatly skilled in the chanting of *znamenny* chant, and many were his pupils, and his chants are famous to this day. From his pupils To Whom I am Known, I have heard that he, Christian, used to tell them about the old masters of Novgorod: Savva Rogov and his brother Vassili, in monkhood Varlaam, Karelians by descent. This Vassili was later Metropolitan in the city of Rostov, a man devout and wise, and greatly skilled in singing, a chanter and creator of *znamenny*, tripartite and *demestvenny* chants. And his brother Savva's pupils, aside from Christian, were Ivan Noss and Stephen, called the Pauper (*Golysh*). They all lived in the reign of the righteous Czar Ivan Vassilievich of all the Russias, being with him in his favourite village Alexandrovo, but Stephen the Pauper was not there, as he wandered about in various towns and taught in the Ussolsk province and in the lands of the Stroganovs,[6] and his pupil was Ivan, named Lukoshka, and he and his master Stephen the Pauper had chanted many *znamenny* chants. And after him his pupil Isaiah has spread and supplied much *znamenny* singing. And from the above pupils of Christian I have heard what he had related to them about the Gospel *Stichera*; someone in Tver, a deacon, a man of great wisdom and piety, had chanted the Gospel *Stichera*: and the Psalter was chanted in Novgorod the Great by a monk named Markél, called the Beardless, who also composed a Kanon of rare beauty for Nikita, the archbishop of Novgorod. And the Triodia were chanted and explained by Ivan Noss who likewise had chanted the *Stauro-theotokia* (Stabat Mater).

From this fascinating account the following approximate genealogical tree of the classic masters of Russian church singing has been constructed.[7]

This array of names has hovered in Russian historians' minds ever since its first publication in the *Moskvitianin* in 1846. What

---

[6] A family of landowners to whose initiative is due the conquest of Siberia. They were descended from Novgorod boyars, maintained themselves on Novgorod territory after the city was subjugated to Moscow and concentrated in their hands vast lands along the River Kama.

[7] By permission of the *Musical Quarterly*. This table was drawn by me in 1940 and has been referred to (and utilized) by the Russian musicologists in their efforts to penetrate further into the old masters.

Generation born in the reign of the Czar Vassili III (1505-33)	1. The deacon of Tver, singer, author of the Gospel *Stichera*	2. Savva Rogoff, famous teacher in Novgorod, born in Karelia	3. Vassili Rogoff, singer and composer in Novgorod, born in Karelia. Metropolitan in Rostoff (1586) under name of Varlaam, creator of the *znamenny*, 3-part, and *demestvenny* chants	4. Markél the Beardless, singer in Novgorod, Chotyn Monastery, author of the Psalter
Generation born in the early part of the reign of Czar Ivan IV (1533-84)	5. Feodor the Christian, teacher in Moscow, born in Novgorod later priest, originator of a chant known as Christian's chant in Alexandrovo settlement with Ivan IV (1564-5)		6. Ivan Noss, teacher in Moscow, born in Novgorod, author of *triodia*, Stabat Mater and *theotokia* in the *menaia*, in Alexandrovo settlement with Ivan IV (1564-5)	7. Stephen the Pauper, teacher in Ussolsk province (N.E. of Russia), born in Novgorod
Generation born in the later part of the reign of Czar Ivan IV (1533-84)	Pupils of his have told the tale of them all to the author of the preface to the *Sticherarium*		8. Ivan Lukoshka (Lukoshkoff), creator of Ussolsk master singing (Lukoshka's singing), in 1615 archimandrite of Vladimir Nativity Monastery under name of Isaiah. Copy of *Octoechos* belonging to him, dated March 1615	

Note: The Deacon of Tver and Markél the Beardless may have been a little younger than the brothers Rogov.

sort of known music did actually go back to them? Up to Malyshev's expedition (Appendix II, i) and its miraculous find, nothing at all could be said, but now over the *Gospel Stichera* there was the clear heading:

Gospel Stichera. Greater chant. Written by the *despotes* Leo, the Wise Emperor, Chanted by Christian.

A ruler was known as a *despotes* in Russian usage. The wise Emperor Leo was Leo VI of Byzantium (886-917), whose contribution to the service books was precisely the Morning Resurrection Hymns (*Gospel Stichera*). The Christian is, of course, Feodor, the central figure in the genealogy. All that needs to be explained is the term Greater Chant, and here Brajnikov, to whom it fell to transcribe these *Gospel Stichera* in the Malyshev anthology, constructs a novel theory:

The Greater Chant is a new epoch in the development of the entire Russian art of singing, a new type of the *znamenny* chant, which did not stop at what had been done by Feodor, but developed further. ... With the patterns Feodor dealt in his own way. He retained the traditional turns to some extent, but created a great many more of his own, very imaginative, patterns, that occasionally have an almost pictorial character in conveying the texts of the *Gospel Stichera*. ... The name 'greater' this chant acquired from its wider expanse (leaps of a sixth and a seventh). While traditional *znamenny* chant contained isolated echos of the folk-song, the folk-song cantilena (*raspevnost, pesonnost*) has now become the very foundation of the 'greater chant'. ... [8]

Compare the example cited by Brajnikov (Example 10) with the traditional sound of *znamenny* chant (Example 8), and we find an almost unbridgeable difference. The church authorities

Example 10. *Gospel Sticheron* by Feodor the Christian, echos I (beginning).

were most intent upon the adherence to the known patterns and when a singer allowed himself too much freedom he was immediately called to order. This is how the Bishop Dionysius reproved the ambitious precentor of the Troizk monastery, Loggin:

Do you not see that over the word 'seed' there is marked one long note only (*statiya*)? And what are you vociferating?

But perhaps what was reprehensible in a performer may have been permissible for a master, which Feodor certainly was. So

[8] Maxim Brajnikov: *Russian Church Singing in the XII-XVIII centuries.* (Report read at the Musicological Congress in Bydgoszcz, Poland, in September 1966), in *Musica Antiqua Europae Orientalis I*, Bydgoszcz, 1966, p. 468 (see Appendix III).

we must eagerly await further confirmation of the Brajnikov theory about the 'greater chant'. If it should be true, endless possibilities arise out of this parallelism between the liturgical chant and the folk-song. As a source of Russian music, as a constant rejuvenating force, *znamenny* chant is all but untapped. The few great works of Russian music that derive from a liturgical source, such as the *Easter Overture* of Rimsky-Korsakov and the *All-Night Vigil* of Rachmaninov, make only a very faint bow in its direction. They revolve around chants of the late seventeenth and eighteenth centuries, which superseded *znamenny* and finally ushered in the official chant of the nineteenth century. This last offshoot, in which the principal feature of a chant—its melody—is almost obliterated, has firmly maintained itself until the present day. With all the theoretical interest in *znamenny* chant, which has obsessed thinking musicians from the time of its partial disappearance, no one dared to approach it or apply it in any practical manner to existing realities. It never dawned on composers who were powerfully swayed by folk-song that the two sources stood surprisingly close to one another and that only one step was needed to cross the boundary.

If Brajnikov is correct—and we must respect his erudition and lifelong dedication to his subject—Feodor must have been equally proficient in church singing and in folk-song. Further references to his work have appeared in Brajnikov's *New Monumenta of the Znamenny Chant* in 1967, and particularly in Uspensky's 1968 anthology, *Examples of the Old Russian Art of Singing*, where a complete *Gospel sticheron* of Feodor's is given in Brajnikov's transcription (No. 76). But not until all eleven of them are published can we really judge of their nearness to the art of the folk-singer.[9]

[9] In 1965, Uspensky brought out his first book entitled *The Old Russian Art of Singing*; in it there is no mention of Brajnikov's theory of the 'greater chant', yet many transcriptions are ascribed to him. Somewhat unconvincingly, Uspensky attributes an eighteenth-century Psalter (No. 382 in the Pogodin collection in the Leningrad Public Library) to Markél the Beardless, the Novgorod Master (see genealogy). After numerous excerpts he concludes that the Moscow School, having exhausted the possibilities of *znamenny*, was turning to other chants, namely *demestvenny* and *putevoy*. This theory ignores that of Brajnikov, and it must be remembered that, while Feodor's authorship of the eleven *Stichera* has been authenticated, Markél's remains unproven.

RUSSIAN POLYPHONY IN THE
LITURGICAL BOOKS

The bulk of *znamenny* and *demestvenny* books show only one line of music above the texts. But towards the end of the sixteenth century there began to appear books, mostly in the *demestvenny* category, with as many as four lines of *neumes*. Transcriptions of these examples of incipient polyphony have so far been unsuccessful, even with the aid of the red-letter marks, and have led only to unresolved discussions as to what this polyphony could have signified. The first Russian theoreticians to deal with it were Odoyevsky and Razumovsky. Both of them rejected the idea that the parts were to be sung simultaneously. Odoyevsky, writing in 1867, says very emphatically:

The assumption that these three parts [he speaks of the Cod. Fund No. 24 in the Lenin Library in Moscow, belonging to the early eighteenth century] were ever intended to be sung together, simultaneously, is out of the question, as there is not the slightest co-ordination in harmony, the parts being completely separate; no human ear could endure a succession of sounds occurring all the while. . . .

Smolensky, on the other hand, spoke of a 'native counterpoint', but did not clarify his thought when, in 1888, he wrote somewhat vaguely:

We, Russians, do not have to seek models for our writing in the church modes of Palestrina, Orlando, and Allegri, or other famous masters. The incredibly rich sonority of our modes, underlined by the clearly indicated part-writing and development of the melodies, is evident from any serious study of them.[10]

Soviet musicologists, however, have embraced wholeheartedly the idea of this native polyphony. This is how Brajnikov put it:

The notations of *znamenny* polyphony require a special approach to their transcription; but when correctly read the music of the 'scores' abounds in harsh sonorities in the form of extended parallel seconds and fifths.[11]

He thereupon cites examples from a series of manuscripts of the end of the seventeenth and eighteenth centuries. Uspensky's

[10] *The Alphabet of Alexander Mezenetz*, Kazan, 1888, p. 42.
[11] Maxim Brajnikov, *Report at the Congress of Bydgoszcz*, 1966, p. 464.

Anthology increases their number and amplifies them. Therefore the latest view obtained of this Russian polyphony is a disturbing one, and we feel almost relieved that its course was interrupted by the influx of foreign harmonizations in the late seventeenth century together with the whole school of partsinging that streamed from Poland and the West.

Russian polyphony, or native counterpoint, as Smolensky termed it, should be similar, or even identical, with what has been termed *heterophony* in folk-song (see Chapter 1, p. 25). It would be extremely hard to accept the possibility of *two* indigenous systems, one for the oral, and another for the written tradition; so that if we hold that there is only one peculiarly Russian way of harmonizing, and subscribe to the theory, likewise advocated by the Soviet musicologists, that folk-song had a great deal to do with the shaping and assimilation of *znamenny* chant, we must needs conclude that the heterophonic manner of singing the folk-song must have *also* affected the singing of the liturgical melodies. However, extant written books, if correctly interpreted, go contrary to this notion. What is worse, they go counter to nature and common sense. Odoyevsky said it clearly, and so did Vaughan Williams (who was another profound student of folk-singing) when he told me in 1956:

Singing is the foundation of what is right or wrong in music. You can make the clarinet and flute play wrong notes together, but you could not sing the C major scale correctly if someone next to you was singing in B major.

This would rule out chains of parallel seconds, or sevenths, though even the infallible folk-singer may let pass a couple of them. The parallel fifths are, of course, basically musical and easily performed. With this we must leave further discussion of this question until a fuller view can be obtained of the books themselves, or a new theory submitted in their explanation.[12]

[12] Since writing the above I have acquired, from M. Brajnikov, his transcription of a Cherubim Song of the late seventeenth century from the Collection of the State Historical Museum, No. 182, p. 1803. This work appears perfectly singable though a few jammed seconds occur in one or two spots. The basis of it being a movement in parallel fifths which is consistent with the practice of the folk-singer, the transcription merely stresses the folk heterophony (*podgoloski*) and may be an important step in solving the riddle of the 'native counterpoint' (Example 11).

Example 11. *Cherubim Song*, anonymous, from MS of the late seventeenth century transcribed by M. Brajnikov.

3

The eighteenth century

THE FORCES OF THE NEW MUSIC

It would be tempting to compare the history of Russian music towards the end of the seventeenth century with that of Italian, and of western music in general, a century earlier. There is a quite extraordinary similarity between the collections of 'kants and psalms' that began to appear in Moscow in the latter part of the reign of Alexis and that of his son Feodor, and the famous *Nuove Musiche* of Caccini (1602) in Florence. Both show a tragic falling-off from the richness and solidity of the preceding polyphonic styles, whether that of the Roman school of Palestrina, or the as yet faintly asserted Russian 'native counterpoint'. Where before there had been a highly elaborate melodic pattern in which *all* voices participated, the 'new music' reduced it to the mechanical juxtaposition of mere morsels of melody—always in the top voice only—and supported by anaemic chains of harmony below.

The marked difference, however, between the West and Russia lies in the fact that the Italian new style was the offspring of a native Italian mentality, growing out of a cogent need to dramatize musical expression, to individualize every idiom, to assert the character of each composer, in short, to make music follow the general emancipation of personality which began in the Renaissance. And while it did unquestionably impoverish music and divest it of its architectural qualities, it also inaugurated the dramatic opera period of Monteverdi and Cavalli prior to its decline at the hands of the Neapolitans. In Russia the need of a stylistic revolution was not nearly as cogent. *Znamenny* chant was drifting into its most effective phase in the works of the masters of the 'Golden Age' and beginning to show its basic and very national connection with folk-art; an indigenous art of counterpoint was gradually being evolved; the red-letter marks of Shaidurov had made the reading of the *znamenny* books immeasurably easier. Into all this the 'new' tumbled almost without warning, a foreign importation rather than an inward command, an enticing way as against the hard labour of conquering artistic matter and acquiring firm mastery.

Events in Russia at the end of the seventeenth century favoured these new trends. Foreigners flocked into the country from everywhere: the Greeks from the south, a motley crowd from Palestine (mostly collectors of alms), and the Dutch and the English through the White Sea and Archangel. They brought with them their own customs and mode of life which many of the Russians found attractive and began to imitate. All this was, of course, a fruitful preparation for the forcible reforms that were to come under Peter the Great. The masses of the people were opposed to the innovations, or, at best, quite indifferent to them, but, as usual, the upper classes, for fear of being behind the times, let themselves be carried away by them, and even the Czars were not slow to set the tone of fashion, as observed by Zabelin, the historian of that period:

After the meal the great Czar was pleased to be entertained by games and the playing of organs and the blowing of trumpets and the beating of cymbals. . . .[1]

The attacks against *znamenny* chant began as early as 1651 when a pamphlet was circulated entitled *The Legends of Various Heresies and Blasphemies against the Lord our God and the Blessed Virgin, which are contained from ignorance, in the znamenny books.* The author was a monk by the name of Euphrosinius. His invective is directed mainly against the behaviour of certain singers and performers of the chant and the corruption of the liturgical texts, but the chant is lumped together with the rest. Euphrosinius found an ally in the deacon of the Moscow Cathedral of the Purification, Ivan Korenev, who put to scorn the adherents of the old:

[1] Ivan Zabelin, *The Domestic Life of the Russian Czars of the Sixteenth and Seventeenth Centuries*, Moscow, 1915, p. 9.

It is not a laughing matter, but one more worthy of weeping, to see how they accuse the new part-singing of heresy and make the clefs of the stave into the work of the devil. . . .[2]

Yet all this might have remained a domestic concern had not Nicholas Diletzky, a clever foreign musician, arrived in Moscow around 1675. He managed to turn the whole issue of the Old *vs.* the New to his own advantage. He arrived in full glory, having been called to Russia by the young Czar Feodor.[3] A native of Kiev, then the capital of the Ukraine, and a graduate of Vilna University in Poland, Diletzky acquired instant fame by translating and advertising his *Musical Grammar* (1679), which was a faithful compendium of the western ways in which he had been trained.

It was the time of the Venetian Baroque. Viadana's *Concerti Ecclesiastici* were part of the past, and the styles of the late Baroque were then shaping, with few traits remaining from such earlier Venetians as the Gabrielis and Monteverdi. In general, the works of the end-of-century masters still had rich sonorities but were less rich in substance. In the process of transition from Venice to Vienna and Warsaw, musical values were further thinned out through processes of imitation, and it was thus a greatly inferior product that Diletzky offered to the Muscovites. His reckoning was correct; the sweet, ingratiating quality of the '*kants*' won easily over the sombre, stately beauty of the old *znamenny* canticles. Lightness and gaiety was what that generation wanted as it turned away from the whole monastic asceticism of the old Russia. Instruments were particularly alluring and, if it had not been for their strict prohibition in church services, they would have penetrated even there. Diletzky contended that:

God would not be pleased if to the traditional tune of the Cherubim Song you should malign and disparage the Cherubim Song itself. On the contrary, will He not be pleased if to the tune of an ordinary song you will let your voice resound with tender emotion in all sincerity towards God?

[2] Ivan Korenev's *Musikiya*, embodied in Diletzky's *Grammar*.
[3] Feodor was a son of Alexis and reigned from 1676 to 1682. Not only was he passionately fond of music, but his name is associated with a chant —Czar Feodor's chant—that has been subjected to later harmonizations.

So the Cherubim Song—the most profound and mystical ingredient of the entire liturgy—acquired such attributes as 'a touching song with tricks', while the different Alleluiahs were referred to as 'the Bird', 'the Jump', or 'From the Attic'.[4] But, along with the enthusiasts for such things as these, there were also people who were shocked by the frivolity, and these not only amongst the Old Believers. The two sides aligned against one another during the seventeenth and early eighteenth centuries form the following diagram:

FOR THE OLD	FOR THE NEW
The inventor of the red-letter marks, the Novgoroder *Shaidurov*	
The last offshoots of the Moscow chanters of the reign of Ivan IV: *Lukoshka*, teacher in the Stroganov lands, and his pupil *Loggin*, surnamed the Cow, a precentor at the Troizk monastery	The monk Euphrosinius (1651), The Patriarch *Nikon* and the Deacon *Meletius* (a Greek) Ivan Korenev and his 'Musikiya'
The Anonymous of the famous Preface	*Diletzky* and *Czar Feodor* (1677)
Alexander Mezenetz	Diletzky's pupils, among whom, however, there was Vassili *Titov* who desperately tried to infuse the old melodies into the new framework.
Tikhon of Makarievsk: the first of the old orientation to use stave and clefs.	

With all the patrons and potentates in the 'new' camp, one can imagine what chances the 'old' had of survival. Things became even worse when Czar Peter attained his majority. But by that time we are already on the threshold of the eighteenth century, that time of rampant western domination, from which we can still miraculously extract one or two consoling facts pointing to the persistent smouldering of *znamenny* chant in the thick of the singing folk.

THE EIGHTEENTH CENTURY

Up to the middle of the seventeenth century, and even in the transitional period of the westernized 'psalms and kants', Russian music was moulded and chanted by the representatives of the entire people. Feodor the Christian and Markél the

---

[4] See references in Preobrajensky's *Music of the Cult*, Leningrad, 1924.

Beardless, though of lowly parentage—the epithet 'Christian' is, in Russian usage, interchangeable with Krestianin, i.e. peasant—are mentioned along with Czar Ivan. Prince Dimitry Krasny is obviously a precursor of Ivan Noss and the virtuoso singer Loggin. Even the deacons Korenev and Titov, pupils of the Kievan Diletzky, were humble but eminently gifted men who rose to positions of authority in the truly democratic structure of the Russian society in the seventeenth century.

But when Titov died around 1715 things had already undergone considerable change. Czar Peter's reforms were to create a deep gulf between the culture of the towns and centres and the life and culture of the villages. Communication between the ruling minority in the capitals and the vast peasant population had been interrupted, and even the suburban popular masses were no longer participants in the great Russian historical drama, but only its speechless spectators. And how could it be otherwise when layer after layer of foreign importations was piled up and when the ruling clique itself was composed almost entirely of Balts and Germans?

Court life, after Peter, was strongly conditioned by servile imitation of the West, and soon the moment came for bringing in the Italian opera. The Italians arrived as a strong body under the leadership of distinguished musicians such as Francesco Araja, but even in their productions, designed mainly for the vocal display of prima donnas and male sopranos, the chorus was an integral part. Reluctant to incur the expense of importing masses of minor chorus singers, the directors looked around nearer home and soon found that the natural Russian voices had by no means disappeared.

A curious testimony to that effect is found in the diaries of a foreign traveller, the Reverend William Coxe, who was in Russia in the later eighteenth century (1772). What he wrote, of course, is characteristic of almost any time:

The postillions *sing* from the beginning of a stage to the end; the soldiers *sing* continually during their march; the countrymen *sing* during the most laborious occupations; the public houses re-echo with their carols; and in a still evening I have frequently heard the air vibrate with the notes from the surrounding villages.[5]

[5] Reverend William Coxe, *Travels into Poland, Russia, Sweden and Denmark*, London, 1792, Vol. II, p. 210.

The main reservoir of this singing was the Imperial Choir and the Chapel to which it was attached. Marvellous material was soon discovered there, and so much must be said for the Italians: their demand spurred on the search for ever new contingents. Not content with training native singers at home, they were dispatched for study to the renowned Italian centres, such as Bologna and Venice. In this way was inaugurated the Russo-Italian reign in the Imperial Chapel and essentially the whole pre-Glinka period in Russian music.

It so happened that the most fantastic voices were found in Little Russia, or the Ukraine, that is around Kiev and Poltava; this had also quite an important political significance since Russia had annexed that territory only in 1652 and was anxious to create stronger ties with it.

Whether it was the political aim or the real musical gifts and charm of the Ukrainians, the eighteenth century presents a veritable chain of personalities connected with music in one way or another rising to fabulous heights and enriching the historical outlook of Russia. But before they could find the opportunity, the foreigners had somehow to be pushed aside, and this came about through the accession to the throne of Elizabeth, the younger daughter of Peter, in 1741.

The new Empress was gay and kind, a perpetual dreamer and scatterbrain. Her love of music was not serious, nor was she a patron of church singing, yet her epoch came to be known as the 'Age of Song'. At her accession—which, in the Roman fashion, took the form of a proclamation by the officers of the guards—she is said to have burst into song:

'Oh, my poor life, I have spent my youth pitifully always full of woe.'

She was over thirty and still unmarried, which may account for the note of sadness. But during her reign, determined to make up for the privations of her youth, she sang and danced, went to Italian opera—but also to church services—she caroused and fasted, and married, morganatically, one of the singers in her chapel, one Alexis Razumovsky.

Alexis was a simple Ukrainian peasant with a superb voice, handsome and clever enough to keep his head and not be carried away by his good fortune. Uneducated himself, he saw to it that his kinsmen should not remain so. Music ran in the Razumovsky family: Alexis's brother, later *hetman* of the Ukraine, went on his foreign travels in the company of Grigory Teplov, collector and editor of the first Russian song album. Alexis's nephew, son of the *hetman*, was the well-known ambassador in Vienna to whom Beethoven dedicated the Razumovsky quartets, Op. 59. And the line did not end there.

The Imperial Chapel was flooded with Ukrainians, or Little Russians as they were known in former times. The choir-boys were thoroughly trained, first at home and then in Italy. Returning from abroad, having distinguished themselves in Venice or Milan, they rose to high positions in the musical life of their own country. A contemporary of Alexis Razumovsky was the Chapel singer, Mark Poltoratzky, whose first appearance in Italian opera by the side of the famous Italians took place in 1750. He rapidly rose to the top to become the Director of the Chapel. The same position was attained later by Dimitry Bortniansky, the most renowned personage in eighteenth-century Russian music, in whom the Italo-Russian style found its most perfect embodiment. Among other Ukrainians occupying important places in shaping the history of Russian church music were Berezovsky and Wedel. The tragic fact remains, however, that all this over-abundant musical talent was expended to create in Russian art a style quite at variance with the country's past musical history and achievements.

TEPLOV'S 'BETWEEN WORK A BIT OF LEISURE'

Although church music was, for these reasons, a lost cause, folk-song tradition continued to develop during the reigns of Elizabeth and Catherine the Great, in a specifically urban manner. It was at this juncture that it began its steady march towards an ultimate position as the central and most persistent influence in the nineteenth century, a position it has maintained in our own times. The original song-book, which was the first printed issue, appeared at the end of Elizabeth's reign, in 1759. We owe it to Teplov who passed it off as something originating during a bit of leisure between more serious pieces of work.[6] The song-book contains seventeen songs, or romances,

[6] *Mejdu delom bordelye.*

as they came to be called in later Russian music to distinguish them from genuine folk-songs.

The Reverend W. Coxe was not the only foreign traveller interested in Russian culture during the eighteenth century. Jacob von Stahlin, the author of a book of observations of Russian musicians originally published in 1769, provides one of the best extant sources of information on Russian musical life in that age. Stahlin said of Teplov that in his youth he had an agreeable voice,[7] sang in the Italian manner and was an excellent violinist. Being one of the exceptional Russians of his time, he was well educated and widely travelled. Moreover he was deeply involved in the various *coups d'état* and changes of government, but miraculously escaped any serious consequences and died a natural death in 1779.

Naturally we do not find in Teplov's collection anything like folk-music, but it would be unfair to deny to his songs all musical value. They are graceful airs, *sicilianos*, *minuets*, or gentle polonaises with love lyrics and a three-part setting that might equally well be sung or played on a harp or cembalo.[8] Yet this is what in the eighteenth century passed for folk-music, was extremely popular, and was included in many publications without any mention of source or author.

TRUTOVSKY'S ALBUMS

With the three Trutovsky albums of 1776-79 (see Appendix I) we make a marked step in the direction of more genuine material. The whole approach had changed. While in Teplov we meet with the grandseigneurial amateur whose sole aim was to provide a little diversion and pass a pleasant hour or two, Trutovsky set about his task professionally. He came from the heart of the people—very probably the Little Russian people. The son of a regimental priest, he started his service at court as a lackey during the short reign of Peter III (1761), but was soon moved to better quarters and appointed court *gooslist* (Lutanist). Courtiers quickly took an interest in him, possibly even Potemkin himself, since his first collection includes several of Potemkin's favourite melodies. He was also to be found in

---

[7] Jacob von Stahlin, *Music and Ballet in the Eighteenth Century*, republished in 1935, Leningrad, p. 90.

[8] A complete listing of them is given by Findeisen in Vol. II of his *Sketches*.

the house of Naryshkins where music was cultivated in a number of ways and where the Princess Marie herself was a performer of folk-songs.

With this sort of music-making in private houses, we encounter for the first time in Russian history something that was to acquire paramount importance in the shaping of the Russian school of composers. In Trutovsky's time the folk-like intonations of the capitals and their suburbs thrived in these salons of the Naryshkins, the Lvovs, or Bezborodkos. All manner of foreign and native musicians were to be found side by side, humble instrumentalists as well as famous prima donnas. And after the sophistication and exclusiveness of the earlier eighteenth century the doors are opened again to the greater simplicity and democratization of the arts in the course of the nineteenth century. To this massive process the folk-song devotees and collectors contributed a lion's share, for among them were to be found representatives of all classes of society, from high state officials to modest school-teachers, from rich landowners to wandering minstrels and tramps.

THE PRACH ALBUM OF 1790

Along with Trutovsky whose last and fourth volume appeared in 1795 we must place the Silesian Czech, Johann-Gottfried Prach. There has been a great deal of confusion about Prach, but it is now established that he had come to Russia some time during the seventh decade of the eighteenth century and that he was a music-teacher in the schools for the children of the nobility. His name has been associated firmly with several editions of folk-songs, especially one that found its way into the hands of Beethoven when the great composer was engaged on his three Razumovsky quartets, Op. 59. Although this takes us already into the nineteenth century, Prach's original collection dates from 1790. However, his role in all the three collections associated with him is confined to the accompaniments. These he was engaged to supply by the actual collector of the albums, Nicholas Lvov.

N. A. LVOV (1751-1803)

Lvov was a heightened specimen of the Teplov type; not strictly a musician, but otherwise an encyclopaedically educated man, a poet, architect, draughtsman, and high-ranking diplomat whose plans were used for the building of a memorial church in Mohilev, where a historic meeting took place between Catherine the Great and the Emperor Joseph II of Austria. All that Lvov did was done with great acumen, and his collections of folk-songs are prefaced by some of his general thoughts on folk-music which are valid to this day. The third and last edition of the Lvov-Prach album was published in 1815, and it was from this that Beethoven selected the Russian folk-songs which he harmonized for voice with the accompaniment of the piano, violin, and cello.

Prach's accompaniments go much further than those of Trutovsky. In place of Trutovsky's single bass line we have here regularly constituted harmonies, obviously in the German classical manner, and ill-suited to the melodies. But since the latter likewise cannot be trusted for accuracy or genuineness,[9]

Example 12. Melody ascribed to Empress Elizabeth, harmonized by Prach, 1790, Findeisen, vol. II, p. 305.

we must be content with those albums as they are—a further step in the right direction, but still a long way removed from giving us an even approximate image of the true folk-song. Among the melodies in Prach's first album there is a tune that is attributed to Elizabeth: *In the village Pokrovskoye.* It would be well to quote this particular example from Prach, since it shows us both the gay Empress and the obscure German musician who set her charming and naïve effusion (Example 12).

[9] The tunes comprising the Prach volumes were questioned by Alexander Serov, a prominent Russian music critic in the nineteenth century.

Russian music

SERF ORCHESTRAS

The Trutovsky and Prach albums are predecessors of innumerable folk-song collections partially listed in Appendix I. In a similar way, and using the very same pseudo folk-song material, the eighteenth century prepared the *Kamarinskaya* of Glinka upon which Tchaikovsky drew for his share of the burgeoning Russian symphonic tradition. The development of musicmaking in the city salons was paralleled by the growth of orchestras on private estates. In western music histories a great deal is said about the splendid residences of princes and noblemen where composers such as Bach and Haydn had ample opportunity to perfect their art. Similar residences developed in Russia after Catherine made her vast grants of land to the nobility. Most musicians in the country were serfs who proved themselves equally as singers and players. That they were highly prized is shown by advertisements and 'wanted' notices when they ran away to freedom:

Arseniev brothers. Distinctive marks: middle height, Nicholas, blonde, grey eyes, can sing and play the fiddle. Feodor, darker, also grey eyes, sings bass and plays the fiddle. . . .[10]

KHANDOSHKIN

Ivan Khandoshkin (1740-1804) was a serf, legally liberated, who became known as a gifted violinist and prolific composer. He was one of the first to transfer folk-song into the domain of pure instrumental music. He was active in St Petersburg and achieved fame in the last decade of Catherine's reign. Thus, in 1780, he was mentioned for his part in a joint concert with the Italian Sartori and the singer Gonzalez. His *Variations on Folk-songs* went through several editions, one having appeared in Amsterdam[11] (Example 13).

Other music-making in the age of the Empresses centred around the theatre. From the national point of view this was its least interesting aspect, for the music was rarely more than a pale replica of Italian *opera buffa* or light French vaudevilles. The heir of Catherine, Paul, had his residence in the palace

[10] Quoted by Y. Keldysh in *Russian Music in the Eighteenth Century*, Moscow, 1965, p. 107.
[11] Discussed by Y. Keldysh, ibid.

of Gatchina, near St Petersburg, and there at one time we find Bortniansky, later director of the Imperial Chapel. The subtly fanciful Assafiev (Igor Glebov)—possibly the greatest Russian writer on music, from whose piercing eye only very few aspects of the entire field remained hidden—has devoted a study to this early Bortniansky and his activity as an operatic composer.

Example 13. Variations on a folk-song, by Ivan Khandoshkin (Keldysh, p. 406).

The charm of these operas of Bortniansky, written to French words, lies in an extremely lovely fusion of noble Italian lyricism with the dreaminess of the French chanson and the sharp frivolity of the couplets. The clever and observing Bortniansky, endowed with unusual musical gifts and a skill which he acquired abroad, could without much trouble plan and develop artistically such seemingly contrasted stylistic elements.[12]

[12] B. Assafiev: *On Two Operas of Bortniansky*, Moscow, 1927, p. 18.

4

Glinka

The beginning of the Nineteenth Century points to a widespread cult of music in the home, both in the country and in the cities. There are few reminiscences of that era without several pages devoted to musical pastimes. It is all dominated by the *song*. The village, the landowner's mansion, the urban residences, the suburbs, the outskirts of the towns, the roadside inns and public houses; the petty bourgeois and merchant circles, as well as the families of the nobility, the houses and palaces of the courtiers, finally theatrical shows with a varied repertoire: all these are saturated by all manner of song. Equally permeated by song-like qualities are the experiments of Russian musicians in composition.[1]

This song-like quality can best be expressed by the Russian word *pesennost* for which there is no exact translation. Somewhere far back it was compounded from the flow of the folk-song and the measured solemnity of *znamenny* chant; and just as a term for this compound cannot be found in any dictionary, so its two ingredients have no parallel in any other system of music. Thus the Russian *pesennost* constitutes a unique and precious domain of general melodic invention.

First and foremost we find it in the folk-songs themselves, and innumerable examples could be cited from the categories of the laments, love-songs, and dirges. Such melodies are the reflection of an eminently musical people whose history was hewn out of a struggle against obstacles: a far from gentle climate, a frequent exposure to enemy attacks, inward strifes and calamities. They are not melodies that bask in the sunshine, like those of Italy, but root-melodies that make their way out of the soil with difficulty (Example 14).

[1] B. Assafiev: *Composers of the First Half of the Nineteenth Century*, Moscow, 1959, p. 3.

For well over a century, from the time of Mezenetz through the eighteenth century and up to Glinka's arrival—that is through the entire period of forced westernization—this Russian *pesennost* was allowed to remain in a dormant state in remote villages. Every move towards the centres brought an inevitable depersonalization, loss of character, and a permeation by current city intonations. The folk-song collectors of the eighteenth and early nineteenth centuries never got below the alien layer. Ivan Rupin and Daniel Kashin followed upon Trutovsky

Example 14. *Loochina* (*The Spill*), from the Kashin Collection, 1833.

and Nicolas Lvov. Rupin, or Rupini, as he was Italianized in the Moscow opera, often composed his own melodies, like the immensely popular *There Races on the Gallant Troika*. Kashin, whose collection of over 100 songs appeared in 1833, was a liberated serf to whom his master had given every opportunity, including study with the famous Sarti. He became the musician-in-residence to Moscow University and figured in every festivity as pianist and conductor. He was often on the point of grasping the true *pesennost*, as Example 14 will show. In fact, he is far more a precursor of Glinka than the often-cited song writers, or composers of the so-called 'romances' with piano accompaniment—Aliabiev, Varlamov, Guriliov, the Titovs—whose common denominator is a tepid and sentimental form of melody. Glinka, who also occasionally indulged in such romances or duets, elevated them to a position of some historic importance, while the infinitely more genuine Kashin is known only as a collector.

All of this is completely overshadowed by Glinka. As Elgar
in England shook hands over the centuries with Purcell, by-
passing legions of imitators and adepts of a foreign culture, so
Glinka stretched over to the Moscow masters of the threshold
of the sixteenth and seventeenth centuries, putting an end to
all doubts about the future of Russian music and creating
works the inherent worth of which is increasing from generation
to generation.

Glinka's learning processes cause wonder and admiration.
His first teachers were the players in his uncle's serf orchestra
who lived just a few miles away from the village of Novospass-
kaya, in Smolensk province, where he was born. Whenever a
particularly honoured guest arrived the players were at once
sent for.

During supper they usually played Russian folk-songs arranged for
2 flutes, 2 clarinets, 2 horns, and 2 bassoons, and it was possibly
from these songs that I acquired my love for our native Russian
music. . . . Above all, I loved the orchestra, and of orchestral works
preferred, after the Russian songs, the Overture to *Ma Tante Aurore*
by Boildieu, *Lodoiska* by Kreutzer and *Deux Aveugles* by Mehul. . . .[2]

Having been sent to a St Petersburg boarding-school, he
managed to take three piano lessons from John Field, but then
passed to a certain Karl Meier, getting as far as a Hummel
concerto (1822). During the holidays he played the violin in
his uncle's orchestra and also tried his hand at composing with
various chamber-music combinations. Thus, through sheer
practice, he gradually acquired his minute knowledge of
orchestral colours. In the *Memoirs* he speaks of all those matters
as if they happened accidentally and were little more than a
diversion in an essentially lazy life; but behind his words one
senses a tremendous will and capacity for work. From instruments he passed to voices, and was greatly helped by something that again sounds like a gay pastime, but was in reality
a wonderful schooling in vocal practices: the singing of summer
serenades, sometimes from a boat, with the Golitzyns and a
certain Tolstoy ('I was agreeably impressed by the sweet voice
of Th. M. Tolstoy in the Venetian barcarolle *Da brava Catina*').

[2] *Memoirs of M. I. Glinka and his Correspondence with Relatives and Friends*,
St Petersburg, 1887, p. 5.

By now he had written a string quartet which was played at the Lvovs'. Now these Lvovs, Feodor and Alexis, were to wield a paramount influence on the destinies of Russian church music. Feodor had just succeeded Bortniansky as Director of the Imperial Chapel; Alexis, a brilliant violinist, praised in Germany by Schumann in the *Neue Zeitschrift für Musik*, was brought rather uncomfortably close to Glinka in the days following the production of *A Life for the Czar*. The casual mention of all those people and their informal music-making in the *Memoirs* gave rise to the legend of Glinka's indolence and pleasure-loving life in those Petersburg years. They were, however, an indispensable preparation for his years of study and wanderings abroad, on which he was just about to embark.

The immediate pretext for departure was what Glinka calls a 'quadrille' of ailments for the cure of which the doctors dispatched him to Italy and Germany in the spring of 1830. He did not return home until four years later, and during that period he had become a mature master of practically all forms of composition. His Italian masters were numerous, but it was in Berlin that he found one who determined his course as a composer: Siegfried Dehn. Glinka, in the *Memoirs*, readily acknowledges his debt to Dehn:

. . . he did not torture me in a scholastic and systematic manner; on the contrary nearly every lesson revealed to me something new and interesting . . .[3]

But this does not exhaust Dehn's role. To define it more fully a little digression is necessary.

Musical composition, as Glinka's precursors and he himself imagined it, fell into two categories: it was *either* a simple melody in the top line, with more or less conventional harmony underneath—such were most operatic arias and chansons, the 'romances' with piano or harp accompaniment, the instrumental works of the Khandoshkin school—*or* it was strict polyphony, such as was taught by the Bologna academicians of the type of Padre Martini. This we find in whole fugal movements of Bortniansky and Berezovsky as integral parts of their *Concerts Spirituels*, sung at many liturgies just before the carrying out of the Host. Neither category was conducive to real music. The

[3] M. I. Glinka, op. cit., p. 93.

Дорогому и высокоцѣнимому Альфреду Альфредовичу
Свану
къ 70-му дню рожденія.
9-го Октября 1960 г.

Specimen of Kriuk notation with cinnabar marks of Shaidurov,
transcribed by Gardner.

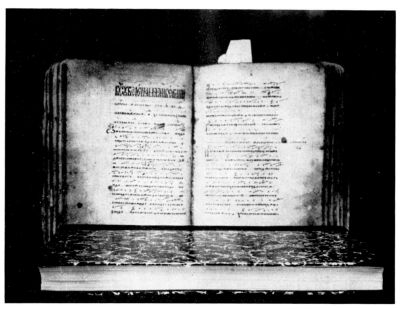

1. Manuscript without cinnabar marks.

2. Group of women singers of Pechory (Maria Spies is kneeling at the right).

3. Russian peasant women singers of Pskov.

4. Piatnitzky choir recording, 1911.   5. Eugenie Lineva.

6. Nicholas Findeisen.

7. Ivan Gardner, 1970.

8. Maxim Brajnikov.

9. Nicholas Lvov.

10. Ivan Rupini (real name Rupin,
    Italianized for Moscow).

11. Prince Vladimir Odoyevsky, 18

12. Mili Balakirev.

secret lay in the way Mozart dealt with polyphonic themes: in giving them a certain *cantabile* curve, e.g. in the Finale of the *Jupiter* Symphony (Example 15a). Glinka took the Mozart manner to heart, and it is not too difficult to imagine that his eyes were opened precisely by Dehn. How near Glinka's manner is to that of Mozart we can see from the opening chorus in his opera *Life for the Czar* (Example 15b). Thus a hybrid form is obtained here that is neither vertical nor horizontal, which was Glinka's way of dealing with Russian intonations and which only he could achieve thanks to a combination

Example 15, (*a*) Mozart; (*b*) Glinka, *Life for the Czar*.

of traits: a highly cultivated and sensitive *ear*, and great opportunities of learning which he handled with the utmost intelligence and discrimination. In addition, one must note his uncanny sense of colour.

Let us see how these combined qualities helped him to attain the unique position that he holds in Russian music. His ear enabled him to hear what was below the surface and what constituted the hidden Russian *pesennost* which the whole preceding period could not hear, excepting, possibly, Kashin and people like him. That Glinka's *pesennost*, though it came near that of the folk-songs, did not coincide with them, is only another manifestation of his genius. Only occasionally, as in the *Kamarinskaya*, does he resort to actual folk melodies. Often he gives some theme that his ear was quick enough to catch, a kind of symphonic transformation. In his *Memoirs* he mentions the song of a Luga driver which stuck firmly in his mind and which he utilized for some of the phrases of his main hero in *Life for the Czar*. His own *pesennost* is consequently the result of the workings of his musical mind. This makes him closely akin to the sixteenth-century Moscow precentors who used the familiar patterns of *znamenny* chant and moulded them in accordance with their musical fancy. In either case the material was of the quality that makes up the Russian *pesennost,* which is devoid of alien features and should suggest to the Russian as well as the western ear a typically Russian sound.

Let us now see how his intelligence and subtle discrimination served him in finding the right forms for his noble material. Above we have heard him confess that *after* folk-song he most enjoyed overtures to French operas. This love determined also the choice for his symphonic forms. Carefully avoiding large constructions and desisting from writing a regular symphony, he cultivated the overture form. In instrumental terms this means *Sonatina,* a contracted sonata with a minimum of development. All his three operatic overtures—those to *Life for the Czar, Russlan and Ludmilla,* and *Prince Kholmsky*—are ideal instances of such an orchestral sonatina.

Finally there is Glinka's sense of colour. In the 'Notes' on orchestration which he put together, late in life, at the request of Serov, he very carefully defined the 'substance' of the orchestra as well as its 'surfeit', meaning by the former the later classic composition of Mozart and early Beethoven, and by the latter the expanded body of Berlioz. While relishing many of Berlioz's innovations and making occasional use of them himself, he nevertheless recommended classic proportions. The brilliant sound of the Russian orchestra—for herein his successors leaned on him—never depends on the number of players, but rather on the application of pure timbres, a strict differentiation of string and wind colours, and, mostly, on a vocal approach which is the result of his *pesennost* being essentially derived from voices, songs, arias, and melodically suffused recitatives.

GLINKA'S FIRST OPERA

When Glinka returned home in 1834 with a definite idea of composing a national opera the general *niveau* of culture in the capitals was already fairly high, as compared with the times of Catherine and Paul. But it was still a very tiny élite at the top that was affected. For a while their minds were too occupied with general and political philosophy; but when they failed to carry their ideas into life with the Decembrist uprising in 1825, the moment had come for an unparalleled wave of great literature. Pushkin was at the height of his powers, Jukovsky was the tutor of the young Prince Alexander (later Alexander II), Gogol had just arrived. Around them swarmed the minor poets of an almost Augustan age. Glinka's endowment, however, was so purely musical that all this literary activity passed by him, though he was 'frequently seeing Jukovsky and Pushkin'. He actually started his opera without any libretto. With complete musical numbers in his portfolio he would come to Jukovsky and ask him to fill in some words. Laughingly Jukovsky sent him to a half-German versifier who provided Glinka with what probably is the most illiterate libretto ever written. But psychologically it was exactly what was needed and, in complete happiness, Glinka spent the better part of a year in the writing of *Life for the Czar*, or *Ivan Sussanin* as it was originally (and subsequently) called. The rehearsing of the work did not pass without the usual intrigues of the theatrical *camarilla*, but the actual production in November 1836 was crowned with success, and Glinka became a national figure.

Having reached the top, he did not quite know where to turn. An appointment at the Imperial Chapel brought no satisfaction since he had to collaborate with Alexis Lvov, a musician with whom he had not a single point in common. He was tempted to tackle the religious domain (Cherubim Song in C), but this was a sphere which he had not encountered during his apprenticeship days and he was therefore not equipped for it. His life was chaotic, partly on account of an unwise marriage. Yet his creative powers were still on the rise and, without even a proper place or home to work, he penned down whole sections of another opera, *Russlan and Ludmilla*. He himself described how the libretto took shape:

I was writing my bits and pieces . . . I had hoped to make a plan under the direction of Pushkin, but his premature death thwarted my intentions. In 1837 or 1838, in the winter, I used to play with great gusto some excerpts from *Russlan*. . . . Amongst my visitors was a certain Bakhturin; he undertook to make a plan and wrote it out in a quarter of an hour, being drunk as a Lord and, just think, the opera was done in accordance with this plan! Bakhturin instead of Pushkin. . . .[4]

[4] M. I. Glinka, op. cit., p. 144.

This description has been challénged by Stassov who says that when he was writing the *Memoirs* (1854) Glinka had completely forgotten that there was originally a rather detailed plan which was not adhered to (Stassov published it in *Russkaya Starina* for 1871). But we can be sure that, from Glinka's life amidst a Bohemian crowd, Glebov is not far wrong when he refers to the manner of work on *Russlan* as a 'friendly dinner-party'.

In *Russlan*, Glinka's favourite intonations attain their most perfect realization. From beginning to end this work is an opera-cantata, where every phrase vibrates and sings in strains that are as different from contemporary western romantic opera as the strains of Chopin were from western piano music.

Example 16. *Russlan*, prologue, Bayan's song, Glinka.

What constitutes Glinka's particular individuality or 'handwriting'? This is harder to determine than in Chopin's case, as the latter's originality is immediately apparent in quite unprecedented turns of melody, unexpected harmonies, and other fanciful whims. This cannot be done with Glinka. Nothing glaringly new appears anywhere, but the sum-total of musical speech is the result of Glinka's taste, measure, and proportion, imbued, moreover, with the hidden accents of the old Russian heritage (i.e. his *pesennost*; Example 16). There is not a single formation here that one could not find in the romantic armoury, yet the whole effect is a revelation. The old sounds are suddenly transformed into a new song of spring. Thirty years later a similar thing happened in Wagner's *Meistersinger,* a work of far greater proportions and filled with a similar *pesennost* deriving this time from a Germanic heritage.

Russlan went down badly. The poor composer could not even decide whether to come out for a bow and had to take courage from a remark by an army general and friend who perceived his doubts. 'Go,' said the general, 'Christ suffered more than you.' After *Russlan* the public interest in Glinka abated still further. A third quasi-operatic venture—*Prince Kholmsky*—took the form of incidental music only. Yet even here Glinka's instinct was of the truest, and the work comes close to Beethoven's *Egmont.*

Then came his journeys abroad. It is as if he wanted to forget his native land and seek inspiration elsewhere. He went to Paris. There he heard that Liszt had departed for Spain and was seized by an irrepressible desire to follow his example. He spent two whole years (1845-7) wandering in various parts of that legendary country, and the musical result was his two Spanish Overtures, *Jota Arragonesa* and *Night in Madrid.* One by one he was supplying classic specimens and landmarks by which the subsequent Russian School was to be recognized. The Spanish overtures differ from those for the operas in being potpourris rather than overtures proper. In spirit and colour they reach out even beyond the Russian School towards the impressionistic canvases of Debussy. Between them came the pivotal *Kamarinskaya* (see Preface), while his wanderings continued through Germany, interrupted by intermittent returns home and prolonged stays in Warsaw. His references to all those vital matters in the *Memoirs* are an almost ludicrous understatement, a sort of flippant table-talk. Later admirers of his, especially Tchaikovsky, could not get over the seeming triviality of his story, but repeated readings induce one to find in it much more than appears on the surface. In the end a kind of sympathy develops that one would scarcely find when re-reading Wagner's *Life.*

The restless existence came to a temporary close during the last stay in Paris when war between France and Russia was declared, in 1854. As if to give the last touch to his peculiar view of life, Glinka recounts a final visit to the Jardin des Plantes to gaze at the small hippopotamus which the Khedive of Egypt presented to Napoleon III. Here the *Memoirs* end, but fortunately Glinka's sister, Madame Shestakova, who will figure prominently in the subsequent pages of our history, has added a brief description of the composer's life in her immediate family (1854-6).

What is valuable in her account is the mention of the people who surrounded Glinka. Most of them reappear later as an integral part of the whole post-Glinka set-up: the singers Karmalina and Leonova, Dargomyjsky, Serov, the brothers Stassov, Vladimir Odoyevsky, and, towards the very end, the newly arrived Ulybyshev and Balakirev. The growing interest in church music also crops up, and it is this that determines to a large extent the direction of Glinka's final departure in 1856: Berlin and his old teacher Siegfried Dehn. His letters from Berlin are full of his studies with Dehn on the Gregorian modes and contrapuntal exercises. Here is truly another case of striving for perfection not unlike that of Schubert, who also embarked on lessons in theory in the last year of his life. Dehn was to write the report of his last illness and death to Russia, and one must give him credit for having done it with tact and warmth.

GLINKA IN THE LIGHT OF CRITICISM

Madame Shestakova, in her account, lets drop the following phrase:

. . . that it was harder for him to compose in Russia than anywhere else is very understandable; there was nothing to admire in climate or nature, while the complete neglect of his talent by the Russian society paralysed in him all inspiration. What would he not have written if he were living now (1870) when his works are so warmly appreciated?[5]

If Glinka himself was not sure where he was going, what could be expected of his contemporaries who could applaud only what everyone else was applauding and who were quite unprepared for a serious musical phenomenon in their midst. So we can only marvel at those minds who quickly realized the great good fortune of Russia in having reared a great composer and got into the fray over his works and their reception.

[5] *Remembrances of Shestakova*, St Petersburg, 1887.

The first was V. Odoyevsky, an exact contemporary of Glinka, a man of great culture whose now-published works reveal a whole panorama of the music in Russia between 1830 and Glinka's death. He reported widely on all the concerts that took place in the capitals (he lived intermittently in St Petersburg and Moscow). His house was the meeting-place of celebrities, and Glinka relates how, in the days of the preparation of *Russlan*, Liszt was invited and given a few pages of the manuscript, which he read flawlessly at the piano to the astonishment of all. But Odoyevsky did much more: he had the prophetic sense of pointing to the sources at a time when they were forgotten. He was one of the first to perceive the polyphonic nature of the Russian folk-song. Even more remarkable was his advocacy of *znamenny* chant which he never tired of explaining to Glinka. These two currents he saw in close interrelation. Here is an excerpt from one of his letters (to I. P. Saharov, a collector of old manuscripts):

... I have finished a book and its title is *Manual of the Fundamental Laws of Melody and Harmony adapted principally to the reading of our Old Church Singing*. A little long, but I cannot help it. For fifteen years I have been involved in this subject and have now, with God's help, reached a stage when Shaidurov, Makarievsky, and Mezenetz [see Appendix II] are quite clear to me ... I have analysed it in detail and can construct a whole theory of our ancient melody and harmony, quite different from that of the West and very profound. ... To interest you further I can tell you that in passing I have discovered the scale of our folk-songs, which, if applied, will sound truly Russian, and by which all distortions of our melodies that have misled the Praches, Varlamovs, and other Germans, can be removed. ...[6]

Odoyevsky was a witness to the composition of *A Life for the Czar* and tells about it in a letter to V. Stassov in 1857. This is where the paths from Glinka cross to his analysts and critics. Alexander Serov, though he rivalled Odoyevsky in education and knowledge, was of too paradoxical a mind to maintain an even keel. He hailed Glinka's works but warned against attaching to them more than a purely Russian significance. This, together with an inordinate advocacy of Wagner, brought him into conflict with his former bosom friend, V. Stassov, and a

[6] V. F. Odoyevsky, *Musical-Literary Heritage*, Moscow, 1956, pp. 514-15.

whole storm broke loose over Serov's article *Russlan and the Russlanists.* All this goes a long way towards showing that Madame Shestakova's words could apply only to the indifference of the masses, while the best minds of the time were profoundly moved. Stassov's role in the propaganda of Glinka was historic, and we owe to him the preservation of many a detail of Glinka's personality as also the first biography. The literature on Glinka steadily accumulated, leading up to the writings of Assafiev (Igor Glebov) whose last exhaustive study was done during the siege of Leningrad by the Germans in 1942.

5

The Balakirev Circle

RUSSIA IN 1855

The fiasco of the Crimean War and the death of Nicholas I deeply affected the flow of Russian life. In the words of the historian Platonov:

The practice of the new government showed important differences from the methods of the preceding régime. There was a whiff of softness and tolerance characteristic of the new monarch (Alexander II). Petty press constraints were removed; the universities breathed more freely; society showed a more vigorous spirit; it was said that the sovereign wanted truth, enlightenment, honesty, and a free voicing of views.[1]

While in the centre of it all lay the liberation of the peasants and their settlement on their own land, the release of the brakes set in the Nicholas era led to a torrential creative outburst in which the arts shone with particular brilliance.

In literature, Tolstoy was about to begin his *War and Peace*, Dostoyevsky his *Crime and Punishment*, and Goncharov his *Oblomov*: in painting, the historical and realistic school culminated in the organization of movable exhibitions (*peradvijniki*); and the greatest things were to come in music. But there was one brief moment when Glinka was living in his sister's house, ailing and inactive, when the fate of Russian music was in jeopardy (1854-5).

The writings of Odoyevsky reflect the general musical activities in Russia for more than forty years. He reviewed concerts in both capitals, contributed articles on musical theory to leading periodicals, and corresponded with the great figures of the

[1] *Istoriya Rossiyi*, Petrograd, 1917, p. 701.

world of music, always breaking a lance for the right cause and taking an active part in the polemics around Wagner, Liszt, Berlioz, and, most of all, Glinka. Of interest is his report on the playing of the Rubinsteins:

> In the older Rubinstein (Anton) one can feel a mature performer; the younger (Nicholas) who is not more than seven is still a child. He knows few pieces from memory and those that he has learnt he never plays the same way twice, but put before him what you wish and he will read it like a book, and what cunning he will use to play the big chords. Since his feet cannot reach the pedal it can be of little use to him. . . .[2]

Towards the end of Glinka's life, Serov and Stassov entered into the fray with endless discussion of his two operas. But who was to succeed him? Strangely enough the same question was being asked at the same time about Schumann's successor in Germany, where the mantle fell on Brahms. In Russia there were several possibilities.

The 'older Rubinstein' had by then established his reputation as a pianist of world renown, but his ideals as a composer led him away from the national path. Like Glinka, he had studied with Dehn in Berlin; but Dehn did not leave on him the mark that he had left on the older composer, nor impress him with the necessity of turning to Russian sources. Thus he sank deeply into the German school of Spohr and Mendelssohn. Out of this morass of imitation he was never to rise for the rest of his life. Rubinstein was a prolific composer with serious intentions. In the early fifties he had written two symphonies—the second, *Ocean*, was popular at one time—and three concerti for his own instrument. All of this was, however, beside the point so far as the Russian school was concerned. This was realized, of course, by Glinka and everyone around him. Thereafter no one pinned hopes on him.

DARGOMYJSKY

But there was in Glinka's entourage another composer not disinclined to assume the role of successor. Dargomyjsky actually possessed certain features that qualified him, but he could not measure up to all requirements, at least not in Glinka's

[2] V. F. Odoyevsky, op. cit., p. 215.

eyes. Only nine years younger than Glinka, and a product of the same seigneurial society, he was never obliged to earn a living. Dargomyjsky moved to St Petersburg early in life, and picked up what musical knowledge he could without serious study. The casualness of his incursions into music and the nonchalant way in which he spoke of the various disciplines were antipathetic to Glinka:

Glinka handed to me the theoretical manuscripts of Professor Dehn which he had brought back from Berlin. I copied them out with my own hand and quickly absorbed the supposed intricacies of figured bass and counterpoint . . .[3]

Dargomyjsky's talent lay in the portrayal of characteristic types and dramatic situations, in the grotesque rather than the lyrical. All of this made him strong in the vocal sphere and rather inept in the instrumental. But any mention of this was forbidden. This is what Glinka's sister says in her memoirs:

When he was writing his opera *Russalka*, Dargomyjsky used to demonstrate bits of it in my house. My brother tried to persuade him to tackle a comic opera when he had finished with this one, saying that he was convinced that it would turn out to be a *chef d'œuvre*. But Dargomyjsky was always peeved by these remarks and told him once: 'You must think that I cannot do anything but comic stuff!' To which my brother retorted that he was aware of the splendid non-comic scenes in *Russalka*, but that for the writing of a comic opera a special talent was needed, the kind that he saw only in him.[4]

The somewhat ironic note in the references to Dargomyjsky persisted even after Glinka's death. Even his surname provoked all sorts of distortions and puns.[5] *Russalka* was staged in 1856, the opera being reviewed and analysed there and then by Serov. In a letter to him the composer thanks him for his 'kind and intelligent words'. Thanks to its various highly dramatic moments—Natasha's despair and suicide, the duet between the

[3] Dargomyjsky, *Brief Biographical Note*, Petrograd, 1921, p. 5.
[4] L. I. Shestakova, *The Last Years of the Life and the Death of M. I. Glinka*, St Petersburg, 1887, p. 338.
[5] The first syllable of the name Dargomyjsky comes from the verb *give* and the third syllable is the word *mouse*. The play on these words was witty but derisive.

mad Miller and the Prince, Natasha's seducer—the work acquired a firm footing in the Russian operatic repertory; yet, as a musical achievement, it cannot stand on its own feet, and any comparison of it with Glinka, or the operas of the younger generation of Russian composers, is out of the question. Most of all, Dargomyjsky's approach to and handling of the folk-song material—and there were ample opportunities for this in the libretto of *Russalka*—is, if anything, a step backward towards Glinka's precursors. Of Glinka's *pesennost* there is not a trace.

Glinka undoubtedly sensed this when he spoke of Dargomyjsky's vein for the comic. But he did not depart for Berlin until fate had confronted him with the musician who was truly made to become his successor—Mili Balakirev.

THE FORMATION OF THE BALAKIREV CIRCLE

In the spring of 1855 Mili Balakirev arrived in St Petersburg in the company of the landowner Ulybyshev, who immediately took him over to Madame Shestakova's house to meet Glinka. Being asked to play, he performed his Fantasia on themes from *Ivan Sussanin* to Glinka's great satisfaction. Undoubtedly the great composer had heard dozens of amateurish improvisations on his opera, but here the young pianist—almost entirely self-taught from childhood—displayed a highly modern piano technique, introducing Glinka's themes with a truly Lisztian sweep and moreover betraying a remarkable kinship to them in touches of his own personal style—his own *pesennost*.

Born into the family of a minor official in Nijni-Novgorod (now Gorki) on the Volga and the eldest of four children, he could scarcely count on support from his parents. Hence it was most providential that he was befriended by Ulybyshev, an enlightened dilettante and author of the first Russian biography of Mozart. Musically Balakirev grew up on the Ulybyshev estate and practised conducting with the local orchestra. Unable to give him systematic training, yet supplying invaluable experience so needed for a lavish natural talent, Ulybyshev also gave him a proper entrée into the musical life of the capital. The meeting with Glinka was most fortunate and determined the whole direction of Balakirev's endeavours.

Meetings! How far-reaching the influence of those between men of genius can become is shown by the next years in the young musician's life. Chronologically his important introductions may be catalogued:

1855	Glinka and his sister
1856	César Cui, Vladimir and Dimitry Stassov
1857	Moussorgsky
1861	Rimsky-Korsakov
1862	Borodin

Here, in essence we have the whole circle. Some of them we have already encountered. Others, like Serov and Lvov, remained aloof. But the focal personalities were all around Balakirev by 1862. He was a born leader and was not happy unless he could criticize, instruct or direct someone. Advise he never did, since his advice amounted to a command, and when this was crossed or ignored, Balakirev's interest faded away no matter how close the relationship to him had been. But when his counsel prevailed, even alien figures, such as Tchaikovsky, were imperceptibly drawn into the sphere of his influence.

His was a fierce battle for supremacy which he finally lost; but the years during which he stood at the helm belong to the most glorious in Russian music. In his humble devotion to Glinka he never wavered. This is what Madame Shestakova says:

Whenever I planned to make my brother's music better known, Balakirev seized on to my idea and, with love, energy, and patience, carried it through to the end.[6]

CUI

César Cui became his closest collaborator. The early life of this musician, whom history has so strangely shuffled in with the makers of Russian music, was passed in Lithuania and Poland, both countries being then part of the Russian Empire. His only teacher was the Polish composer Moniuszko (author of the first Polish national opera) and his first notes in music were songs to Polish and French words. In all of this he did

[6] Quoted by E. Garden, *Balakirev, A Critical Study of His Life and Music*, London, Faber and Faber, 1967, p. 70.

not go very far, as he was bent on the career of a military engineer, preparation for which took him to St Petersburg. There, after graduation, he settled, first as an instructor, and later as a professor of fortification, rising to the rank of general and continuing throughout his life to contribute to the literature on this subject.

Cui's ideology must have been strong and clearly defined in those formative years, although we hear nothing of it until his providential meeting with Balakirev. He impressed his slightly younger colleague with his ready knowledge of opera—he was working on Pushkin's *Caucasian Prisoner*—and Balakirev, whom opera interested but slightly, henceforth relied on his judgment in musico-dramatic matters. Thus the two of them exercised a joint control over the initial efforts of all who came into their midst. Cui's gift was in the small forms, bordering on the salon. He never touched either folk-song or liturgical music, and yet his aspirations were towards grand opera and grandiose symphonic forms such as those of Berlioz and Liszt. Unsuccessful in all but the intimate song and a kind of minor lyricism, he assumed the role of critic, often failing to grasp essential things, but rendering service to those of Balakirev's orientation as against the conservative Rubinstein camp and the Wagnerism of Serov.

Having formed their partnership and clearly divided its functions, Balakirev and Cui began to look for a suitable location. With Glinka out of the picture their gaze was turned to the house of Dargomyjsky on Mokhovaya Street. They were unsure as to how Dargomyjsky would fit into their ideas, being puzzled also by the kind of society that used to assemble around him, with all those women singers whom he taught and accompanied, and his old father sitting motionless in a huge armchair against the wall. But when his father died Dargomyjsky moved to another apartment and the musical gatherings suddenly stopped. However, it was in that motley assembly at Dargomyjsky's that one day two young officers in the uniform of the Preobrajensky regiment approached Balakirev and Cui, anxious to make their acquaintance. One of them was Feodor Vanliarsky to whom Moussorgsky later dedicated a song, 'Not like thunder from Heaven', and the other was Moussorgsky who, as they soon learned, was a skilful pianist.

Balakirev was delighted to find someone to join him in playing the classic and romantic composers in four-hand arrangements. In this way began Moussorgsky's turbulent apprenticeship with Balakirev. Remembering it much later, Balakirev wrote:

Not being a theoretician, I could not teach Moussorgsky harmony, but explained to him the form of compositions.[7]

He had found an object on which to impose his stubborn will, but it worked only so long as the 'object' obeyed implicitly. Five years later he was to write, 'Moussorgsky is almost an idiot'.[8] But through their meeting another stone was laid in the foundation of the new Russian school.

VLADIMIR AND DIMITRY STASSOV

To cement those stones was the function of the brothers Stassov, more particularly the older one, Vladimir. Dimitry and Vladimir had been given a first-class education by their father, the famous architect of various Moscow churches and St Petersburg buildings. Vladimir studied art and archaeology, served in a number of official government capacities, travelled widely in Europe in the company of Count Demidov-San Donato, and in 1854 joined the staff of the St Petersburg Public Library as archivist and assistant to the Director, Baron Korff. His task was to catalogue all the holdings, in the process of which he read voraciously, accumulating a vast knowledge of Russian antiquity and history, the subjects which interested him most.

Having also had musical instruction from the leading St Petersburg pianists (Henselt and Gerke), he made Glinka's acquaintance in 1849. From that moment the course of Russian national music became his prime concern. After Glinka's death his enthusiasm was automatically transferred to Balakirev, leading to an endless solicitude about the perpetuation of the Glinka heritage. What Balakirev effected by means of editing, correcting, conducting, and arranging, Stassov proclaimed, publicizing his exploits by means of press notices. He also supplied him with data from the library archives. Their voluminous correspondence, which began soon after their

[7] M. D. Calvocoressi, *Modest Mussorgsky*, London, 1956, p. 24.
[8] *Letters of M. Balakirev with V. Stassov*, Petrograd, 1917, p. 183.

meeting in 1857, touched upon all that was dear to both of them: the cult of Schumann, Berlioz, and Liszt, the collection of folk material, the performance of the new music, and the encouragement of fresh talent. For Stassov this meant painters and sculptors, as well as composers. Thus the difference between the partnerships Balakirev-Cui and Balakirev-Stassov is immediately clear. The former remained official, unquestioned, and polite: the latter was tumultous, full of contradictions and disputes, yet warm and deeply affectionate. Their friendship lasted all through their long lives, although Balakirev's unbending will and often tactless stubbornness was responsible for many a strain. Witness a note from Stassov at the age of 79 (1903):

abandoning on the way all petty transient things, a 79-year-old man came to thank his old friend Mili for this—that the friendship is not over and that it is rich and beautiful forever. V. S.[9]

Dimitry Stassov played a lesser, though very necessary, role. He was a high-ranking lawyer, later a senator, and all matters requiring a judicial procedure, such as copyrights, contracts, etc., were entrusted to him. But he played 'nurse' even in a more intimate sense, as he looked after Balakirev when, in April 1858, he fell ill with brain fever (in those days many ailments were referred to as *goryachka*, an untranslatable term). It is to him that the *Overture on Themes of Three Russian Folk-Songs*—one of Balakirev's earliest and best orchestral works—is dedicated. In his family, various members of the Balakirev circle found the warmest welcome and hospitality.

BALAKIREV AND THE FOLK-SONG

The period of suspense between Glinka and Balakirev was very brief, for the latter upon arriving in Petersburg plunged into the thick of things and came out simultaneously as a composer of piano music, songs, and orchestral works. There was no immaturity in all this in spite of Balakirev's youth. His style was compounded from the Glinka intonations, his inherent love for the Russian Orient (Caucasus) common to most Russian

[9] E. Garden, *Balakirev*, op. cit.

14. Modest Moussorgsky.

13. César Cui in the mid 1870s.

Anton, the elder;

15. THE RUBINSTEINS:

Nicholas, the younger.

17. Alexander Borodin.

16. Nicholas Rimsky-Korsakov.

18. Ludmilla Shestakova.

composers, and his assimilation of the best romantic music of the west. All this was held together by a tremendous vitality and a strong infatuation with the dance.[10] The Glinka intonations meant, of course, a permeation by the folk-song. Here Balakirev leaped ahead and tackled the whole problem in a way as yet untried.

After Kashin and Rupini the collecting of folklore passed, for a while, into the hands of literary figures, novelists, scientific explorers of antiquity, and poets. As a result many collections came out without the melodies and were texts only. But these expeditions pointed out the proper way of doing the job: travelling to the villages, into the thick of the country, and noting down the material on the spot. By the early fifties the musicians were again at work, and in 1855-6 the great Volga expedition took place. One of its main participants was the famous dramatist Ostrovsky who, for musical reasons, took along the guitarist Villebois. The latter was a convivial person and preferred to pass the time with the Volga merchants on their barges, while Ostrovsky laboured day and night with the peasants, trying to memorize the melodies which he later sang to the gay Villebois. Yet the collection appeared under the latter's name in 1860, the texts having been edited and revised by the critic and poet Apollon Grigoriev (1822-64), one of those highly talented and shiftless people of the Russian nineteenth century whose potential achievement was ten times greater. The truly epoch-making collection appeared a little before that of Villebois. It was made by Michael Stakhovich, a genuine and most scrupulous precursor of later collectors whose motto was:

In writing down songs one must not ignore the least variant of them: even if two melodies appear almost identical they must both be recorded.[11]

With such momentous things in the air it is no wonder that Balakirev took the first opportunity to get out himself towards the Volga regions. He was hampered by overwork and lack of funds. He wanted to combine the journey with a cure at the

[10] Remarkable is his love of the Polonaise *alla pollacca*, the Mazurka—Chopin is here the prime influence—and the wild Cossack dance.
[11] M. Stakhovich, *Russian Folk-Songs*, Moscow, 1964, 2nd Edition, p. 17.

watering place, Essentuke, so he took the boat from Nijni-Novgorod and, getting out at the various stops down the river, noted the songs of the bargemen and haulers. One of these acquired world-wide fame as the *Song of the Volga Boatmen*. In his circle it provoked universal astonishment and was ranked by Cui with Beethoven's greatest.

Balakirev's album of forty songs—it came out in 1866—is as new a page in Russian music as Glinka's *Kamarinskaya*. Here were newly collected melodies; the collector himself was a musician of genius, who set about the task of harmonizing them in an utterly unprecedented way. His aim was to make accompaniment an autonomous work of art, like the melody. In all previous collections there was a rampant discrepancy between the precious stone of the original song and the utterly unsuitable instrumental part. Even Beethoven's stylizations, though expert, are done merely in the spirit of the times and have little intrinsic artistic value. Not so Balakirev's; here the precious kernel is displayed against an equally precious foil, and the inspired though unknown maker of the melody encounters an artist of commensurable stature. Balakirev's English biographer has put it very aptly: 'the songs are really original compositions in miniature, which make some of them even lovelier than they originally were'[12] (Example 17).

With this album, as with his first *Overture on Themes of Three Russian Folk-Songs*, Balakirev placed himself side by side with Bach, who so treated German chorale, and with Brahms, who took up German folk-song in similar fashion. Further links in that chain of interpreters were Grieg and Dvořák, and, in our times, Vaughan Williams. Before the album itself appeared, Balakirev had extracted from it three more melodies and incorporated them in his second overture on Russian themes, *A Thousand Years*, later called *Russia* in commemoration of the thousandth anniversary of the official existence of Russia as a State (1862). The enthusiasm for folk-music was mounting and went to the point of Stassov's writing out for Balakirev what he imagined to be English folk-music, when the latter was about to compose his incidental music to *King Lear*.[13]

If we add to this rich output the twenty-odd songs that

[12] Garden, op. cit., p. 301.
[13] *Letters of M. Balakirev with V. Stassov*, op. cit., pp. 16-19.

Example 17. *Roundelay*, Balakirev folk-song collection of 1866.

Balakirev wrote in the decade of 1855-6, among them such masterpieces as Pushkin's *Song of Georgia*, Lermontov's *Song of Selim*, *Song of the Golden Fish*, and *Hebrew Melody*, we shall realize what a flowering this was in his life and that of Russian music. Unfortunately it was also during this decade that certain traits of his character were intensified: intolerance of musical views and preferences opposed to his, and a resultant irascibility and harshness of criticism. The first to be subjected to peremptory treatment was the young Moussorgsky. At first he seemed entirely to Balakirev's liking, and their letters are full of the most intimate confidences. But gradually differences began to crop up, the roots of which lay even beyond purely musical points; they touched upon the whole ideology of the time.

The men of the sixties (*Shestidesyatniki*) were ignorant of the Church and, generally speaking, hostile to it. Their ideal was not the Gogol of the *Selected Correspondence with Friends*,[14] but Gogol's attacker, Belinsky.[15]

In so far as he was ignorant of the intonations of the Church, Balakirev was a typical representative of this generation. All he knew was the artificial Italo-German atmosphere of Lvov and the Imperial Chapel, and for this he naturally had no use whatever. His perception of the folk-song was, likewise, coloured by his own intonations, eminently valid and artistically justified, but excluding any less romantic approach. This is where he ran into trouble with Moussorgsky who previously, while he was still in the officers' school, had experienced stronger influences:

Frequently visiting the teacher of religion, Father Kruptsky, I could, thanks to him, penetrate deeply into the substance of the old church music, both Greek and Roman.[16]

How different Moussorgsky's approach to both folk-song and the chant was from that of Balakirev was fully revealed only

[14] In 1847 Gogol, in a fit of remorse and self-castigation, published this confused book in defence of orthodoxy and autocracy. It was attacked by friends and foes, most bitterly by Belinsky.

[15] *Letters of M. Balakirev with V. Stassov*, op. cit., p. 43. He adds: 'I want you to get to know his [Belinsky's] wonderful, unswerving, and firm nature'.

[16] M. P. Moussorgsky, *Letters and Documents*, Moscow, 1932, p. 422.

later in *Boris Godunov*. But there was a decided presentiment of
his method in the compositions of the early sixties, which he
dutifully submitted to his master. The latter, impatient, criticized sharply, and when Moussorgsky still went on his own

Example 18. *Prayer*, Moussorgsky, 1865.

way lost all interest in him. The works that must have irritated
Balakirev particularly were, no doubt, the Fragment from
Oedipus Rex—Balakirev once referred to him as the absurd
author of the Phrygian Choruses—some of the Salammbô
music, and certainly such songs as *Prayer* (Example 18) and
Sleep, O Peasant's Son.

RIMSKY-KORSAKOV

Rimsky-Korsakov was brought to Balakirev in 1861. The progress of their sessions was interrupted by Rimsky's departure on his world cruise which lasted until well into 1865. But a lively correspondence continued throughout that period. Having discarded Moussorgsky, Balakirev transferred all his hopes on his new eighteen-year-old pupil:

I am lonely without you, the more so, as with the exception of Cui, I do not expect anything from anybody . . . of you I expect a great deal and dote on you as an old aunt on her favourite nephew. . . .[17]

This relationship, too, was to deteriorate tragically, finally ending with a catastrophic rupture far worse than anything that had happened in the case of Moussorgsky. The troubles may be traced to the same source: the unwillingness of the pupil—by then himself a master—to submit to the teacher's directions which always were given despotically and very insistently.

The only member of the circle who seems to have escaped the 'iron mitten'[18] of Balakirev was Cui, who, all through the sixties, was at work on another opera: *William Ratcliffe* (from Heine). The musical ideas making up that work are a most perfect expression of the collective thinking of the circle. Without being striking or even memorable, these ideas are nevertheless maintained on a remarkably high level and attain some degree of expressiveness in the manner of the lesser-known works of Schumann (e.g. his opera *Genoveve*). Tchaikovsky was known to have admired some sections of *William Ratcliffe* which offers at least partial explanation for the fact that Cui was thought of as one of the founding members of the 'mighty little band'. Even though he had created nothing solid, Cui was always unhesitatingly referred to as one of the Five—*Les Cinq*, as the French were to call them.[19]

Meanwhile highly important forces were operating outside the Balakirev coterie. These had no direct bearing on the

[17] A. N. Rimsky-Korsakov, *N. A. Rimsky-Korsakov, Life and Works*, Moscow, 1933, p. 91.
[18] An expression used by Moussorgsky.
[19] The Russian *moguchai kuchku* is best expressed as 'mighty little band', though there have been many other terms used.

creative forces of the Russian school. The persons involved, if anything, were hostile to any pronounced manifestations of Russian nationality, and openly advocated the ways of the West. But, in so doing, they were also influencing the flow of musical life and helping to produce enlightened artists upon whom the task of carrying on both national and anti-national traditions later developed. One of these, a powerful shaper of western elements, was Anton Rubinstein.

ANTON RUBINSTEIN

Born in the province of Podolsk in south-western Russia in 1829, Anton was trained as a prodigy by his remarkable mother as was his brother Nicholas, born in Moscow in 1835. Under Russian law the members of the family were confined to the pale so long as they held to the Jewish religion. But the grandfather had had the whole clan of the Rubinsteins christened, and then had dispatched them to Moscow. There Anton took some instruction from the piano pedagogue, Villoing. In 1840 teacher and pupil set out for Paris, and the young Rubinstein played for Liszt. In 1844 the mother took both boys to Berlin and apprenticed them to Dehn. When the disorders of 1848 broke out in Europe, Anton returned to Russia and found a generous patroness in the Grand Duchess Helen Paulovna. Another prolonged stay abroad established his fame as a pianist so that, when he came back, his prestige was enormous and he was entrusted with responsibilities in Russian musical education on a large scale. The courses under the Imperial Russian Music Society were expanded into a Conservatoire of which Rubinstein became the director in 1862. St Petersburg, already seething with German musicians, now attracted a host of theoreticians and teachers who, without having the slightest idea of the Russian musical past and often ignorant even of the language, were to train professional musicians, educating composers as well as performers.

Russian music has had many a tragic turn, but one of its exceptionally lucky strokes was that the first composer to come out of Rubinstein's institution was none other than Peter Tchaikovsky. He learned from the German masters what he needed, then went on his own path. This brought him face to face with the same problems that had confronted Balakirev:

what to do with the legacy of Glinka, of which he never lost sight, and how to make use of the rich fount of folk-songs. True, his conservatoire training left him with a certain veneration of western technique from which Balakirev, who went entirely by instinct, was relatively free. But it was precisely this technique that enabled him to mould the larger forms of composition as he produced a whole succession of great works. But Balakirev, after a volcanic outburst, would suffer a series of relapses and for want of the needed tools would be unable to bridge the gaps that every composer has to face between fits of inspiration.

The appearance of Tchaikovsky—a direct pupil of Rubinstein—confused the issues at stake and paralysed the thrusts of Balakirev and his associates against academic discipline. If a creator of Tchaikovsky's stature could come out of conservatoire; if he, moreover, could turn voluntarily to the national sources and consult his would-be enemy (Balakirev) about thematic material and its use in symphonic forms,[20] what could possibly be the wisdom or sense of dissuading the younger men from entering the institutions? This question gained special force since, by the side of Anton Rubinstein's St Petersburg conservatoire, there arose four years later, in 1866, a similar school in Moscow, led by Anton's brother Nicholas. This muddled situation which no doubt contributed to Balakirev's eclipse induced Rimsky-Korsakov, on whom all his hopes for the future of Russian music were pinned, to seek a solution within the very walls of the conservatoire his first master so detested.

SEROV

Between the conservatoires and Balakirev stood a third power —the already famous and feared critic, Alexander Serov. Born in 1820 and educated at the Imperial Law School, at which he and Stassov met and struck up a fast friendship, Serov throughout most of his life never disentangled himself from the bonds of government service. How irksome these were to him is evident from the constant changes of his career and domicile, and from the frequent interruptions occasioned by trips abroad.

---

[20] When composing his *Romeo and Juliet* overture, Tchaikovsky sent thematic material to Balakirev for criticism (December 1869).

His whole heart lay in music. Possessor of a keen mind and a brilliant analyst, he conquered for himself a firm position as music critic. However he wrote in a caustic and vehement manner, losing thereby many friends, among them the oldest friend he had, Stassov. Nevertheless he commanded respect by means of his great erudition and insight into what was still an almost closed book to many Russians—the folk-song. Until the death of Glinka and even for some years afterwards, Serov vied with Stassov as a champion of the works of Glinka, and especially of the two operas. To both of them the subject was one of sublime importance, but Serov's writings gradually acquired a note of resentment and showed badly concealed irritation. The reasons for this were very subtle, but are partially explained by the fact that he already had great ambitions as a composer and yet could not bring himself to espouse wholeheartedly the cause of Russian music. On the contrary, he made an idol of Wagner and set about paving the way for his operas in Russia. This implied a certain disloyalty to Glinka, at least in the eyes of Stassov. The result was a total break with these two former friends.

Balakirev stumbled into the strife when it had already gone very far. Finding himself entirely in Glinka's camp and virtually perpetuating the direction of his genius for native music, he aroused Serov's ire and was subject to his attacks in the press. Thus, instead of becoming a force in the development of the Russian school, Serov actually hampered it. Then, somewhat unexpectedly, he made his great début as a composer—in his opera *Judith* (1863). No wonder that the attitude towards it of the Balakirev group was largely negative! A fair idea of their feelings we find in a letter that Moussorgsky wrote to Balakirev on 10 June of that year.

I want to impart to you my impressions of Serov's opera . . . it would seem that such a capital work should be heard more than twice: and yet Wagner's *Kindchen* does not bring anything that would affect you deeply, in all its five-act life, not one stage episode over which you could ponder. Withal the libretto is exceedingly bad, the recitation pitiful, un-Russian: only the orchestration is interesting in spots, though often too complicated. . . . Yet after *Russalka*, *Judith* is the first serious venture on the Russian stage. . . .[21]

[21] M. P. Moussorgsky, op. cit., p. 85.

We find a perplexed note in the detailed analysis that follows: on the one hand some outright weaknesses and lapses of taste, on the other acknowledgement of the grandiose intentions of the composer. The same perplexity is apparent in the lines that Rimsky-Korsakov devotes to Serov's second opera *Rognyeda* (1865).

In the Balakirev circle *Rognyeda* was chuckled at. . . . But I cannot but own that it intrigued me greatly and I even liked a number of spots . . ., even its coarse but colourful orchestration. I was afraid to speak up about this in the Balakirev circle. . . .[22]

Viewed as works of art Serov's operas cannot hold their own, but historically they cannot be denied an important place between Glinka and Dargomyjsky's last opera *The Stone Guest*. With the public they had an invariable success thanks to their strong sense of drama and some effective if blatant pages of writing which Serov had transposed from his hero, Wagner.

BORODIN

While Rimsky-Korsakov was away on the cruiser *Almaz*, the last member of the Balakirev circle made his entry into it in the autumn of 1862: this was Alexander Borodin. A learned chemist and already professor in the Medico-Surgical Academy, Borodin entered with weight and authority, as his knowledge of music was both practical—he played several instruments— and theoretical. The latter he had acquired by reading German textbooks and by study of the literature of chamber music. Musically all this had already come to fruition in the composition of a piano quintet which Borodin had demonstrated abroad, so far, however, only in amateur groups.

Under such circumstances Balakirev naturally could not function as a teacher in the proper sense of the word. Yet the impact of the meeting was enormous and resulted in Borodin's undertaking a work of big proportions: his first symphony in E flat major. The work progressed slowly and was not finished until 1869, but the composition of the circle was now complete and, collectively, it constituted a tremendous force which neither Rubinstein's professionalism nor Serov's opposition could seriously challenge.

[22] Rimsky-Korsakov, *My Musical Life*, Moscow, 1926, p. 88.

6

Moussorgsky and Rimsky-Korsakov 1868-81

The different ways of Moussorgsky and Rimsky-Korsakov at this juncture are indicative of a struggle between imagination and discipline—struggle that has conditioned the arts since time immemorial. In such a struggle the two conditions for the emergence of musical works of art are fulfilled, and the end result may vary as we know from the music of Bach, or the Viennese classic. In Russia the perfect balance was yet to be achieved, and its achievement came in a strange, roundabout manner. The case of Glinka caused some confusion, for here was a man who for long had groped his way forward and had disdained longer periods of self-discipline, reaching the top as if by intuition. Balakirev modelled himself after his idol, but his imagination was undisciplined; hence his creative achievements were sporadic. Nevertheless he advocated the same course for the members of his circle and was surprised at the utterly divergent results for the two youngest members.

MOUSSORGSKY'S FORMATIVE YEARS

Moussorgsky was incapable of subjecting himself to the slightest constraint, despite the fact that he had been exposed in his young years to the rigours of an officers' school, where he had been sent from his parents' estate to prepare for a military career. He did well at school, but his musical talents were so outstanding in those surroundings that he developed undue confidence, which later became pernicious and dangerous conceit.

There is no information at all about his childhood in the country and very little about his early education. When he came to Balakirev at the age of eighteen (1857) he had just obtained his commission, was an accomplished pianist, and possessed a pliable, very expressive voice. The meeting led to momentous decisions. Before a year was up his resignation from the regiment had been accepted. The far-seeing Stassov assiduously tried to dissuade him from this step: 'Look at Lermontov', he said; 'he could remain an officer in the hussars and become a great poet, regardless of duty in the regiment and all the parades'.[1] Moussorgsky's only reply was that the service prevented him from occupying himself as he wished. His musical occupations, however, were fitful and uncertain: a few operatic projects, instrumental pieces, songs. All this went through Balakirev's hands, provoking nothing but exasperation in the process.

The idea that haunted Moussorgsky from the start was that music should reproduce the accents of human speech, raising it to a higher plane of course, but always following its natural flow. Like a red thread this notion runs through all his creations forming a counter-focus to his innate lyrical vein, his instinct to 'melodize' all that he touched. It is in the fusion of these two opposing impulses that the highest originality of Moussorgsky lies. But such a fusion was not always achieved in his music, where one can often observe a desperate struggle between lyrical and realistic elements. This disparity puzzled Balakirev in the first years of their acquaintance and caused Rimsky-Korsakov's notorious 'corrections' in *Boris* and *Khovanshchina*, and made even Stassov turn away from the last song-cycles. Small wonder that Moussorgsky, in the autobiographical note which he wrote in the last year of his life, placed himself apart from 'any of the existing musical circles'.[2]

In the early period a number of things went well. A composer of the strongest convictions, and with a firm faith in himself, but lacking in sureness of touch which comes largely from schooling, Moussorgsky alternately delighted and repelled his colleagues. Balakirev, who set himself up as teacher, quickly discovered how unteachable this pupil was, and with his

[1] *Collected Works of V. Stassov about M. Moussorgsky*, Moscow, 1922, p. 10.
[2] M. P. Moussorgsky, op. cit., p. 424.

habitual impatience upbraided him. When Moussorgsky showed resentment:

In any case your letter is prompted by a mistaken annoyance, as it is time to stop seeing in me a child that must be supported so as not to fall.[3]

Balakirev washed his hands and let him go his own way. However, Balakirev's attitude was not shared by the others; in fact, there was a growing discontent on the part of many with his insistence on certain minor matters, such as the choice of tonalities, and disregard for substance.

MOUSSORGSKY'S SONGS (1864-8)

The few years preceding *Boris* saw Moussorgsky at work on his most remarkable songs. It was at that time that Dargomyjsky drew quite close to the circle and busied himself with *The Stone Guest*. The difference between that work and *Russalka* is so striking that one wonders if it was not precisely Moussorgsky who finally urged Dargomyjsky towards a style in which the intonations of human speech are so strongly in relief. The first performance at Dargomyjsky's house of all the tableaux of this opera took place in November 1868 shortly before the death of the author, with Moussorgsky doing the parts of Leporello and Don Carlos. Moussorgsky was already deeply involved in his *Boris* at that moment.

Moussorgsky's songs threw all, except Balakirev, into paroxysms of delight. Stassov bubbled over—made a noise (*shumel*), as his friends termed it. Rimsky-Korsakov later wrote in his *Chronicle*: 'Moussorgsky, having returned from his summer stay in the country, brought the newly composed *Svetik Savishna* and *Hopak*, and thereby opened his series of vocal works of unparalleled genius and originality.'[4] Towards the outside world, however, this whole group of enthusiasts were impeachable. Aside from being attacked by ultra-conservative critics, who never tired of singing the praises of Serov and Rubinstein, westerners of all types subjected them to their invective. It so happened that, at one of the concerts of the Free Music School

---

[3] M. P. Moussorgsky, op. cit., mentioned in a footnote about a Moussorgsky letter to Balakirev in 1861, p. 42.
[4] A. Orlova, *Works and Days of M. P. Moussorgsky*, Moscow, 1963, p. 126.

when Moussorgsky's chorus *The Defeat of Sennacherib* was performed, Turgenev was present. His only comment was: 'What self-deception, what blindness, what a way of ignoring Europe.'[5]

The successful realistic trend of the songs—those scenes from life, like the love of the village idiot *Savishna*, or the *Orphan*, *Kallistrat*, and the *Lullaby of Yeriomushka*—drove Moussorgsky to attempt a setting of Gogol's *Marriage*, a hilarious satire in prose. But having done one act, he relinquished the work. Reactions on the part of members of the group was mixed. Dargomyjsky said that the composer had gone too far, while Borodin called it a curious and paradoxical thing, full of new and very humorous ideas, but as a whole '*une chose manquée*' and impossible for performance. Moussorgsky knew this himself, and plunged without reservations into *Boris*. This was the great moment of his life.

Outwardly, there had been very little change since he left his regiment. But his family resources had disappeared, and after the sale of their property he had to enter government service as a civil clerk in the Engineering Department (1863). During this period he shared lodgings with some friends, but after a nervous breakdown moved in with his brother's family. What dismal turns his non-musical existence was taking we know from the accounts of Stassov and Rimsky-Korsakov, with whom he also shared lodgings in 1871-2, and others. All efforts to rescue him failed. Only occasionally would he emerge from his solitary haunts to take part in musical gatherings with former friends. 'Moussorgsky came in a dreadful state,' wrote Madame Shestakova to Stassov, and he in turn informed Balakirev that 'Moussorgsky is going down' in 1878.[6]

RIMSKY-KORSAKOV'S FORMATIVE YEARS

At about the same age as Moussorgsky, only five years later, Rimsky-Korsakov was dispatched from the provincial town of Tikhvin, in the Novgorod province, to the Naval School in St Petersburg, and stayed there about the same length of time as did Moussorgsky in the Officers' School. Thanks to the *Chronicle of my Musical Life*, which Rimsky compiled at various periods, we know much more about his years of military schooling than

---

[5] A. Orlova, op cit., p. 131.
[6] Discussed in greater detail by M. D. Calvocoressi, op. cit., pp. 194-210.

about Moussorgsky's. We know how he went on cruises during the summers, how he spent his weekends, and we learn of his growing interest in music and of his passion for Glinka. In the last year at the School his music teacher led him to Balakirev who was immediately fascinated. This posed the first serious dilemma for the young midshipman, for upon graduation he was expected to take a three-year voyage to distant lands and learn his *métier* in practice. He has told us how hard it was for him to part from music and his newly won friends at Balakirev's —Cui and Moussorgsky. And yet his decision was to go—a course so very different from that taken earlier by Moussorgsky, against the advice of Stassov.

After nearly three years of cruising to places as far as Rio de Janeiro—this port is fascinatingly described in the *Chronicle* —Rimsky returned to the musical life of Petersburg (1855) and to the beloved circle which had now been extended by the inclusion of Borodin. Partly during his travels and partly upon his return, he managed to put together his *Symphony in E Minor* which was rehearsed and performed by Balakirev at a concert of the Free Music School. Cui, who had already begun his journalistic activity, pronounced it, the next day, the *first* Russian symphony, forgetting all about the existence of at least three of Rubinstein's works. Such was the self-admiration of the circle and its complete contempt for the *Conservatoire* forces!

The momentum gained from the formation of the circle and the inspiring relationships between its members happily lasted for several years. Each composer brought his own particular contribution which was demonstrated, discussed, and often subjected to alterations and re-orchestrated. It was then that Rimsky acquired the reputation of a great orchestral expert and worked on the poem *Sadko* and his second symphony *Antar*. Dargomyjsky, Cui, and Balakirev belonged to the upper chamber, and their judgments, especially those of Balakirev, were listened to with bated breath. Real cordiality existed only among Moussorgsky, Rimsky, and Borodin over whom the fiery Stassov spread his magic cape. Feminine influence came from Madame Shestakova and, after 1868, the sisters Alexandra and Nadejda Purgold, the second of whom eventually became Rimsky-Korsakov's wife.

It is difficult to discover who learned from whom. All shared a kind of collective growing up, original teachers being left behind. After the happy years the gradual loss of the authority of these teachers led to the somewhat tragic dénouement of the musical clique. There were losses on both sides and the notable victims—first the unprotected Moussorksgy and then Balakirev himself, with his love of authority and his unsociability. The immediate products of the abundant era, however, were the great operatic projects of Moussorgsky and Rimsky: *Boris Godunov* and *Pskovityanka*. Moussorgsky worked at white heat and by July 1869 the first version of his opera was finished. Rimsky took longer, but because of delays and several revisions of *Boris*, the two operas were produced almost simultaneously in 1873-4.

Though the two composers inevitably influenced each other, especially during the time they lived together, their works differed widely. In these years Moussorgsky had reached his pinnacle, Rimsky his limits. *Boris* was a living work of art of unprecedented originality, every bar of which startles, delights, moves one to the quick. Even where the composer used somewhat familiar materials, as in the choruses built on folk-tunes, he transformed them into something novel. Rimsky's themes are derived from Balakirev's store, memories of songs heard in childhood, and folk-song collections. These, attached to a well-knit dramatic story and presented with care and wisdom in a series of historic tableaux—Glebov called the work an opera-chronicle—make a deep impression; yet the work does not overwhelm one. The indelible accents of Rimsky's style were to come much later after he had attained his apogee with *Snegurochka* (1880).

Both operas underwent radical alterations. But while Moussorgsky revised under constraint, his 'Ur-version' having been censored by the operatic committee, Rimsky was inwardly devastated by the first performance, having realized the insufficiency of his entire training under Balakirev. Thus he was confronted by the second dilemma: must discipline take over where intuition was failing? As the acknowledged master in orchestration, he had already been invited to Rubinstein's conservatoire in 1871. And now the teacher himself—who was, moreover, the seemingly successful author of an accepted operatic work—decided to join his students on the benches of the theory classes. Again he had chosen the way of rigid discipline as opposed to free imagination, somehow realizing that he reached his limits in the *Pskovityanka*. The next ten years proved abundantly how right he had been.

The reaction to his course was decidedly negative in the Balakirev circle, Borodin commenting, as usual with good humour, Balakirev and Stassov wryly, and Moussorgsky with vehemence, calling it outright treachery. But Tchaikovsky wrote from Moscow: 'All these innumerable counterpoints that you have performed, the sixty fugues and a mass of other musical tricks—all this is such a feat for a man who eight years ago composed *Sadko* that I would like to shout about him to the whole world.'[7]

TOWARDS THE PINNACLE

Several years were needed for this colossal readjustment. Rimsky-Korsakov was now married. He held two parallel posts, that of a Conservatoire professor and an inspector of all choirs of the Marine Ministry, which necessitated trips to the Black Sea; and he had also been asked to replace Balakirev as conductor of the concerts of the Free Music School. The rival concerts of the Imperial Russian Musical Society were conducted, after Balakirev's removal, by Napravnik, the main conductor of the opera. However, whenever anything new was put on the programme, Napravnik dodged it and called in Rimsky. Around all this bustle of daily duties the composer was busy with two folk-song collections.

FOLK-SONG COLLECTIONS

Into the first he put many of the songs of the Prach and Stakhovich vintage, songs that he had heard in childhood, and those that he picked up from anyone around him.[8] He tells us, for instance, how he spent endless time in catching a tricky rhythm from the singing of Borodin's maid, a native of one of the Volga provinces. All this was divided by categories and supplied with

---

[7] *P. Tchaikovsky's Complete Collected Writings*, Vol. V, Moscow, 1959, p. 412.
[8] *One Hundred Chants Nationaux Russes*, collected by Rimsky-Korsakov (1875-7), Op. 24.

new harmonizations, which are simpler than those of Balakirev, yet true stylizations which find the essence of the melodies and surround them with a precious framework. The second collection was notated from the singing of Tertius Filippov himself,[9] the famous collector and preserver of Russian antiquity (see Chapter 10). This work on folk material was, of course, a wonderful antidote to his theoretical studies. While the mind acquired the much-needed discipline, the composer's soul revelled in the lovely intonations of the people, and the result was a new opera—*The May Night*—after Gogol, a many-faceted work in which antagonistic tendencies of author and composer are held in check. Rimsky's happy vein balances Gogol's inexhaustible humour.

May Night (1877-8)

No greater contrast can be imagined than between the austere and measured *Pskovityanka* and the gay, exuberant *May Night*. It is as if the composer needed a playground for all the variegated powers hidden in him and had given them free rein, being also, at last, relieved from the heavy authority of Balakirev. Amongst comic operas *May Night* is one of the most enjoyable. One would not call it a masterpiece, because of the still unamalgamated elements, not the least of which is the romantic pair of lovers treated in the customary western way with duets and arias in the high vocal register. The brilliant orchestra is also made to conform to the usual trappings of the romantics with their deliberate tone-painting: harp glissandi, tremolos and French horns à la Weber. The realistic recitatives are not free from imitation of Moussorgsky. All in all, the hands of the composer are in the process of being untied, but the final outcome of this liberation through folk-song and discipline alike came only in Rimsky's next opera, *Snegurochka*.

Snegurochka

In *Snegurochka* Rimsky-Korsakov created a genuine masterpiece and proved to himself, as to the critical world around him, that

[9] Tertius Filippov, *Forty Folk-songs*, harmonized by Rimsky-Korsakov (see Appendix I).

his course in search of perfection through retraining at the Conservatoire had been the right one. Over the composition of this work a bright aura shone. On 18 May 1880 the Korsakov family, now blessed with three children, moved to an estate beyond Luga, about 150 versts south of St Petersburg and situated in a ravishing countryside of forests, lakes, and rivers. The composer found himself reverting to the days of his childhood in Tikhvin. Ideas for the Ostrovsky dramatic fairy-tale which had haunted him ever since *May Night*—he had recently visited the poet to obtain the libretto rights—flooded into his head irrepressibly. He found his usual way of writing in orchestral score too cumbersome and resorted to a vocal score with piano, so that by 12 August he had finished the whole opera, leaving the orchestration for the coming winter in Petersburg. As in *May Night*, nature forms a constant background and again the ritualistic element is ever-present. But now these are transferred to Russian pre-history—into the realm of the *Berendeis*, a fairy-like Utopia ruled over by a loving, warm-hearted Czar in whom we may recognize Rimsky-Korsakov himself with his pantheistic, aesthetic outlook on the world. Neither the Ukrainian folk-songs of Rubetz (used in *May Night*) nor the realistic accents of Moussorgsky were needed any longer. The Russian folk-music that was poured into *Snegurochka* produced Rimsky's own intonations, so that in the end we cannot tell what is his and what he took from the people. The archaic setting of the tale furthered the use of the old modes, and in some of the reed patterns of the shepherd Lel we seem to hear snatches of the pastoral (fourth) echos of *znamenny* chant. The fragrant spring-like poetry of the music, ending in the melting away of the Snow-Maiden under the rays of the first summer sun, could be compared to the delicate colours of Botticelli. Indeed the whole opera is a unique portrayal of spring, from its early stages of the melting snows and the awakening of nature, to its merging with the warmth of a northern midsummer day in June.

While Rimsky-Korsakov thus achieved, through rigid discipline, supreme freedom of construction on a large scale without in the least impairing his inborn gifts for scoring, his friend Moussorgsky was writing scene after scene of the great music drama *Boris Godunov*.

Boris Godunov

A vast chapter of Russian music history centres upon this work, and again one can recall Tolstoy's *War and Peace* and Dosto-yevsky's *Crime and Punishment*. We are told that Tolstoy with his own artist's discipline reworked pages and pages of his historical epic, but that Dostoyevsky wrote as the spirit moved him, sending in the chapters to the publisher with the ink still wet on them. We may wish for greater stylistic purity in Dostoyevsky, but nobody dreams of applying a pedantic rule to him and insisting on corrections. In fact, his thoughts on his way of putting them constitute his whole personality, its singleness and fantastic image. But alas, with Moussorgsky a different view was taken. The harping on his lack of schooling and ignorance of musical orthography never stopped, and in this respect his nearness to Rimsky-Korsakov proved his undoing. Here, critics argued, were two equally talented musicians, of whom one was wise enough to learn from the bottom, while the other flaunted his contempt for discipline and vaunted himself above the others. As if to give more weight to this reproach, the composer's own best friend came to his rescue after his untimely and tragic end, and brought law and order into a seemingly chaotic mass of glorious ideas.

All this may very well be so with the fragments that Mous-sorgsky left at his death, where the friendly interference of others was needed to preserve great scraps of musical thought, but with *Boris* the case is different. Moussorgsky himself had put all the finishing touches to it. The work was at least played and sung, and produced an immense impression on people un-concerned with matters of harmony or orchestration. The stupendous ideas spoke for themselves and the force of their impact was immediate. These were not stylizations of folk-songs, although intonations from the latter are scattered all over *Boris*. This was an outpouring of the sources themselves through the workings of an individual genius, the concentrated essence of music hurled at the masses of people who had already detached themselves from the soil and had begun to forget the natural expression of a whole musical race. It was a powerful reminder of the beauty, the vigour, and the abandon of Slavonic popular art, particularly in its Russian aspect. Conservatoires and schools of the Rubinstein brand had very little to do with it, and it was only the narrowness of the critics and the slavishness of western imitation that could measure Moussorgsky's achievement by such standards. People like Stassov realized this to the full and never stopped proclaiming the greatness of *Boris*. Rimsky, in his heart, felt it also, but the course he had chosen for himself, and for which he was so supremely fitted by his special endowment, overawed his natural feelings and unfortunately convinced him of the need to come to his friend's aid on all fronts, including that of the fully accomplished work of art, and trimming his utterance to fit the requirements of orthodox technique. The curious outcome was a new and totally unprecedented form of art in which two opposed musical mentalities are merged into one—the compound image of Moussorgsky and Rimsky-Korsakov.

Moussorgsky was acting on his own. His canvas was Pushkin's drama. Some bits of it he used verbatim, others he tore to pieces according to his needs. Together with Karamzin and Pushkin, he treated the Czar Boris as a usurper and murderer, yet imbued him with pity and remorse, dwelling with particular pleasure on his noble traits—his devoutness, his love for his family, his deep thoughts of the Russian realm. In the best Shakespearean tradition, Moussorgsky was not concerned with any scenic conventions but went straight to the root of the matter, and followed the Czar's fate through the seven years of his wise but tragic reign: the people's supplications for his assumption of power and his coronation (Prologue); his first accuser—the chronicler-monk with his tale of Boris's crime; his next accuser—the Pretender—who contrives to flee across the border and establish his claim to the throne (First Act); the Czar's family assembled in the Kremlin and the frantic struggle with the next accuser—Prince Shuisky (the Second Act, central to the whole terse drama); finally the encounter of Boris with the people themselves in the guise of the simpleton —the last and fatal accuser—leading to his collapse and death (Third Act).

Moussorgsky finished the opera within one year (Dec. 1868 to Dec. 1869) and immediately submitted it to the repertoire committee. The strength of the music lay in the choruses and in the wonderfully expressive recitatives that bound them together. While the choruses were familiar, Moussorgsky's recitative style remains unique. Here he speaks with the melodies and accents of a true creator, a chanter of the type of those who made the *znamenny* chant or the singer who narrated the *bylinas* and spiritual verses. Weaknesses—if one can speak of weaknesses here—arose only in the adaptation of Moussorgsky's material to the routine resources of the opera. Singers were accustomed to grateful tenor and soprano roles, and orchestral players had been brought up on Verdian figures and accompaniments. None of this was understood by the bewildered committee who returned the score to the composer with the remark that there was not even a female part in it.

REVISIONS

This is where the surgical work on Moussorgsky's ideas first began. He himself set to work and produced a partly rewritten manuscript, keeping, however, the Prologue and First Act. He conventionalized the palace scene by including episodes irrelevant to the main action—for example, the story about the parrot—thus seriously weakening the dramatic force of the original. Then he added new Polish scenes, creating an artificial female part and providing the customary love duet at the end. It is astonishing how even for this forced inclusion Moussorgsky was able to write splendid and effective music, although everything inside him must have been rejecting the thought of it. The last act dramatized the death of Boris and ended with the inclusion of the simpleton scene transplanted into the now famous forest scene. All this was far less direct and logical than Moussorgsky's original draft, but the committee's main objections had been removed and a number of women singers were now to be found among the enthusiastic supporters of the composer. Chief of them was Platonova who, as *prima donna*, had a right to a benefit performance with her own choice of the opera. Without hesitation she demanded *Boris* and even threatened resignation if crossed. But the directors proceeded cautiously and tried at first only three scenes; the two Polish ones and the frontier inn scenes (Acts one and two) in February 1873. The success was so overwhelming that it was then decided to go ahead with the whole opera (27 January 1874).

AFTER 'BORIS'

Five whole years passed after the completion of the first version, and during this period Moussorgsky's furious inspiration did not rest. Into the midst of his readjustments of *Boris* fell extensive sketches for his next opera *Khovanshchina*, with Stassov finding the historical material and Moussorgsky writing the libretto. Also in those years he completed *The Nursery* and published a great number of the earlier songs. These were the richest harvest years of Moussorgsky's career. But some serious cracks in his genius had already appeared.

The most far-reaching development was the dissolution of the Balakirev Circle. This must not be viewed as a sudden or even very definite event. The optimist Borodin says in a letter:

You have probably heard a lot about the dissensions in our Circle, even its dissolution: I don't see it in the same way as Ludmilla Ivanovna (Mme Shestakova), or others. To me it seems natural. While all were like eggs under a brood-hen [he meant Balakirev] we were all alike. When the chicks came out they were covered by different-coloured feathers, and when the wings had grown each flew to where he was drawn by his nature. The absence of similarity in taste, etc., is, if anything a positive factor.

But he adds: 'Balakirev somehow could not understand this,'[10] and it was this withdrawal of the leader that was the beginning of the end. He estranged himself for four years, just those years when Rimsky had decided on his re-education in the conservatoire and Moussorgsky saw the production of *Boris*.

In fact Balakirev's defection was of no consequence to Moussorgsky. What hit him much harder was the fate of *Boris* after that first historic performance. There was, to begin with, Cui's condescending and even hateful review in the *St Petersburg Journal*. Then came performances with cuts, greater intervals between performances, and finally disappearance of the work from the current repertoire. Connected with this mutilation of *Boris* was the decay of Moussorgsky himself. This is how Stassov complained about it to his daughter:

Moussorgsky has changed completely. He has begun to drink, his face is swollen and dark in colour, his eyes are dull, and he spends

[10] *Letter of A. P. Borodin*, Moscow, 1936, Vol. II, p. 89, to L. I. Karmalina, 15 April 1875.

days on end in the Marly Yaroslavetz [a Petersburg restaurant] with a cursed bunch of boozers. . . .[11]

Stassov made a heroic effort to drag him out and proposed a journey, at his own expense, to Weimar to visit Liszt, whose great love for the new Russian school was talked of everywhere. But Moussorgsky would have nothing of it under one pretext or another.

LAST SPARKS

Only sporadically did his genius become stirred in this last period of his life. His touch can still be felt in parts, but the mighty current of *Boris* and the flashes of great music in *Khovanshchina* could not be recaptured. Into this time, nevertheless, fall three major works: the piano cycle *Pictures at an Exhibition* and the song cycles *Sunless* and *Songs and Dances of Death*. To relieve the gloom of the latter he began work on a Gogol subject, very similar to the one used by Rimsky-Korsakov for *May Night*. Into the *Fair of Sorochintzy* he wrote for the last time music that radiates humour, poetry, sunshine, and finds true, realistic accents to delineate the racy Ukrainian Gogol types. All these works were found in a heap of paper scraps when the composer was taken to the St Nicholas Military Hospital. It was there that Repin painted the monstrous but no doubt life-like portrait of his that is known the world over. Death came to Moussorgsky at the age of 42, in March of 1881, leaving the first gap in the ranks of the Balakirev Circle—a gap that was never closed.

[11] A. Orlova, op. cit., p. 380.

7

Tchaikovsky and Borodin

TCHAIKOVSKY (to 1881)

Having been concerned so far mainly with St Petersburg, let us take a view of the musical life in Moscow in the crucial years of *Boris* and *Snegurochka*.

There was a world of difference between the two capitals. Moscow was scarcely more than an overgrown village, and its whole approach to the arts was deeply provincial. Speaking of a considerably later period, the Muscovite musician and writer, Leonid Sabaneyev, describes the nineties as follows:

Moscow was, after all, a provincial town with its patriarchal mode of life, with its quiet streets and little houses, which were only beginning to be replaced by many-storied modern buildings. Besides, Moscow was inveterately conservative in its tastes and tendencies; narrow in its horizons. Of the Russian National School, i.e. of Rimsky-Korsakov, Borodin, and particularly Moussorgsky, even the musicians in Moscow had only a remote idea. Wagner was viewed as a sort of musical Antichrist. . . .[1]

What is so extraordinary is that a whole pleiad of conspicuous artists was affected by these old-world notions: Ostrovsky, Mey, Grigoryev, Stakhovich. When Tchaikovsky, following the invitation of Nicholas Rubinstein, settled there in 1866 he, too, fell under their sway and could not quite shake them off to the end of his life.

Tchaikovsky was born into the family of a factory director in the Urals, far from civilization. In the manner of his time, he was brought up by a staff of governesses and teachers until

[1] *S. I. Taneyev*, L. Sabaneyev, Paris, 1930, p. 101.

he was taken to St Petersburg where he entered first a prepara-
tory *pension* and then, in 1850, the School of Jurisprudence—
the very same that twenty years earlier had moulded Serov and
Stassov. While there he experienced several shocks, the worst
arising from news of the death of his mother from cholera.
Though outwardly regaining his equilibrium as he developed
into a very likeable young man, he harboured these experiences
deep in his soul. Graduating from the School, he put on the
uniform of an official of the Department of Justice. He was
already nearing his transformation, yet, for the time being,
continued to lead the empty life of Petersburg society, attending
theatres and balls, but remarkably few musical events. The
seeds of tragedy which played so heavy a part in his subsequent
life were sown precisely in these Petersburg years. Thus history
links him with Gogol, Dostoyevsky, Moussorgsky, and all those
whose careers were somehow shattered in those ghost-like
autumn days and equally unreal white nights of the northern
capital.

In 1851 he lightheartedly undertook a trip abroad and thereupon abruptly began rebuilding his life. He entered the newly
founded Rubinstein Conservatoire in Petersburg, put an end
to his social distractions, and plunged headlong into musical
studies. His capacity for work was enormous, and his musical
tastes, though catholic, focused on Mozart, Glinka, and
Schumann. Herein was his meeting-point with the Balakirev
group. After three years of concentrated study with Rubinstein's German professors and with Rubinstein himself for
orchestration, he departed for Moscow to take up his duties
there as professor of theory. Very few extant works or fragments date back to those Petersburg years.

His first piano compositions and songs (Opp. 1-10) appeared
in Moscow, and are a refraction of Tchaikovsky's personality
through the typical Moscovian intonations. Not a trace here
of any folk-song roots as in Balakirev or Rimsky-Korsakov, or
of their oriental leanings, and still less of Moussorgsky's whimsi-
cality. All is trim and well ordered—and immediately accessible,
like that *Souvenir of Hapsal* which brought him immediate
popularity. All tendencies of this period culminated in the
First Symphony in G Minor, which set up a pattern fully in keeping
with the strange psychology of the composer: an intimate

dreamy streak, as witness the inscription 'Winter Dreams' over the first movement, yielding to a wild riotousness in the finale. Tchaikovsky would refer to it as the Two Peters, his dual, almost schizophrenic nature, and equally a reflection of Moscow life with its sharp transitions from mournful brooding to noisy antics, from elegy by day to nights among the gypsies, from old-time sedateness to revelries with sleigh-bells and road-side inns.

Tchaikovsky's life in Moscow in the late sixties and early seventies is full of this duality. Hard work alternated with endless talk, disputes in diverse company, and, alas, dissipation! It could easily have become a rehashing of his pre-conservatoire Petersburg ways, except for his creative urge. But with the same suddenness as before he turned to the folk idiom (1872), finding what he wanted in the Prokunin collection (see Appendix I) and arranging the material for voice and piano, and for piano with four hands. These efforts take us far away from Balakirev's stylizations and pianistic accompaniments. Tchaikovsky wrote simply and directly and, because of that, possibly came much nearer in spirit to the originals (Example 19). The fact of his turning to folk-music is as remarkable as the reform of his whole mode of life ten years earlier. It would have been only too easy for him to continue drowning his despondency in the soul-stirring romances of his youth to words of Pleshcheyev, *Not a Word, O My Friend*; Mey, *Why*; and Apukhtin, *So Quickly to Forget*.[2] But for him it was important not to revel in such moods but to struggle against them in torrents of work and discipline. From then on folk-song influence persisted for a long time, though never achieving the preponderant role it played with Rimsky-Korsakov or Balakirev. His first surviving opera *Oprichnik*—two earlier ones were destroyed by him— shows many borrowings from Villebois, Stakhovich, and Balakirev, while in the *Second Symphony in C Minor* and *First Piano Concert in B flat Minor* he built finales on Little Russian—i.e. Ukrainian—melodies from the Rubetz volume (Appendix I).

[2] Pleshcheyev, Mey and Apukhtin were well-known Russian poets in their time. Pleshcheyev was perhaps more famous for being a member of the revolutionary Petroshevsky Circle than a great poet, while Apukhtin was a friend and schoolfellow of Tchaikovsky whose later poetry was based on regret for the days of his youth. Mey, one of the 'image' poets, wrote the *Maid of Pskov* drama which Rimsky-Korsakov used for his opera.

Example 19. Russian folk-song from the Prokunin, 1872-3, harmonized by Tchaikovsky.

Already on settling in Moscow Tchaikovsky shared rooms for some years with Nicholas Rubinstein. To gain freedom, he ultimately moved into his own lodging, but even then he was irked by all sorts of professional connections which he tried to shake off by frequent trips abroad. These too failed to bring the desired results. He thereupon blunderingly took a fatal step and persuaded himself to marry a young lady whose overt infatuation with him he had not the heart to repulse.[3] Two

[3] In the story of Eugene Onegin by Pushkin the hero was unmoved by a girl's passionate confession of love. The subject was floating in Tchaikovsky's mind and with his usual hypersensibility he was reliving the romance.

months after the marriage he suffered a nervous collapse and was whisked off abroad by one of his brothers. This crisis terminated his official position as teacher at the Conservatoire, but the fates were kind to him, and as if to make up for this loss of income a wealthy admirer appeared on the scene, bestowing on him a substantial yearly pension. This was Madame Nadejda von Meck, whose correspondence with Tchaikovsky fills several volumes, revealing him as a most subtly psychological and refined stylist.

The year of the crisis—1877—marks the first peak in Tchaikovsky's creative life. He had just finished the ballet *Swan Lake* and the tone poem *Francesca da Rimini*. His thoughts were occupied with the opera *Eugene Onegin*, which he finished soon after his flight abroad, and this whole period of activity, somehow unaffected, even aided by his crisis, came to a culmination in the *Fourth Symphony in F Minor*, a work laid out on a scale as yet untried by any Russian composer. It shows, perhaps better than any other composition, the peculiar way in which Tchaikovsky viewed folk-song material. When he lets it resound in the final movement on the tune for '*In the field stood a little birch tree*' the old melody serves solely for rhythmic and dynamic purposes, forming but a pretext for a grandiose symphonic development out of all proportion to the humble, unpretentious role of the folk-song. The symphony is another example of Tchaikovsky's passage from the inward, purely personal experiences reflected in the opening movement to his submergence in the crowds of the market-place in the *Finale* which represents complete abandonment in mad revelry.

The next few years saw no slackening of this unparalleled production. His marriage was liquidated and he was free to live where he pleased, to travel, to spend his time between Russia and Europe, but, above all, never to pause for a moment in his arduous artistic toil. A whole string of capital works resulted: a new opera, *The Maid of Orleans*, the *First Suite in D Major*, *The Italian Capriccio*, *1812*, the *Serenade for Strings*, the *Violin Concerto*, and so we arrive at the year 1881 with its accumulation of the tragic deaths of Dostoyevsky, Alexander II, and Moussorgsky. These afflicted the composer with yet another, the untimely end of his great friend and benefactor, Nicholas Rubinstein. This event was mirrored in the great *Trio in A Minor* for piano, violin and cello. Who can forget the theme for the long set of variations into which the composer poured out the whole of himself, and together with this the warmth, cosiness, and sentiment of the songs so popular in Rubinstein's circle?[4] Joy and tears are mingled, exuberance and a lugubrious ending go hand in hand, a panorama of fleeting dances and dirges. In short we find there the entire gamut of Moscow life, which so affected Tchaikovsky and at the same time deterred his Petersburg colleagues.

BORODIN (1833-87)

The career of Alexander Borodin, running parallel with Tchaikovsky's, was one of the strangest ever lived by a man of genius. A historian of music is hard put to record Borodin's musical achievement, for he had actually very little time for music. Burdened by his professorial duties as chemist at the Medico-Surgical Academy, he was often dispatched abroad to attend scientific congresses. A man of influence besieged by innumerable requests on all sides, a friend and counsellor of medical students, and a protagonist of higher education for women in Russia, he still contrived to inscribe his name in the annals of music by a handful of works of such brilliance as both to set a course in his own country and indelibly affect the minds of European musical leaders from Liszt to Ravel. It is this latter aspect of him that is most astonishing, and it would not be an exaggeration to say that the impact of Russian music on the West began not with Glinka, nor with Tchaikovsky, nor with Rimsky-Korsakov, but with Borodin's scattered works.

Everything about him, from his birth on, was unusual. The illegitimate offspring of an elderly Georgian prince and a humble widow from the shores of the Baltic, he was given a solid education by all manner of private tutors, music playing a large, but not preponderant, part in his education. When he was twelve, a young playmate was taken into his mother's house, and it is largely to the initiative of the two boys that we

---

[4] A delicate attempt to trace and explain the soul-states of Tchaikovsky was made in various writings on him by Assafiev (Glebov), but an even deeper insight into the path of the composer is shown in a recent article on him by the philosopher Karil Zaitsev (now Archimandrite Constantine), in *The Orthodox Way*, Jordanville, N.Y., 1965.

must attribute Borodin's early musical training. They selected their own instruments—Sasha Borodin playing flute and cello, and Misha Shchiglyov playing the violin—found other partners, and set out on the classics. What could not be played on strings and wind they tackled as piano duets. But if the house was filled by the sounds of music it was also filled by the smell of chemical acids and crystalline solvents contained in flasks that graced every window. By the time he was sixteen, Borodin was ready to enter the Medical Academy. There his progress was rapid under such famous teachers as Zinin. Several years later he received his doctor's degree and was sent abroad to do prolonged work in German laboratories.

While living in Heidelberg he fell in with a group of Russians, made music with them, and tried his hand at composing. His models revolved around Mendelssohn's works. It was at this time that he also met his future wife, Catherine Protopopov, a pianist of excellence who was the first to introduce him to the music of Schumann. On his return to St Petersburg he was presented to Balakirev and an almost overnight transformation took place (1862). All that was musically pent up in him exploded, fragment by fragment, and took shape in the four movements of his *First Symphony in E flat,* one of the most striking symphonic works of the entire Russian school.

The symphony matured slowly, and with it matured Borodin's genius, under the influence of Balakirev and his circle. The young genius imbibed all that Balakirev conducted at the concerts of the Free Music School.[5] The result, however, was a personal idiom of such originality that, with Stassov, one can marvel yet only say vaguely that the national element forms the mightiest ingredient in it. But to try to find its concrete source in any folk-song collection is vain. The performance took place, finally, in January 1869, under the baton of Balakirev, a few days before the death of Dargomyjsky. The success was moderate, but even this is astounding, since the novelty of the work precluded any intelligent reaction from an unprepared

[5] This institution was inaugurated by Balakirev in 1862 to counteract the teaching at the Conservatoire and to oppose the unenterprising concerts of the Imperial Musical Society. Balakirev's programmes were invariably drawn from such composers as Berlioz, Schumann, and Liszt, as well as from the works of his Circle.

public. Nevertheless, Borodin was sufficiently stimulated to begin on a second symphony and, simultaneously, an opera. The subject for this was found in the *Tale of Igor's Host*, a lament for the fate of Russia during the twelfth century, which Stassov there and then worked out in all detail for the composer.

Meanwhile Borodin found a happy marriage with Catherine Protopopov. The young couple lived in a fashion that defies all explanation. Catherine, who suffered from asthma, was afraid to settle in St Petersburg with its damp climate, and continued to spend winter after winter with her mother in Moscow. So Borodin had to live by himself in his immense quarters adjoining the laboratory at the Academy. Meals were served as the spirit moved servants; people came and stayed for days on end, got sick and even went insane there. All was reported daily to Moscow. To this state of things we owe the four volumes of Borodin's letters, which incidentally rank very high in epistolary literature, and also the fact that *Prince Igor* remained unfinished at his death.

But he did complete the *Second Symphony in B Minor*, which, if anything, even surpasses the *First*. The quality of the material is again pure gold and the national element as conspicuous, yet independent of any known sources. All four movements are now equal in splendour whereas in the *First Symphony* the finale was somewhat below the other movements. In keeping with his own non-dramatic nature Borodin contrived in both symphonies developments which are static; like folk-dances they show a cumulative amassing of energy not unlike a persistent stamping on one spot and are the complete opposite of developments found in Beethoven or Tchaikovsky. The symphony was finished in 1867 and first performed the next year, now under the baton of the conductor of the Imperial Opera, Napravnik, and at one of the concerts of the rival series of the Music Society. It did not score even the moderate success of the *First Symphony*, but in the same year Borodin went to visit Liszt in Weimar and found the grand old man to be an enthusiast both for his own works and the whole Russian school. For the first time he was made to feel that his reputation abroad as a composer exceeded that as scholar and scientist. Between 1881 and 1886 he made three further journeys abroad and the circle of his admirers was increased, especially in Belgium. This late recognition served as a sort of consolation for the indifference of the Russian public which had been brought on by ignorant and biased critics.

The last decade of Borodin's life continued in the same atmosphere, so highly unsuitable for the pursuit of music. For his Belgian friends he composed a few songs and the *Petite Suite* for piano. The note of epic grandeur is almost gone, having given way to a most ingratiating salon quality. The same applies to his only symphonic poem, *In the Steppes of Central Asia*, a kind of musical portrayal of the peaceful colonization by the Russians of territories occupied by Asiatic tribes. The Russian and oriental elements in Borodin's make-up were firmly blended, and nothing could express this blending better than his uncanny knack of letting two long and independent characteristic melodies flow along in counterpoint. Into this last decade fall likewise the two string quartets.

RUSSIAN CHAMBER MUSIC

Russian chamber music was only beginning at that time. Apart from a few early works by Glinka there were but a few unimportant contributions by Cui and Rimsky-Korsakov, Balakirev, Dargomyjsky, and Moussorgsky. For the most part, Russian composers remained cool towards what they considered an academic type of music. But in the seventies Tchaikovsky produced his three string quartets, and Borodin soon followed suit. He had always been affected by the classic sonata form. The dynamic contrast of themes fascinated him, only, instead of making them compete and struggle in antithesis, he preferred to combine them in synthesis. In this peaceful coexistence Borodin's psyche is reflected as in a mirror. His fundamental good-humour, his lack of rancour and his equability all speak eloquently in everything that he wrote. All the Russian self-torture, love of sacrifice, soul-searching are exorcized by Borodin's immense loading of sheer primeval force and joyous optimism. Extremes were intolerable to him, and he embraced wholeheartedly the quiet flow of Haydn's forms. Of this balanced serenity the two quartets are the finest example. The *First Quartet in A Major* begins with an echo of a Beethoven theme, from the finale of Op. 130. It continues with a Scherzo,

not unlike a Mendelssohn movement, but with a very spicy
Borodin harmonization, and a slow movement, closely related
to native folk-song laments, but interrupted by a western fugato.
The Second Quartet in D Major, which he timed for the twentieth
anniversary of his engagement to Catherine (1881), he finished
more quickly than any of his other works. It reflects his senti-
ments of that early period: 'O Lord, how much I lived through
then! What a mixture it was of happiness and bitterness!' The
happiness is far more prevalent, and it would be vain to seek
even one drop of bitterness in the succession of the four movements: the serenity of the first, with just a touch of capriciousness, the turmoil of the scherzo only as a preparation for the
lyric, waltz-like second theme in the manner of Johann Strauss,
the languid Nocturne, and the, possibly somewhat jerky and
hurried, finale. Of the heroic, sweeping images of the symphonies there is nothing in these genial works, the bright sunset
of a strange yet perfectly balanced life.

Unfinished there remained a *Third Symphony in A minor* and
his grandiosely conceived opera, *Prince Igor*, the glorious
material of which inspired Stassov, Rimsky-Korsakov, and the
young Glazunov to make it into a coherent work, one of the
most popular and picturesque of the whole Russian school.
Death came suddenly to Borodin during a gay party at his
house on the last day of Carnival Week (1887). The following
morning the greatly distraught Stassov rang the bell at Rimsky-
Korsakov's door. 'You know what has happened?' he said with
great excitement, 'Borodin is dead.' With this the whole Balakirev period of Russian music—the flourishing 'mighty five'—
already long on the wane, received its *coup de grâce*.

8

Church music and the Imperial Chapel

When Nicholas Rubinstein opened the doors of the Conservatoire in Moscow he established a chair for religious music, appointing archpriest Dimitry Razumovsky, who along with Odoyevsky is reckoned among the leading Russian musicologists of the nineteenth century. He was entirely devoted to church music and less than a year after his appointment in 1866 published books on church singing in Russia. Historically this was an important milestone, and modern musicologists still praise his solid scientific foundations.[1] But as for the course that church singing had taken in Russia since the eighteenth century Razumovsky seems to have been less than indifferent. To him the *znamenny* chant, with its gorgeous melodic lines, belonged in the museum and should never again be a part of actual life:

To the sacred musical achievement of the Chapel belongs . . . the so-called Court Chant. This began in the first quarter of our century when the Imperial Chapel reached great heights in the execution of singing in parts. The early nineteenth century is especially remarkable for its concern with the old liturgical melodies [*sic!*]. The singers of the Chapel, collected from all corners of the Empire, brought to the Chapel, aside from their natural vocal gifts, an excellent knowledge of their local varieties. These were actually amalgamated within the Chapel into one whole and formed what is now known as the Court Chant.[2]

[1] See M. Velimirovïc: 'Stand der Forschung über kirchenslavische Musik' in *Zeitschrift für slavische Philologie*, Band XXXI, Heft 1, 1963.
[2] D. Razumovsky, *History of Russian Church Singing*, Moscow, 1886, pp. 246-7.

The complete cycle of Court Chant was compiled in 1846 by Alexis Lvov and duly published. By order of the Synod it was introduced in all the churches of the land. Razumovsky must have known what a confused generalization he had uttered in the above definition of the Court Chant, for he later modified it somewhat. But such was the rigorous authority of the Chapel that no voices were raised to oppose Razumovsky, and his views were repeated in all subsequent histories up to 1915.

COURT CHANT

Lvov's edition was revised in 1869 by his successor Bakhmetev who established the monotonous Court Chant even more firmly in universal use. Bakhmetev's harmonizations are barbarous, what with their heavy doublings in the basses and extreme poverty of the chords supporting what in itself was already poor enough melody. That this compendium is still in general usage can only be explained by the age-old stasis of Orthodox Church legislation. For preservation of dogmatic purity these policies in the end were a blessing, but aesthetically they proved a downright evil influence upon church services. In fact, of the most effective artistic ingredients, the singing of the choir almost equals in importance the holy ikons. While marvellous music, built on genuine popular intonations, was flowing from the pen of great secular masters, the Church continued, and in part still continues, to revel in the German harmonies of 1830-40, so beloved by Lvov, to whom even the music of Glinka was alien. Even more astonishing was the *laissez-faire* attitude of such a connoisseur as Razumovsky who apparently did not appreciate the vast distance separating these two examples (Examples 20(a) and 20(b)).

LOMAKIN AND POTULOV

This difference the Russian nineteenth century could not fully take in. And it is this same inability which indirectly affected the great composers also. After three years of trial Glinka left the Chapel, expressing his dissatisfaction with his own settings. At the end of his life he reverted to the problem of church singing and even went to Berlin to try other ways with his old teacher Dehn. But since even Glinka had nothing to impart to Balakirev or the Chapel in this domain, less competent people became involved in it, and Lvov ensured that they would do nothing independent or adventurous. There was Gabriel Lomakin who collaborated both with Lvov and with Balakirev at the Free Music School and tried to keep both in

Example 20. (*a*) Nineteenth century court chant from the Bakhmetev Ordinarium 1869. (*b*) *Znamenny* chant of the seventeenth century from the synodal square note notation Obikhod.

the dark with regard to this ambiguous collaboration. One Potulov was another who dared to go counter to Lvov by publishing a whole set of *znamenny* melodies harmonized with modal chords in the root position (one chord to each note). One can imagine the devastating outcome of such a procedure!

TCHAIKOVSKY AND CHURCH MUSIC

Finally—and by now it was already 1878—Tchaikovsky began
to appreciate the depth and importance of church music and
wrote to Madame von Meck:

I want to try and do something for church music. It is here that we
have a hardly touched field of action. . . . Do you know that composing for the Church is the monopoly of the Chapel, that it is
forbidden to print or sing in churches anything that had not been
published in the edition of the Chapel, and that this monopoly is
jealously guarded by this institution and will not permit anyone to
write to sacred texts? My publisher Jurgenson has found a way to
circumvent this strange prohibition, and if I should write anything
for the Church, he will publish the music abroad. It is not unlikely
that I will set the Liturgy[3] of St John Chrysostom.[4]

And he did set it, in May 1878 (Op. 41). The director of the
Chapel vetoed its publication. But Jurgenson won in the St
Petersburg District Court, and Tchaikovsky's liturgy became
the first free Russian liturgical work.

That Tchaikovsky was equally inhibited by the existing
restrictions there is no doubt. He was trying his hand in a
forbidden field. But he was also in the midst of his greatest
inspirations, the *Fourth Symphony* and the *First Suite*, and by
their standards the Liturgy is but a timid and uneven work.
Yet we do run into bits of splendid writing and the craftsman-
ship never abates, so that the step taken by this composer and
his enterprise marked a decisive movement in church music.
Three years later he returned to the subject and this time
plunged into the study of the old melodies and their harmonization, but these melodies were still far removed from the *znamenny*.
What is so typical of the prevalent mood of all Russian composers of that period is their viewing the work on liturgical
themes as hardly worth the trouble. Listen to this:

I am now dragging on a grey, uninspired, joyless life, but I am well
physically and have even begun work. I am setting for full chorus

[3] There are three patterns for the Liturgy (Mass) in the Russian Church:
the one most used is that of St John Chrysostom; the others are that of
St Basil the Great and the one known as the Presanctified, used during the
Great Lent.

[4] *Letters to Madame N. von Meck*, Academia, 1934, Vol. I, p. 314.

the chants of the All-Night Vigil[5] from the Obikhod[6] . . . I would like to preserve the old melodies, but as they are built on unusual scales, they are unadaptable. . . .[7]

What a travesty! And yet Tchaikovsky was among those who went about his tasks faithfully, who did not turn from such solace as can be given by religion, in fact would stand through long services, unnoticed, somewhere in a village shrine. His thoughts about church singing clung to him. In 1888 he wrote:

A Messiah is needed who with one stroke should destroy all the old, and go along a new path which lies in the return to hoary antiquity and the resurrection of the ancient chant in the proper harmonization. . . .[8]

But he was to die without finding this Messiah, and his remaining works for the Church do not show that he came nearer a solution than in his Liturgy.

THE BALAKIREV CIRCLE AND CHURCH MUSIC

Looking at Balakirev's group we find even less concern. Balakirev experienced a real transformation from a sceptic to a fastidiously devout person; but his preoccupation with the ritual and the formalities prevented him from penetrating to the core of the matter by taking up the music of the Church. Like Glinka, he was given a singular opportunity of coming to the rescue when he was appointed Director of the Chapel in 1883. But he had never been much of a choral composer and preferred to teach the choir-boys how to play instruments. Choral composition he left to Rimsky-Korsakov who came in as his assistant at this juncture. Rimsky-Korsakov never did things by halves, and began to apply to the liturgical melodies the same principles that he had used with folk-songs. But the result was not the same.[9] Folk-music was his very life, but with the old chants he did not quite know what to do. Thoughts

[5] A combination of Vespers and early Matins.
[6] See p. 34.
[7] *Letters to Madame N. von Meck*, op. cit., Vol. II, p. 513.
[8] Letter to K. M. Konintsky published in the *Russian Musical Gazette*, No. 2, Moscow, 1899, p. 51.
[9] Balakirev and Rimsky-Korsakov laboured in the Chapel for twelve years and the results were disappointing for so long a period.

on church music never bothered him, as they did Tchaikovsky, though with great conscientiousness he left a group of compositions (Op. 22 and Op. 22bis) which were on a high level but fail to move. If the chants ever touched him it was when he was creating such canvases as the *Russian Easter Overture*, or the prayers of the people in the *Legend of the Invisible City Kitej and the Maiden Fevronya*.

The remaining members of the Circle created nothing for the Church and thereby underlined the hopelessly secondary position occupied by religious music in the gorgeous panorama that was unfolding itself in opera, symphony, and ballet. As time went on under the leadership of secular composers, the monopoly of the Chapel over religious music naturally disappeared and compositions poured in from a host of musicians, some of whom could hardly be called composers at all. Nearly every choir-master was bold enough to try his hand at some liturgical canticle, and the number of valueless harmonizations was equalled only by a seemingly endless stream of free compositions quite devoid of any character. The Petersburg Court Chant degenerated into a sterile body of intonations, such as even Lvov could not have imagined. Russian church singing had nothing to hope for from Petersburg, but towards the end of the nineteenth century a new movement arose in the Moscow Synodal School.[10]

[10] Isolated examples of the exploitation of liturgical melodies for instrumental works do, however, occur, as e.g., Arensky's Quartet Op. 35 in memory of Tchaikovsky. Two of its movements are based on *motifs* from the Requiem service (*Pannikhida*), but these motifs, in themselves, are only of eighteenth- or even nineteenth-century origin.

9

Secular music in the eighties— the Belaieff Circle

'When the history of Russian Music comes to be written the name of Belaieff[1] will mark a notable and honourable page.' So wrote Stassov in 1895 on the tenth anniversary of the Russian Symphony Concerts called to life by Belaieff, about whose career very little is known before 1886 when at the age of 50 he became a dominant figure in Russian music. Born in St Petersburg in 1836, he received his education in the School of the Reformed Churches,[2] had travelled widely in his youth, learning business methods and visiting abroad, mainly England and Germany. In due course he became a partner in his father's enormous timber concern. He was married but had no children, although he eventually adopted a daughter. Throughout these years he devoted all his spare hours to the pursuit of music. He was a dedicated viola-player and an assiduous member of various amateur orchestras and chamber ensembles. Always he tried to find ways to substantially serve the cause of Russian music. In 1882, Liadov[3] took him to a concert in which Balakirev conducted the first symphony in E major of the 17-year-old Glazunov, and this proved a decisive moment for Belaieff, who was enormously impressed by what he heard. At once the rich merchant decided to invest in a music-publishing enterprise.

[1] The proper transliteration of this name would be Beliayev, but the name of his business has been affixed for all time as M. P. Belaieff, Leipzig, and now Bonn.
[2] One of the four German Schools (Gymnasia) in Petersburg, considered superior to the Russian institutions.
[3] See p. 127.

He developed procedures unknown in Russia up to that time, entrusting the printing to a single firm, that of C. G. Roeder in Leipzig which was one of the best in Europe. He saw to it that the composers were well paid but demanded strictest accuracy from them in proof-reading, marking *tempo* indications and generally 'delivering the goods'. Glazunov headed the list of publications. After him came Liadov, Rimsky-Korsakov, and a host of minor men, all born within the Russian Empire. Since they comprised a great variety of nationalities, Belaieff became, in a sense, a musical empire-builder. From publishing he proceeded to planning concerts devoted to the performance of the works published—these became the Russian Symphony Concerts—and to the bestowal of annual prizes for works deemed especially significant by a jury. Though Belaieff relied on the judgment of his committee on publications, he sometimes went against its recommendations. Often later events vindicated his judgment, as in the case of Scriabin, whom the committee had rejected.

The new musical hierarchy differed considerably from that of Balakirev's time. The leading figure now was not a professional musician, though he did have clearly defined views on music. Moreover he combined in one person the practical and the artistic approach. Understandably, he was not totally successful in winning over all members of the old fraternity. Moussorgsky, of course, was dead by this time and Borodin was scarcely to be reckoned with, since his medical duties more and more hampered his musical activities. With Balakirev a clash was inevitable. Both he and Balaieff were forceful, strong-minded individuals. Cui preferred to stand aside and observe, lending help here and there only with reservations. Rimsky-Korsakov came over to Belaieff, but only after being wooed jointly by Liadov and Glazunov. Of two available despots Rimsky-Korsakov infinitely preferred Belaieff who would not 'correct' his music or make suggestions of a musical nature; and by the middle eighties—the time when the two former friends worked together in the Imperial Chapel—Rimsky-Korsakov's rift with Balakirev had become almost irreparable. V. Stassov and Madame Shestakova remained aloof, remembering former heroic times which had now given way to a steadily more conservative course.

Supporters of the Belaieff Circle consisted of a host of minor composers, among them a few prominent performers such as the brothers Blumenfeld. Belaieff was lukewarm towards opera and passionately fond of chamber music, a preference which influenced the general trend of his publications. Among the first of these to appear were the two string quartets of Borodin, followed immediately by the early chamber music of Glazunov. However, publication of operas was not totally eliminated: first came Borodin's *Prince Igor*—'I have bought a diamond', Belaieff said of this acquisition for his catalogue—then a number of Rimsky-Korsakov's operas, and finally Taneyev's *Oresteia*.

One great lacuna is noticeable, in the complete absence of any works for the Church.[4] In his aversion to the course taken by the Imperial Chapel, Belaieff went so far as to exclude all compositions of a religious nature. There is even a report of a clause in his will that forbids such works to be included in his catalogue.[5] His indifference to the folk-song left another gap also. The notable exceptions were the Balakirev Album of 1866, which somehow landed in Belaieff's hands, and the first Liadov collection of 1898.

GLAZUNOV (1865-1936)

The backbone of the Belaieff Circle was Alexander Glazunov, as everyone agreed. Even Stassov, who had encouraged the anarchic thrusts of Moussorgsky and of the realists in painting, was completely captivated by the organized art of Glazunov and never ceased singing his praises. He called him fondly 'Orel (the eagle) Konstantinovich'.

Glazunov came from bourgeois stock. His father was a book-publisher with a rather narrow outlook, his mother an amateur pianist. Every encouragement was given to the boy's musical propensities, but he was also sent to a regular school, though not a classical gymnasium. With Balakirev and Rimsky-Korsakov as instructors, his composing, from the start, was

---

[4] A partial explanation lies in the general apathy of the Russian composers setting liturgical texts. This was prior to the efflorescence of the Synodal School.

[5] This I was told by Alexander Tcherepnin, now one of the directors of the Belaieff firm.

strictly instrumental. The composer who affected him most was Borodin, and the reasons are clear, for Glazunov also showed a penchant for abstract symphonic material. Neither the combinations of Balakirev, in the form of folk-material[6] nor the 'colouristic' scheme of Rimsky-Korsakov were of great interest to him. He looked for layers of purely symphonic construction such as we find in Borodin's symphonies and quartets, and for ways of systematizing and expanding them. Later he turned to Tchaikovsky—from whom his masters had duly quarantined him—and still later to Wagner and Taneyev. His love of symphonic lay-out, his delight in successions of superimposed blocks, and his preference for a dense, strictly polyphonic texture for building up his tonal plateaus, all marked him as a symphonist first and foremost.

Glazunov had been dubbed an *epigone*, i.e., one who comes after others stronger than himself, only to say more mildly what had been already said. True, he could not be compared in originality with the most prominent figures in the Balakirev group, nor was he the passionately subjective romantic like Tchaikovsky. Yet his contribution is quite clearly significant and quite original within the confines of the tradition. He put the finishing touches to what already was there, but as yet lacked final coherence and gave the Russian symphony an ultimate harmony and a massive consolidation.

With the powerful and generous support of Belaieff, his life flowed uneventfully and, at least during the first decade and a half of his maturity, quite peacefully. His peace, however, was to end in the first years of the new century, when he was caught up in the stream of unrest and was called on to safeguard and direct the course of the St Petersburg Conservatoire. The tenor of the early part of his life is reflected in the catalogue of his works which by 1890 included three symphonies, a number of symphonic poems and arrangements, three string quartets, the well-known *Cinq Novelettes*, a good deal of piano music, but only a few scattered songs. Although he played several instruments, he never attained virtuosity. As a conductor he fared even worse.

[6] His teachers' unique preoccupation with the folk-song did not touch him in the slightest. Only in the orchestral poem *Stenka Razin* do we encounter a paraphrase of the Volga Boatmen Song.

RIMSKY-KORSAKOV

In Rimsky-Korsakov's career the eighties signified at first a downward trend, but eventually a surge to new heights, more splendid and exciting than ever. The lull after *Snegurochka* was perhaps normal, but was accentuated by his preoccupation with teaching and with new duties imposed by his appointment, together with Balakirev, to the Imperial Chapel. His ever-active mind seemed never to rest. Moussorgsky's death prompted his work on the unfinished *Khovanshchina*, the orchestration of which took most of the summer of 1882. But before he was done with it, he jotted down, in passing as it were, his enchanting one-movement piano concerto, founded on a mournful soldier's melody from the Balakirev collection of 1866 (Example 21). How such a very pianistic exposition could be

Example 21. *Russian soldier's song* from Balakirev album, 1866, by Rimsky-Korsakov.

created by a composer for whom the piano essentially was alien puzzled everyone including Balakirev, who genuinely admired the work.

But relations with the erstwhile leader of the Circle deteriorated from year to year. As Belaieff began to draw nearly everyone into his own orbit, Glazunov included, the rift became complete. The death of Borodin in 1887 dealt an irreparable blow to Russian music. *Prince Igor* was in as bad a state, as was *Khovanshchina*, and the task of putting it in order was shared by Rimsky-Korsakov and Glazunov. It is difficult to discover just how much of this gorgeous music is actually Borodin's. Assafiev (Glebov) published some of his conversations with Glazunov during long summer walks in the environs of St Petersburg in 1906-7. In recounting one of these he recalled that Glazunov had spoken of the Overture to *Prince Igor* discounting the legend that he remembered it note for note from

Borodin's playing. Borodin had sketched the work but never brought it all together. Actually the overture was the work of Glazunov on Borodin's themes, another proof of the guild-like methods of the Russian composers and of their calling themselves with customary humility mere 'editors'.

Rimsky-Korsakov recalls that while working on *Igor* he had thought of an orchestral piece on some episodes from *Scheherazade*, and an overture on liturgical themes. The former is another projection of the Russian-Oriental line, the line that had its inception in Glinka's *Russlan* and is clearly traceable in Balakirev's *Tamara* and Borodin's *In the Steppes of Central Asia*, as also is Rimsky-Korsakov's *Antar*. In *Scheherazade* it reaches its apotheosis. Rimsky-Korsakov dwells minutely on its subject-matter and tells us what he had in mind when he picked this or that episode from the *Thousand and One Nights* and how the four parts of the suite are permeated by certain *leitmotifs*. Quite a few western composers of the Romantic era had been swayed by a desire to paint the wonders of these Arabian tales, but only the Russians were able to capture some genuine strains of the near-eastern world of intonations. This they achieved partly by being brought up on the idea of a multicoloured realm, partly by actual excursions into the Caucasus (Balakirev) and the Crimea, where the muezzin's prayers at sunrise and sunset were still everyday realities. Though just only discernible in the brilliant orchestral refraction given them by the Russians, those mournful, yearning sounds are the common ingredient of all Russian orientalism. Borodin, in whose vein this blood was alive, gave it the most lasting and haunting realization in the Polovtsian acts of *Prince Igor*. But *Scheherazade* comes very near to achieving the same poignant expression. Rimsky-Korsakov said that it was one of the works where he reached his greatest virtuosity and sonority without resorting to a Wagnerian supersize orchestral score.

The *Overture on Liturgical Themes* (Easter Overture) might well have become the cornerstone of a new instrumental tradition based on ancient chants, had these old melodies been more readily accessible. As matters stood, however, Rimsky-Korsakov was not altogether at ease in trying to resurrect childhood impressions of the Easter service. He was quite right in sensing in this liturgical corpus powerful elements of early pagan rites, especially those which combined worship with strong dance-rhythms. For his principal motto Rimsky-Korsakov took a melody of one of the *echoi* of the Novgorod chant originally derived from *znamenny*. But neither he himself, nor Glazunov, nor any of his other pupils, dared to explore further into the domain of the liturgical sources. Hence, as a fusion of the religious and the rampantly secular,[7] the *Easter Overture* occupies a unique position in musical literature.

After these purely orchestral works Rimsky-Korsakov obeyed his urge to return to opera by reverting to the sketches that he and his old friends had supplied more than ten years earlier for the abortive Mlada project.[8] Just as he found himself entangled in this ill-fated idea, a great many other nerve-racking events beset him with the result that he succumbed to something resembling a nervous breakdown. Once before we have seen how this great man handled vital decisions in his life and how they usually proved right in the end. Now, though prolonged uncertainty and doubt assailed him for reasons which one can only guess, the superficial causes seem to have been, first, the *première* of Wagner's *Ring* in Petersburg in 1889; in connection with this he mentions how he and Glazunov attended all the rehearsals with score in hand. Secondly, there were the extensive visits of Tchaikovsky to the northern capital, which brought on a painful reappraisal of the whole Balakirevist orientation, especially as, along with Tchaikovsky, the Moscow critic Laroche appeared on the horizon. Laroche, a clever and eloquent writer, had always taken a hostile attitude to the Circle and in much the same measure he always extolled Tchaikovsky. At this time he attached himself both to Glazunov and Liadov, an action which was bound to hurt the sensibilities of so forthright and logical a person as Rimsky-Korsakov.

[7] Another such fusion exists in Balakirev's *First Symphony* in 1898.

[8] In 1871-2 Gedeonov, Director of the Imperial Theatres, arranged a co-operative project of Rimsky-Korsakov, Borodin, Cui, and Moussorgsky for a stage spectacle based on a libretto by Krylov. Only Cui had finished his part when Gedeonov lost his post and the opera ballet was aborted. Rimsky-Korsakov reworked the libretto with an increased Wagner-like orchestra for over a year, but in spite of an initial successful performance with Stravinsky's father in the leading role, the work was eventually dropped from the Maryinsky Theatre repertoire.

But deeper causes for his malady arose from the rift with Balakirev, and from illness and death in his immediate family. Strangely enough, a deep-seated urge for self-criticism also contributed to the difficulty:

And lo! one fine morning I felt an extreme fatigue, combined with a rush of blood to the head and a confusion of thought. I got a great shock and even lost my appetite. When I spoke about it to my wife, she told me to stop all work, which I did. But when left to myself, disagreeable and haunting ideas incessantly piled up. I thought of religion and a humble reconciliation with Balakirev. . . . Towards music I remained utterly cold. . . .[9]

Fortunately he was distracted from utter gloom by the production of *Mlada* and various other concert events. How heartening it is to read about this recuperation as having come of its own accord, without the aid of psychiatrists! He was fully recovered some time in 1894.

TCHAIKOVSKY, THE LAST YEARS

By then a staggering event had shaken the whole musical world, for Tchaikovsky suddenly died. During the twelve years following the composition of the Trio in memory of Nicholas Rubinstein he had had a calm but productive period. In the decade of the entire sixties events in his life were quite tranquil. At least they seemed so by contrast with the intense crisis of the preceding period. Poignant agony seemed still to haunt his music—witness the *Manfred Symphony*, the opera *The Enchantress*, and finally the *Fifth Symphony in E Minor* (1881)—but a relatively serene attitude towards the world and towards himself prevailed. This tendency towards peacefulness was crowned in 1888 by the ballet *The Sleeping Beauty*. By then he was an acknowledged master in the West, as well as in Russia, and was free to shape his life and work as he pleased. He had even found a haven in his house in Maidanovo.[10] But peace rests with inner, not outer circumstances of life. Tchaikovsky had achieved merely a semblance of this peace, as the last five years of his career were to show.

His relentless labours never abated. Like Schubert, he could say: 'When I finish one song I go to the next'—and what

[9] N. A. Rimsky-Korsakov, *My Musical Life*, Moscow, 1926, p. 309.
[10] A village near the town of Klim, some fifty miles north-east of Moscow.

devastating and strength-consuming songs they were! Remarkably, even during his travels, and while living uncomfortably
in foreign hotels, his work did not stop. For instance, in the
year 1887 he spent the second half of January and February
in Maidanovo working feverishly on *The Enchantress*. In early
March he conducted a concert of his own compositions in
Petersburg, where he saw the first performance of his *Second
Suite*. Then he hurried back to Maidanovo to finish *The Enchantress* and in May travelled down the Volga, embarking
also by sea to Tiflis and Borjom. There he wrote his *Mozartiana
Suite*. In July he left Batum, travelling by sea to Odessa and
from there without delay to Aachen to visit his dying friend
Kontratyev. In Aachen he finished the suite and then by
September appeared again in Maidanovo. In October he rehearsed and conducted *The Enchantress* in Petersburg and in
November performed the suite in Moscow. By the middle of
December he was again on tour, this time visiting Berlin and
Leipzig, where he appeared as conductor for the first time at
a *Gewandhaus* Concert. One must remember that conducting
did not come easily to him; there had to be perpetual effort
to overcome his natural shyness. In spite of all obstacles and
difficulties new ideas flowed into creation in a wild torrent,
and by the end of the next year the *Fifth Symphony* was already
an accomplished feat.

The remaining years of Tchaikovsky's life steadily accentuated the feelings of gloom and premonitions of death that had
been his constant companions all along. Outwardly he was successful, as always, in deluding his friends behind a mask of
happiness. But his last works tell a different tale, most of all the
opera *Pique Dame* and the *Pathétique Symphony*. From Florence,
as he was composing the *Pique Dame*, he wrote to Glazunov:

I am very much in need now of friendly concern and a constant
communion with people. I am going through a very curious stage
on the way to the grave. Something is happening within me that I
cannot fathom. A sort of fatigue from life, a disillusionment: at
times frightful despair, but not the kind at the bottom of which
there is the anticipation of a fresh upsurge of life's joys, but something hopelessly final. . . .[11] (1890)

[11] M. Tchaikovsky, *Life of Peter Tchaikovsky*, Moscow, 1902, Vol. III,
p. 375.

Tchaikovsky's inner life can only be surmised. Did he, or did he not, achieve a state of peace before dying? There are witnesses to the fact that just before his last journey to St Petersburg, to conduct the *Sixth Symphony in B Minor*, even in the first stages of his illness, he felt happy as never before. Maybe it was granted him to overcome that terror of death that lurks in his final musical bequest. What sort of a language does he speak towards the end?

The substantial presence of folk-song intonations and actual folk-songs that can be traced in the works of his early period disappears almost entirely after the finale of the *Fourth Symphony*, the *Overture 1812*, and some scattered and very unimportant places in the operas of the middle period, *Mazeppa*, *Tcherevichki*, and *The Enchantress*. Neither the suites, nor the last two symphonies reveal any recognizable folk-song patterns. *Pique Dame* is about as far from the folk-song idiom as Taneyev's chamber music or Scriabin's *Poem of Ecstasy*. His reliance on the chant is faint, even in his liturgy. There is a vast capacity for moulding his own melodic formations, penetrating, haunting, impregnated in one's memory for good and all. His harmonic language speaks with utmost force and consequence— witness the expanding chords in the third movement of the *Pathétique*—yet never achieves the force of a revelation as do Borodin and Moussorgsky in their idioms. Tchaikovsky's greatest strength lies in his uncanny faculty for symphonic construction and development—a faculty which underlies his masterly handling of polyphony, witness the Fugue from the *First Suite*. His orchestral eloquence is phenomenal. Instead of bewitching in the manner of Rimsky-Korsakov, he grips and shatters. His deep melodies and sombre timbres are unforgettable. When his music penetrated into the western capitals it caused complete consternation. This is what John Ireland told me in 1956 at the lowest ebb of Tchaikovsky's popularity among musicians:

I still like Tchaikovsky, believe it or not. When we were at the College [Royal College of Music] we all thought he was the last word in music. I heard the first performance in England of his Sixth Symphony. It simply swept us off our feet. We had never heard such music before. . . .

As the impact of Balakirev waned, the colossal force of Tchaikovsky's music made itself felt in every phase of Russian music, becoming almost obsessive in its influence through the rest of the century and even beyond.

SERGE I. TANEYEV (1856-1915)

The first to be affected was Taneyev, who came from the town of Vladimir, some ninety miles north-east of Moscow, where his father, a highly cultivated and art-loving man, was a civil servant. Music played a leading role in his life as a child, but already at the age of ten he was entered for the newly founded Moscow Conservatoire. He stayed there nearly ten years, and his teachers at the advanced stage were Nicholas Rubinstein and Tchaikovsky. For his graduation Taneyev played the Brahms *D Minor Piano Concerto*, a work hardly known in Moscow at the time. When Tchaikovsky resigned his professorship, Taneyev was retained to take over some of his classes. Neither by temperament nor by his discipline was Taneyev akin to his teacher, yet it was precisely the romantic side of Tchaikovsky that left the indelible mark on him. It was this discrepancy between a highly original mentality and a derivative way of expressing himself musically that stamped Taneyev and prevented him from coming into his own as a composer of influence. Only by ignoring this discrepancy and by reading into Taneyev's scores deeper meanings—by finding, as it were, idealized relationships between idiom, mode of thought, ways of thinking, and manipulation of materials—can admiration and enjoyment of his music be found. Not many arrived at such attitudes, least of all his master and idol, Tchaikovsky, who was frankly puzzled by Taneyev. He could not understand why his disciple should plunge headlong into detailed study of the Netherlands masters, nor why he would strew his notebooks with fanciful contrapuntal combinations, only to achieve naïve results. Tchaikovsky was critical of his faculties as an orchestrator: 'This is your weakest spot', he told Taneyev, with some acerbity.

But, along with such intellectual sport, Taneyev was moved by truly penetrating ideas about music and the importance of the role that he assigned to Russian composers and ancient musical tradition. As early as 1879 he had grasped the importance of Russian song in the modernization of Russian music in the nineteenth century:

The task of every Russian composer consists in furthering the creation of national music. The history of western music gives us the answer as to what should be done to attain this: apply to the Russian song the workings of the mind that were applied to the song of western nations and we will have our own national music. Begin with elementary contrapuntal forms, pass to more complex ones, elaborate the form of the Russian fugue, and from there it is only a step to complex instrumental types. The Europeans took centuries to get there, we need far less. We know the way, the goal, we can profit by their experience. . . . Let us master the art of the old contrapuntists and undertake a difficult but glorious task. Who knows what we shall bequeath to the next generation—new forms, new music? Who knows but within the next few decades, early in the twentieth century, Russian forms will have been evolved. It does not matter when, but they must come.[12]

No better light could be shed on Taneyev, the musical thinker, even the composer. The more one reads in his extensive diaries, the greater becomes one's admiration for this truly rare personage who attained the highest originality by renouncing any search for it, and by steeping himself in the imitation of old masters such as the Netherlanders, Bach and, last of all, Handel, with whom Taneyev revealed the greatest affinity. Handel's influence is overpowering in his last and most inspired work, the cantata *Upon the Reading of a Psalm.* In calling this work Handelian we encounter an archaic phenomenon: for who does not know that in the Middle Ages the pupil who came nearest to his master elicited the highest praise?

But, in the last analysis, Taneyev was a false champion, for he failed to accomplish what he had preached in 1879. Looking at works composed after his graduation from the conservatoire (1876-9), we found that they were mostly unpublished and therefore are now inaccessible. But in those which are extant we find Russian motifs lurking everywhere, mainly in the form of fugal themes. There is a *Netherland Fantasy* on a folk-song from the Balakirev collection of 1876 which Rimsky-Korsakov used with such insistence for the whole Tartar Act of the opera *The Legend of Kitej*; there is also a whole set of liturgical choruses among his papers. All these are thickly interspersed with a variety of notes revealing occupations of a purely intellectual

[12] From a Memorandum Book reproduced in Vassili Yakovlev's book of Taneyev, Moscow, 1926.

type: the writing of textbooks of harmony and instrumentation, translations from the German, etc. Hence the total picture is blurred and we are at a loss to follow the composer's notions, except in terms of massive intellectual computation of such abstraction and complexity, as to lose all contact with his original purpose of 'the creation of national music'. Furthermore, the eighties for Taneyev were filled with administrative affairs, stemming from his post as Director of the Conservatoire. Only in 1905, when he relinquished this directorship and finally withdrew altogether from teaching at the institution, did he seriously begin to publish his works. This factor alone explains their small number—thirty-six in all.

The word 'WASTE' is writ large over all Russian endeavours, achievements, projects, and actual contributions to all fields of knowledge. One would think that this waste might be least applicable to someone of such vast erudition and industry as Taneyev. But for the cause of Russian music, and especially religious music, for the chants and the folk-songs, for national operas and symphonies, destiny acted in the most wasteful manner by producing this *Russian Netherlander*, this polyphonic master, comparable to Josquin, Palestrina, or Bach, this compiler of learned books on western counterpoint and fugue, this writer of a monumental operatic work on an ancient Greek myth, the *Oresteia*, just at a time when the immense riches of the old chants clamoured for a 'national' counterpoint, when the art of the old ikon painters was suddenly revealed in all its mediaeval austerity, and when a backward gaze of so great a mind as Taneyev's into the Russian, instead of the western, sources would have been of paramount importance. Yet who can blame an artist for choosing the one path that suits him? And have not two of Taneyev's greatest pupils—Scriabin and Medtner—travelled in even more remote paths? Have they not wandered in even denser western forests?

It is strange that nearly all published works of Taneyev belong to the last twenty-five years of his life. There is only one published symphony (the other three have remained in manuscript), six quartets and other chamber music, many songs and choruses, and above all the opera *Oresteia* and two big cantatas which begin and end his whole output as Op. 1 and Op. 36, respectively. All these works are saturated with music of the highest calibre—works moulded with consummate mastery, though moving within predictable spheres. Practically nothing occurs that is unexpected either emotionally or reflectively. One marvels at the deft and expert handling of the parts, the perfection of the overall form, the safe and invariably effective sonorities. But one waits in vain for a touch of the unreal or mysterious—for a startling row of chords, or a volcanic rhythm. In melody, that ultimate test of the greatness of the music, one finds in Taneyev two extremes: either abstract, Palestrina-like formulations, or expressions of gushing sentimentality—expressions moreover which lack Tchaikovsky's utter sincerity. But when, as in his songs, he was challenged by verbal images or psychological states, he at times succeeded in an uncanny fashion, as in that superb anthology from Ellis's *Immortelles* (Op. 26). But with this collection, as also with the name of Ellis, the poet and philosopher, we arrive at Taneyev's last years which coincide with the period of symbolism in literature and the general search throughout European music for exotic colours and sounds. In those times Taneyev was one of the most remarkable figures of old Moscow. He lived with the greatest frugality, disdaining the conveniences of civilization. Most of his life he had been cared for by the nurse who had been with him since childhood. When she died, leaving him forlorn, he was surreptitiously looked after by friends and pupils. He caught a cold at the funeral of Scriabin in the spring of 1915 and died two months later from a heart complication.

10

Return to the sources

PRECURSORS

The steadily rising passion for the collection of folklore in nineteenth-century Russia became a wave of enthusiasm for a rich past that had been veiled in darkness. The period of romanticizing, typical in the early stages of any movement, had waned by the end of the century, giving way to a yearning for the real thing, the unadorned art, even the crude sounds of the southern Russian steppes as these were rediscovered during the Kerch excavations. Along with the folklore movement came renewed interest in genuine, untouched folk-song. The two towering figures in Russian music at this time, both active since the middle fifties, were V. Stassov, whom we have already encountered as the protagonist of the Glinka-Balakirev group, and Tertius Filippov. The latter, though not as vocal as Stassov, was no less enthusiastic about ancient Russian culture, especially its religious manifestations.

FILIPPOV (1825-99)

Filippov came from Rjev in the Tver province, north-west of Moscow, and after obtaining a solid education at Moscow University disappeared for a while within the maze of a bureaucratic career. But in 1856 he was dispatched to the Don and the Azov Sea for what today would be called ethnographic study. A few years later he entered the Department of Control, soon rising to the highest position. His main interest centred upon the struggle between the Slavophiles and the Westerners, in which all his sympathies were with the former. While Stassov was in a way but a half-hearted Slavophile who admired Belinsky and Tchernyshevsky, Filippov shied away from this school of thought, espousing the pre-Petrine organization of Russia, with its Patriarchate and Church councils. His proselytizing took a strange form: instead of talking, he carried on his propaganda by means of singing the old folk-songs, with consummate mastery and knowledge. His aim was to disseminate the ideals of native culture to a smaller circle of Muscovites by means of the periodical *Moskvityanin* and from there into ever wider areas of Russian society.

Around 1880 he sang some of his songs to Rimsky-Korsakov who delighted in harmonizing them (see Appendix I and Chapter 6), still in the manner of romantic stylization, although with deep insight into the melodic nature of the raw material. But at that very time Melgunov published his two albums (Appendix I), in which all stylization is summarily abandoned. They were called 'barbaric' by Rimsky-Korsakov, an epithet which brings us to the core of the new search: the sources were barbaric and their first impact on the more refined romantics produced shock. Melgunov's was the first attempt to fix on paper not just one of the voices or lines of melody, but as many as the ear could catch. In the very first song of his collection Melgunov lists five separate variants (*podgoloski*) of the same tune just as if he had extracted a line from each of the singers in a chorus. Where he failed, hence earning the epithet 'barbaric', was in his attempt to reduce all the variants so that they might be accompanied by the piano. A mechanical pianistic version of what the peasants intone with such perfect blending and minute nuance is, of course, impossible, and only the early gramophone, some twenty years later, could roughly approximate the tonal picture.

A year or two after Melgunov's publication the Palchikov collection from the Ufa province (Appendix I) appeared: Palchikov avoided Melgunov's mistake and listed only separate lines, sometimes ten or twelve of them. The Melgunov and Palchikov collections proved what had been suspected as early as the time of William Coxe and was probably known to Glinka, Odoyevsky and Serov—that Russian heterophony was a very real thing.

ISTOMIN AND DYUTCH

Meanwhile Filippov procured funds from the Imperial Treasury and dispatched two specialists, the ethnographer Istomin and the musicologist George Dyutch, to scour the northern provinces of Olonetzk and Archangel for remnants of musical antiquity. This they accomplished to perfection, bringing back close on two hundred songs ranging from the most ancient Spiritual Verses, so dear to Filippov, to the comparatively recent soldiers' songs. Filippov's instinct that the North was replete with precious music was then as sound as it would be today—witness the Malyshev Expedition of 1955 (Appendix II). The collectors penetrated deep into an untouched region, covering nearly five hundred miles by boat, even at times by rowing-boat, and travelling on horseback or by carriage on land. Since the time at their disposal was limited and the area immense, they had to proceed with speed and frequently resorted to the Czar's money. The very arduous task of taking down the songs from the actual performance fell to Dyutch.

A former pupil of Rimsky-Korsakov and a fellow-student and inseparable friend of Liadov, Dyutch became a conductor who was mentioned with high praise in all the reminiscences of the period. Soon after the expedition he fell victim to consumption, dying prematurely in 1891 without having seen his collection in print. Making all allowance for the approximate character of his notations—he rarely attempted more than one line—we find in them a rich fount of melodic beauty. One of the first composers to be inspired by this material was Balakirev, who stylized thirty of the melodies for the accompanied settings which form the second Balakirev album (see Appendix I). Undaunted by Dyutch's death, Istomin took part in another expedition to the Russian North in 1894. His new collaborator was Liapunov, a musician very close to Balakirev. This time they did not confine their search to the extreme northern provinces, but touched on Vologda, Viatka, and Kostroma as well. As the movement south continued, they discovered that the Spiritual Verses began to disappear. Dance songs and roundelays came in abundance, as well as laments and wedding songs. These two Istomin volumes were published by the Imperial Geographic Society at the instigation of Filippov and are unique in the high quality of the material, as well as in the care and exquisite art bestowed on the publications.

---

[1] The fascinating description of their procedure upon arrival in a village has been given in Chapter 1.

SMOLENSKY (1848-1909)

While intensive activity in folk-song preservation was to be expected in the Russian milieu of the time, the appearance of a protagonist of ancient church music in full view of the static Imperial Chapel was definitely a surprise. This was no other than S. Smolensky, the daring editor of the Mezenetz *Alphabet* (See Chapter 1, p. 32). Like Filippov, he was a graduate of several university faculties in his native Kazan. Music he learnt within the family of a gifted dilettante much in the manner of Balakirev. For years he was active in the Kazan High School for the Tartar population where he helped to promulgate effective teaching methods. But all the while he was also making careful studies in the Solevetzky Library of his city, famous for its collection of old manuscripts containing the old kriuk (*neume*) notations. Smolensky raised an uproar over the need to study these notations in order that the true foundations of Russian music might be restored. He thus became an ardent follower of Mezenetz and, like him, claimed that the kriuk alphabet and its unknown canticles were of Russian origin.

When Razumovsky died in 1889, Smolensky had been called to succeed him as professor of church music at the Moscow Conservatoire. Simultaneously he took over the post of director of the Moscow Synodal School, an institution which up to then had led an inconspicuous existence. With incredible energy he lifted its standards, musically and pedagogically, trained intelligent singers and instrumentalists, and succeeded in making world-famous the choir which appeared in Vienna in 1899. He had in this the advantage of being free from the tyranny of the St Petersburg Chapel and of collecting around himself some of the more gifted church composers of the time. At the Conservatoire, likewise, he advocated the study of old notations and incidentally implanted in Rachmaninov, his most prominent pupil, a deep love for ancient melodies.

Seeing the splendid success of Smolensky in Moscow, the St Petersburg court circle lured him to the Imperial Chapel in 1901. Probably they acted on advice from the still powerful K. P. Pobedonostzev, who had always actively shared Smolensky's views. But here progressive reforms fell on totally arid ground and Smolensky preferred to withdraw after a brief period, to devote himself to a variety of cultural, pedagogic and scientific projects. Among the activities arising from these was an expedition which led to Mount Athos for the reproduction and photographing of old Byzantine manuscripts housed at the famous monasteries there. He died during a journey to his native Kazan in 1909.

All that was natural in the domain of folk-music needed a seer and prophet in church singing, that most woefully neglected and misguided sphere of activity. Such a seer Smolensky most assuredly was and, like all seers, was ahead of his time. His theories of a 'native counterpoint', different from that of the West, were long looked upon as chauvinistic and unfounded. Only recently have his views broken through to be seriously studied by modern scholars. The work of Smolensky in transcribing old notations and developing a theory about native counterpoint was being paralleled by the *peradvijniki* (wandering artists), who were just rediscovering the colours, designs and motifs of peasant art and beginning to restore old frescoes and icons. In religious art Vassnetzov and Nesterov, inspired painters and designers, were carrying forward the same sort of tasks as was Smolensky in music. To them as to Smolensky, appreciation and recognition are just beginning to come.

THE MAIN SWEEP

To one growing up in early twentieth-century Russia, musical life seemed but an expansion of the romantic period—part of a continuation of the past with Schumann a central figure and the northern poet-musician Grieg supplying all one could imagine in novel and romantic harmonic sensations. Mozart had not yet become an idol, and the first impressions of Bach were still vague and unassimilated. The patriarchs of Russian music were still alive, and it was quite common to see such figures as Stassov, Cui, and Rimsky-Korsakov in the St Petersburg Concert Hall of the Nobility.

Of the great discoveries and changes going on behind this romantic scene only a few initiates were aware. The public had not an inkling, and yet it was precisely in these momentous years that the massive movement towards song and chant sources became universal. Of course, this was not merely a

Russian phenomenon, for similar trends existed throughout Europe. In Western art the Byzantine mozaics of Ravenna and Sienese primitives worth only a shrug of the shoulders in the nineteenth century suddenly became objects of devout pilgrimages; here, too, Gregorian Chant, restored by the monks of Solesmes among others, was now carried into actual services throughout Europe by the famous papal Bulls *Nos quidem* and *Motu proprio* in the years 1901-3. It was precisely at this time that the collector Eugenie Lineva returned from her first expedition to the Ukraine with the recordings of the singing of the peasants.

Filippov had meanwhile died, and Lineva, not supported by the Czar's money, found it much more difficult than before to persuade singers to perform. She tells how she had had to settle for longer periods in the villages and gradually take the peasant women into her confidence in order to find informants. Although she made only infrequent trips and managed to collect far less than Istomin, she could now prove with finality, by means of her records, that Russian *podgoloski* (variants) were fixed Russian phenomena.

Some facts of this remarkable woman's life are worth telling. Trained to become a concert singer, her artistic sensibilities were touched to the quick by the singing of a band of pilgrims in Kiev. From that moment on she abandoned all her ambitions and devoted herself entirely to the collection of the art the pilgrims revealed to her. When fate directed her to America she was already in possession of priceless material and, once settled in New York, managed to inspire a group of Russian singers to perform the folk-songs chorally. At one such concert the great Russophile industrialist Charles Crane happened to be present, and he immediately invited Lineva and her singers to the Chicago World Fair of 1893. On their return to Russia the Linevas—her husband was an engineer—tried to refund Crane's money; but this enthusiast, instead, sent double the amount to the Imperial Geographical Society expressly requesting that it be used for Lineva's next expedition.

All told she undertook three such trips: that into the Ukraine already mentioned, and two others—in 1904 and 1909—into Great Russian territory (Vladimir, Novgorod, etc.). These augmented her collection immeasurably, with sixty-five items in print and hundreds still unpublished. Her use of recording equipment lends an authenticity to her volumes which makes up in quality for what they lack in quantity. They are moreover supplied with most valuable prefaces in which the collector's problems are discussed from various angles.

How much of this did Russian composers know in 1900? Perhaps more than we think. It is certain that Lineva's recordings would have disturbed them greatly. Rimsky-Korsakov's whole ideology was built on the folk-song. He relished its modal structure; its unsymmetrical rhythms, even the unstable tonic must have intrigued him, and in his strictly organized musical world he would find the proper moment to apply all these touches. But touches they must remain; they never aspire to a self-sufficient role. This is why all through his output a modal cadence is gently modified, a wayward rhythm tamed. Above all, the classic-romantic code of part-writing must be clung to religiously. Rimsky-Korsakov's code prescribed uniform four-part harmonizations. It had its simple laws of melodic leading: conjunct progression was the rule, disjunct the exception; it determined the spacing of chords, forbidding certain doublings in a manner completely contrary to the practice of the folk-singer. As for consonances and dissonances, the style can only be described as 'Palestrinan' with preparations and resolutions managed in a manner only slightly less strict.

Much of this code was permitted by authentic folk-song so long as folk-melodies could be controlled where discrepancies occurred. Russian composers were only too delighted to deal with it; with only these few compromises they allotted to it a leading position. Lineva, however, proved that many of its most salient characteristics were different from the classic-romantic ideal, just as the figures and proportions of the *trecento* were opposed to those of the Renaissance. On the eve of that revelation the folk-songs collected on the expeditions of Istomin, Dyutch, and Liapunov absorbed the attention of Liadov.

LIADOV (1855-1914)

From the point of view of the old Russian heritage the first twenty years of Liadov's activity as a composer might not have existed at all. The son of the conductor at the Imperial Opera, he was drawn into a chaotic Bohemian way of life from early childhood. Entering the Conservatoire on a scholarship, he idled away his time until eventually expelled. Readmitted after some years, he wrote a brilliant graduation exercise—*The Overture to Schiller's Bride of Messina*—and thereafter was retained as a teacher. Though he groaned under the weight of it, this pedagogic task saved his life, since without appointed duties he would have gone down in utter melancholia. Even his secret and supremely happy marriage did little to urge him to action.[2] Aside from Belaieff, Liadov was a friend of the folk-song collector Dyutch who had been expelled from the Conservatoire with him, the church composer Avdeyev, and the chorus master at the opera, Pomazansky, his brother-in-law.

Liadov's attitude towards music was at times lacking in confidence. It seemed to take him an age to tackle a composition, and then when he finally did get busy he spent another age working on the piece like a jeweller, touching up, polishing and at last putting in all dynamic marks. Models dear to him were Chopin, Schumann, and Glinka, and only through the music of the latter was he influenced by something of a folk idiom as manifested in Glinka's *pesennost*. Beyond this in the great wilderness of folk-music Liadov was afraid to venture. So for years nothing but little piano pieces amused him. He delighted in the miniature, whether a musical box or a nursery rhyme, wrote preludes and studies, waltzes and mazurkas; and so it went on until that magic moment when Balakirev threw into his lap some of the recently collected folk-melodies (1897). Liadov was greatly inspired, and the result was some 150 precious stylizations for voice and piano, for women's chorus and, finally, for orchestra (*Eight Russian Folk-Songs*).

Liadov's art stands as the ultimate vindication of folk-song material incorporated into classical music with academic perfection. Tastefully and with infinite refinement, he touched upon peasant intonations, removed rustic husks and penetrated to untold accents of beauty and warmth (Example 22). This led, of course, to stylistic beautification and, therefore,

---

[2] Insisting that his marriage concerned only himself, he tried to keep it a secret, but the curious Belaieff penetrated into his lodgings when he knew that Liadov was not at home and there made the acquaintance of a most charming and devoted woman.

away from the untarnished raw product; but to Russian art-music Liadov managed to give one of its most exquisite ornaments without completely betraying the peasant's way.

Liadov's *Ten Settings from the Obikhod*, Op. 61, his sole contribution to the religious field, was just as delicate a piece of

Example 22. *Fifty Songs of the Russian People*, 1902, Liadov.

work and possibly a direct outcome of his massive preoccupation with folk-song. With true instinct, Liadov chose genuine *znamenny* melodies and invented most fitting harmonies; but even here he shrinks from giving up the academic workmanship altogether, and slips in the occasional unauthentic turn of phrase. Musicians of the nineteenth century could never fully reconcile themselves to exploitation of the ancient tonalities upon which *znamenny* chant is solely based (Example 23).

KASTALSKY (1856-1926)

Quite free from any academic approach was Liadov's opposite in Moscow, Alexander Kastalsky. When it came to careful workmanship, he was wholly uninhibited and was in the habit of dashing down pages only roughly sketched. In short, he was not over-burdened by schooling. If this was a defect, he made up for it by a genuine feeling for antiquity and eagerly joined the ranks of those who clamoured for a return to the sources.

Example 23. *Ten Arrangements from the Obikhod*, Liadov.

He was born in Moscow in 1856 into the family of a learned arch-priest and professor and grew up surrounded by books and literature of all kinds. Music played a very minor part in his upbringing, but with his naïve improvisations on the piano he intrigued even connoisseurs. They sensed in him something new and induced him to enter the Conservatoire. He was by then nearly 20, and so did not fit comfortably into the traditional framework. Hence, his Conservatoire years were haphazard, particularly since they were interrupted by military service. Gradually his interest turned towards the Moscow Synodal School, just before Smolensky took it in hand. Here he developed his very original ideas on choral singing and, at the suggestion of Orlev, the conductor of the Synodal Choir, began his series of stylizations of the old *znamenny* chant. These

20. Steven Smolensky.

19. Tchaikovsky in the 1870s.

22. Herman Laroche.

21. Tertius Filippov, Folk-song collector.

24. George Dyutch, Anatole Liadov, Nicholas Lavrov.

23. Alexander Glazunov, a portrait by A. M. Lubinov, 1928.

25. Maxim Gorky, Vladimir Stassov, Ilya Repin, Mrs Repina, 1904.

26. Boris Assafiev (pseudonym, Igor Glebov).

won immediate approval and were published by Jurgenson.[3]
The historic role of Kastalsky was clearly revealed in these
settings which marked a complete departure from the official
style of the Imperial Chapel, a return to the old Russian
canticles, into which melodic turns from the folk-songs had
been infused (Example 24). Thus the first attempt was made
to restore to the Orthodox Church its proper musical heritage,
just as a similar attempt on the part of the painters was made
to restore the virginal beauty of the icons.

Example 24. *Christmas Kontakion*, Kastalsky, *znamenny* chant harmonized in 1902.

To the realm of the folk-song proper Kastalsky turned somewhat later. In 1912-13, he was still trying to find a bridge
between church and folk-music:

I am studying the materials for my coming work—summarizing
the various characteristic aspects of the Russian song and at the
moment scrutinizing old manuscripts of church singing, which no
one has as yet read or transcribed on to the stave.[4]

In another letter of this period, Kastalsky encouraged Listopadov to undertake folk-song research. His epoch-making
collections (see Appendix I) began simultaneously with those
of Lineva and continued through the entire revolutionary and
post-revolutionary period. But in this domain Kastalsky's role
remained that of observer, adviser, summarizer. He did not

---

[3] Peter Jurgenson began his own publishing house in 1861 with little
capital, but through a friendship with Nicholas Rubinstein met Tchaikovsky
and had the foresight to publish his works from the beginning with Opus 1.
He was also famous for the first Russian publications of Chopin, Schumann,
Mendelssohn, and Wagner. In the last two decades of the nineteenth
century, he published almost one hundred stylizations of Kastalsky, many
of which were of the *znamenny* chant; for example, Nos. 3, 6, 10, 24, 28, 31,
54, etc.
[4] Article on Kastalsky by Zhitomirsky, Moscow, 1950.

attempt folk-song compositions such as those he left for the Church. In fact, his main work on folk-music, *Foundations of Popular Polyphony*, remained unpublished until after his death in 1926. His own compositions in the secular field were little more than frescoes, although an opera of his was performed in 1917.

All of this had but little bearing on his wonderful accomplishment at the Synodal School, where he was the direct successor of Smolensky to whose ideals in the use of folk-song and chant he gave a practical direction.[5] The tragic end of the whole movement came after the Revolution when further discoveries in the religious field were halted. Most of Kastalsky's collaborators at the School, among whom the principal was Paul Tchesnokov,[6] were forced to write secular choruses.

[5] One other name should be mentioned in connection with the inception of the revolt against the Imperial Chapel: that of Nicholas Kompaneisky (1848-1910), the author of harmonizations of the eight *Theotokia-Dogmatica* of the *znamenny* chant. Kompaneisky, incidentally, also the writer of *Reminiscences of Moussorgsky*, was deeply interested in the origin of the *znamenny* chant and combated the theory that it was constructed on the western modes.

[6] Tchesnokov (1877-1944) was a pupil of Smolensky at the Synodal School. This is what he wrote to me in 1933: 'I have devoted my life to choral work, have written about 500 religious and 100 secular choruses. But the central labour of my life is a book on choral conducting . . .'. Assafiev commented on him in *Russian Music from the Beginning of the Nineteenth Century*, op. cit., p. 304: 'The choral works of Tchesnokov have an excellent sonority, but they are more superficial and less rich in content than those of Kastalsky. Tchesnokov's style is but a craft *par excellence*, a gorgeous technique.' But Michel Ossorguine, one of the greatest connoisseurs of the *znamenny* chant in our time, placed Tchesnokov very high. In my view, he is more consistent and professional than Kastalsky who, however, loses some of his ingenuous beauty when he moves away from the sources, rather than towards them, in his hunt for prettiness (*à la* Arensky or Gretchaninov).

Scriabin and Rachmaninov
1886-1903

As we have seen, outwardly the nineties seemed but an extension of the preceding period. In St Petersburg the scene revolved around the three dominant figures in Belaieff's circle: Rimsky-Korsakov, Glazunov, and Liadov. By this time Rimsky-Korsakov was becoming more involved in opera. Through the transitional *Mlada*, and *Christmas Eve*, his second comic opera on a work by Gogol, he prepared himself for his next major work, *Sadko* (1896). Glazunov's symphonic output was rising steadily up to the time of his Sixth Symphony and his first ballet *Raimonda* (1897).

THE ZVEREV 'PENSION'

But in Moscow things moved in new directions. There was then a curious establishment in the old city for the preparation of young pianists. It was run by an elementary teacher of the Conservatoire—one Nicholas Zverev. Here was the epitome of the old-time Russian eccentric. Having lived well and squandered a sizeable fortune, he was forced to apply for a job at the Conservatoire. In his youth (he remembered) he had studied the piano with Dubuque and Henselt and later he had begun to take talented pupils into his household to train them for entrance to the Conservatoire. Board and lodging and tuition were all gratis, but students were not allowed to go home at any time during the first two or three years. Even during vacations, they had to go with Zverev to the country, or even to the seaside in the Crimea. Every day began at six a.m. when the boys had to clean their rooms, clothes and shoes. Then work began, each one practising in his room, while Zverev, too, sat in a separate room smoking his pipe and occasionally stopping them with ejaculations such as: 'no fancies', 'stick to the music', 'stop smearing'. All this might have been suitable only to the pen of a humorist, had not two youthful geniuses strayed into the hands of Zverev, thus immortalizing the institution. These were Scriabin and Rachmaninov. Although Rachmaninov along with other boys submitted to the Zverev régime until he left in revolt, Scriabin by merit of his sheltered childhood was exempted. It was typical that the pampered Scriabin was allowed to go to Zverev only on Sundays for lessons and demonstrations while continuing his studies at the Moscow Cadet Corps.

Their apprenticeships coincide with various periods in the careers of the most prominent musical figures of the time. Here are a few recollections:

ON SCRIABIN

Once in spring General Nikiforov called and asked me if he could bring a talented musician. A young cadet was brought in, small, very thin and fragile. I tested his ear: flawless. I started working with him, showed him some elementary things: forms, phrases, periods. By September he had written a few pieces, all delightful . . .

Taneyev (1886)

It frequently happened that he played at my home, while I was taking a rest. Once I fell asleep and suddenly woke up to the most delicious sounds. I was afraid to stir so as not to break the enchantment. 'What was this?' I asked. It was a new Prelude in D-flat major. This is one of the loveliest memories of my life. Scriabin possessed in the highest degree what I always impressed on my students: the less like itself a piano is under the fingers of the player, the better it is.[1]

Safonov (1888)

Rachmaninov himself recollects:

In connection with the arrival of Anton Rubinstein, there was a soirée at Zverev's at which I played along with Scriabin and Joseph Lhevinne. After the concert, there was a reception and Zverev bade me go to Rubinstein, pull his coat, and show him his place at the table. After supper, Rubinstein played for us the Sonata Op. 78 of Beethoven.

[1] The Taneyev and Safonov recollections appear in Julius Engel's biographical sketch of Scriabin, *Musical Contemporary*, 1916.

When I was passing into the top form at the Conservatoire, the examiners told me to play several pieces in 3-part-form. When I had done it, they were so pleased that they gave me an 'A+' mark in the journal. One of the examiners was Tchaikovsky and, seeing this, he added three more pluses to the 'A+', surrounding it in this way with the pluses.

(*1889*)

And then of his studies with Taneyev in his typical humorous fashion:

What a wonderful man Taneyev was! How he laughed! He would go into peals of laughter, like a happy child. He was incapable of the slightest insincerity. He was so upset by our laziness. There were four of us in the class, but I remember only Scriabin and myself. We never did any work at all.[2]

Though Rachmaninov seems to have suffered no ill effects from this laziness, the same fault was to cost Scriabin dearly, after the two had gone off on their separate careers. From Taneyev's class, they both passed to Arensky to study 'free composition'. The course was supposed to last two years, but Rachmaninov managed to persuade Arensky to pack it all into one. Scriabin was not slow to ask for the same privilege, but was roundly refused. Deeply hurt by Arensky's attitude, he threw up the idea of receiving a composer's diploma. His only consolation was the gold medal that Safonov had given him for piano, but this was in no way comparable to the double gold medal Rachmaninov had won in piano and composition (1892).

EARLY RACHMANINOV

It must be admitted that Rachmaninov's beginnings were considered more brilliant than those of Scriabin. Rachmaninov's graduation project was the one-act opera *Aleko*, the score for which he finished in seventeen days, having it copied and bound in a purple binding with gold lettering. It was promptly produced, and the publisher Gutheil bought it from the composer

---

[2] For the recollections of Rachmaninov see Alfred J. and Katherine Swan, *Musical Quarterly*, January-April 1944, and The Note (actually a big biography) on Rachmaninov, written by his cousin Sophie Satin, first published in Moscow in 1961.

for five hundred roubles. This news rapidly spread through Moscow, and the composer, like Byron after *Childe Harold*, found himself famous overnight. It gave him wings, and in the summer of 1893 he completed no less than five big works covering all the principal genres of composition: songs, piano pieces, a symphonic poem, and even a *'Concert Spiritual'* for chorus *a cappella*, which was performed by the Synodal Choir under Orlev. Gutheil paid well for all this, but Rachmaninov's successes in Moscow society necessitated an expensive social life and his money ran short. He resorted to giving lessons, which bored him. His piano recitals always drew a big public and the Moscow reviewers were enthusiastic. But, all in all, his existence was precarious. The fundamental difficulty was that he lacked a home, since his father and mother had been separated, and had to live off relatives. Especially during the summers, he moved restlessly from place to place.

EARLY SCRIABIN

The life of Scriabin shaped itself quite differently. His first ventures as a composer were anything but formidable. He wrote only for the piano and even had to pay Jurgenson for the publication of his first works. They passed quite unnoticed. He still lived in his aunt's and grandmother's home where he enjoyed privacy and was given every care. Nothing important happened until spring 1894 when he went to give a recital in St Petersburg and there met Belaieff, who was so impressed that he encouraged Scriabin to publish in his series and even organized for him a tour abroad in 1895-6. Many of Scriabin's preludes, études, and impromptus of that period were composed as he moved from one hotel to another in Switzerland, Germany, Holland, Belgium, and Paris. In Russia, however, his main propagandist was his devoted teacher Safonov. In 1897, Scriabin finished his piano concerto which Safonov, a very active and capable conductor, immediately put on many of his programmes. In that same year, Scriabin had married and, to help him financially, Safonov, now director of the Moscow Conservatoire, offered him a professorship there. Through Belaieff, he met all the members of the Petersburg circle and managed to make a deep impression on some of its most influential musicians, particularly on Liadov and the family of Rimsky-Korsakov. In fact, his following in Petersburg became much stronger than in his native Moscow.

DIFFERENCES OF STYLE

It is interesting, at this stage, to compare the idiom of these two composers. We have already seen how much more diversified and comprehensive was the sphere of Rachmaninov, as against the narrower limits imposed by the fact that Scriabin specialized in piano music. Rachmaninov was a born songwriter, had splendid gifts as an orchestrator, and could also write for liturgical choir. His way of presenting his ideas was intended for a large though not always a very discriminating audience. In his forcefully original style both good and bad elements were mixed. The good were derived from his love of folk-song and liturgical chant, of church bells and strong rhythmic beats. But his creations were all slightly tainted by 'everyday' intonations, so common to the Moscow world. No truer characterization of Rachmaninov can be found than the following recollections left by Alexander Goedicke, his contemporary and fellow musician:

He loved church singing and frequently, even in winter, he got up at seven and, taking a cab in the darkness, drove off to the Androniev monastery, where he attended early liturgy, listening to the old chants sung by the monks in parallel fifths. It could well happen that in the evening of the same day he would go to a symphony concert and from there to the restaurant Yar or Strelna and stay there till after midnight listening to the singing of the gypsies. . . .[3]

The successful, acclaimed, performer was always uppermost in him, whether it was playing or conducting. He knew well what was effective and would reach his audience. So his compositions were fashioned accordingly. One need think only of the Prelude in C-sharp minor which actually belongs to that Moscow of the nineties. His songs struck fire immediately and were sung by the worthy and unworthy alike. In short, there was greatness and accessibility: two qualities that are rarely compatible.

The young Scriabin presents an entirely different picture. His first works strike one as Chopinesque in style. He had

[3] A. F. Goedicke, 'Memorable Meetings', in *Reminiscences about Rachmaninov*, ed. Z. Apetan, Moscow, 1961, Vol. II, p. 13.

immersed himself so completely in the world of Chopin, both as pianist and composer, that all those who heard him, except Safonov, expected little else. There is the lyrical Chopin of the ballades, as well as the heroic composer of the *Allegro Appassionato Op. 4*, the first sonata and some preludes and studies. But soon a new subjective note creeps into his harmonies, and already some of the works written during the trip with Belaieff are quite a distance from his idol. What is so eminently attractive is the melodic line, highly original and never showing the slightest lapse into 'everyday' formulations. Here again the 24 Preludes of Op. 11 stand out as the epitome of a noble and refined art. I suspect that the one that awakened Safonov was that in D-flat major from this series—one of the loveliest conceptions by anyone in the whole Russian School. It is difficult to trace the imperceptible growth of Scriabin's own language, but with *Sonata No. 3 in F-sharp minor* and the *Mazurkas*, Op. 25, his style had become both unique and mature. Strangely, there are no typical Russian idiomatic expressions anywhere, either from folk-song or from chant—a fact which clearly reflects the hothouse atmosphere of his upbringing. Wrapped up as he had been in his favourite western composers, he apparently ignored all earlier developments in Russia.

Soon after his marriage, Scriabin had also embarked on orchestral writing, finding in Safonov an ardent performer of his first two symphonies and the little *Reverie*, Op. 24. At this point, the influence of Chopin had waned, and that of Wagner began. But never could an orchestral influence even from such a genius as Wagner sway Scriabin's love for the piano or cause him to forget that he was a Russian reincarnation of Chopin.

With the symphonies of Scriabin and the world-famous second piano concerto of Rachmaninov we pass into the twentieth century. While Scriabin's progress was uninterrupted, for Rachmaninov the year 1897 marked a severe crisis that left a trace on all his compositions since it affected his faith in himself *qua* composer. His inner security was never fully re-established for the rest of his life. The fatal occurrence was the failure of his *First Symphony in D-minor* in St Petersburg, where he had made the mistake of entrusting it to Glazunov, instead of conducting it himself. The disheartened composer withdrew the work from further public hearing or publication and it was not revealed to the world until after his death. During the Second World War, the parts were discovered in the Leningrad Conservatoire as it was known by then, the score reconstructed, and the work performed anew.

The whole coruscating scale of Rachmaninov's idiom is given full play in this early symphonic work, and it is further ennobled by the seriousness of the composer's intentions in moving away from the familiar habitual adoration of Moscow. Rachmaninov knew the condescending attitude towards the so-called provincialism of Moscow which prevailed in St Petersburg and strove to do his best. But Petersburg was itself not ready to accept anything so unusual as these religious overtones or the broadly flowing melodic undercurrent untouched by folk-song, or Rachmaninov's occasional excursions into rhetoric. All these qualities moreover were travestied in Glazunov's obtuse performance. The composer must have anticipated a fiasco, for all through the performance he stayed outside the concert hall, running up and down the stairs to the balcony and holding his ears. César Cui's review was devastating in its mockery. The lasting result of this experience was a prolonged lull in compositional activity which lasted almost three years. His Moscow friends came to his aid. He was appointed assistant conductor at the private opera of Mamontov, and it was here that he first encountered Chaliapin. This led to their joint concerts, Chaliapin singing and Rachmaninov accompanying, unforgettable events in Moscow musical life. To shake him out of his depression, it was arranged that he should visit Tolstoy, but the great writer failed to take any real interest in him. Finally he underwent treatment by the hypnotist N. V. Dahl. When this brought him back to his former state, he gratefully dedicated to the doctor his *Second Piano Concerto* (1900). Immediately after this work came the *Cello Sonata*, Op. 19, the Cantata *Spring*, Op. 20, and the *Ten Preludes for piano*, Op. 23. A period of great happiness also ensued in his private life: in April 1902 he married his cousin Natalie Satin.

Thus musical events in Moscow during the early years of the new century centred around Rachmaninov. He was active in three areas, as composer, pianist, and conductor at the opera. Scriabin, on the other hand, was largely shut up within himself. Even his symphonies aroused little attention although Safonov prepared and performed them with the utmost care and devotion. The truth was that people, if they knew him at all, regarded him solely as a pianist, and when the symphonies were announced considered him presumptuous to have published them. Instead of a follower of Chopin they sensed here a kind of Wagnerian.

However, the development of Scriabin's harmonic language progressed rapidly. In the *First Symphony in E-Major* the public could still recognize some echoes of Tchaikovsky, but in the *Second Symphony in C-Minor* it heard only dissonant chromaticisms. The whole direction of the composer, away from everything that was familiar and dear to the Muscovites, in fact everything that made Rachmaninov so attractive to them, repelled all but a few individual enthusiasts. Moreover, Scriabin, whose early life was spent at the piano, was an awkward orchestrator, and this made the trend of his ideas towards the grandiose and superhuman appear all the more disproportionate. Great revolutionary ideas were stirring within him. He moved into regions that included many things besides music; philosophy, aesthetics, religion and mysticism. But what he had to express took shape only in a musical language; only here he was at home, only here he was endowed with the genius to conceive great themes, new harmonic forms, exciting, incantational rhythms. All that hampered him in the realization of his thoughts he detested and rejected: above all, his teaching duties at the Conservatoire. After the *Second Symphony*, he buried himself in a mass of piano works, in order, as he said, to earn enough to make a break possible, and go abroad for purely creative purposes. At this 'mercenary' objective one can only smile, since that mass of piano music included such utterly unheard-of and perfect inspirations as the Fourth sonata, the *Poems*, Op. 32, and the *Tragic* and *Satanic Poems*.

He laboured at this all through 1902 and 1903, but even the liberal fees of Belaieff were not sufficient to offset living expenses. Only when a patroness appeared in the shape of Margarita Morozova, of whom we shall have more to say later, did he and his family of four children depart for Switzerland. As for the Moscow public and musical world at large, at this juncture he was all but forgotten.

12

The Third Renaissance
1903-15

About the time of Scriabin's departure to Switzerland, when Rachmaninov was just beginning to recover from his breakdown, there began the most glittering period of Russian music. Though short-lived, it might still be termed a third Russian Musical Renaissance, equal to the second which developed under the aegis of Balakirev, and the first in the times of the Novgorod and Moscow masters of the early seventeenth century.

It is, of course, possible to look at the flow of Russian music in those fateful years as a simple and natural prolongation of the process which had started in 1855 with Balakirev's arrival in St Petersburg. For was he himself not still alive and at the height of his powers as a musician? And was not Rimsky-Korsakov's star on the rise, shining more brilliantly than ever? And was not Tchaikovsky's music conquering all Europe and America even though the great composer himself was no longer alive? All these questions may be answered affirmatively. Yet there was a vital difference between the outlook of the Balakirev era and that of the turn of the century. Rimsky-Korsakov characterized the former as a period of 'storm and stress' and the latter as a 'steady march onward'. It was this 'steadiness' of the Belaievists, their essential conservatism and eclecticism, their interest in all types of music save the religious, that gave the nineties the look of a recession, a consolidation of positions rather than a conquest of new heights, a scattering of strength through a division among too many participants, many of whom were mere *epigones*, followers, routine imitators.

A resurgence, a search for new heights to scale, a daring departure from accepted values—all these can occur only when, either consciously or instinctively, a new ideal is embraced. Such an ideal emerged in the early years of the century, involving the search for original sources, the examination of historic and prehistoric antiquity, the reversion to folk-music, which the Belaievists had neglected, and the sudden appreciation of the riches of church music and of the whole religious culture behind it such as the moderns had never possessed. All these factors make it possible to speak of the last decade before the outbreak of the First World War as a separate and distinct period. The new aesthetic rested on the new type of folk-song collectors, on the Moscow Synodal School and Choir, as well as on the non-Christian movement into the mysteries of the East, the last two vividly personified in the antipodal figures of Rachmaninov and Scriabin. Moreover both capitals had reached their highest productivity. Formerly Petersburg had taken the lead, Moscow gently trailing behind. Tchaikovsky's lifelong connection with Moscow had given its musical life a strong momentum, and since he and Taneyev had been influential, even if indirectly, in shaping the situation which made possible the emergence of Rachmaninov and Scriabin, Moscow could now rival St Petersburg's musical culture. Here was Russia's potentially most significant period; but its several luminaries were all too suddenly to be extinguished by the world-shaking events of 1914.

ST PETERSBURG

Rimsky-Korsakov's career continued its strange, unpredictable course. Moving from one musical discovery to the next, he struck a rich vein of gold in the recitatives of his opera *Sadko*, for which he had prepared technically in the hybrid *Mlada* and Gogol's *Christmas Eve*.

Sadko

This recitative, says Rimsky in his *Chronicle*, is not the ordinary language of speech, but a sort of stylized epic narrative or chant, the prototype of which can be found in the declamation of the Riabinin *bylinas*[1] (Example 25).

[1] Rimsky-Korsakov, op. cit., p. 353.

He claims with justice that this musical phenomenon is unique not only in his operas, but in the whole history of opera. *Sadko* (1895-6) is a tale of the exploits of a legendary Novgorod, hero and artist, which displays most of Rimsky-Korsakov's attractive features. Essentially the orchestra was his most potent force of expression; he was a masterful, persuasive orchestrator.

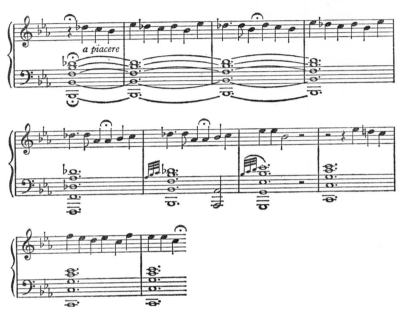

Example 25. *Sadko*, Tableau One, Rimsky-Korsakov.

But he developed with equal eloquence his big choral scenes with their splashing array of types—merchants, pedlars, buffoons, Sadko's companions—a vast population moving swiftly, all intoning their appropriate motifs, and held together by fascinating refrains in the manner of a huge rondo.

After *Sadko*, the direction went downward again so far as concerned aesthetic quality. A fatal voice prompted the indefatigable master to try his hand at non-Russian subjects: Polish in *Pan Voyevoda*—his homage to Chopin—neutral in *Servilia*, an unconvincing story of a noble Roman woman converted to Christianity. Both were failures, though the orchestration aroused even more than the usual admiration as we know from Rachmaninov's remarks:

When I was conductor at the Bolshoy Theatre in Moscow, Rachmaninov once said, I put on Rimsky's *Pan Voyevoda*. The music is poor but the orchestration—stupendous.[2]

The little stage piece *Mozart and Salieri*, on the other hand, is a genuine work of art. The inspiration lay in the exquisite verses of Pushkin (Dargomyjsky had the same experience in his *Stone Guest*) which Rimsky leaves without alteration, finding the exact musical counterpart for them.[3] The upward direction of the zigzag line began with the *Czar's Bride* (1898), moved swiftly in *Czar Sultan* (1899) and led him to the *Legend of the Invisible City Kitej and the Maiden Fevronya*. There were to be no more reverses, and thenceforward the 53-year-old composer continued to ascend even greater heights.

KITEJ LEGENDS

About 1902 Rimsky-Korsakov focused his attention on the 'legends' of Kitej, which recount that the venerable city was miraculously rendered invisible when the Tartars were on the verge of entering it. Into this legend Rimsky-Korsakov's librettist, Vladimir Belsky, worked that of Fevronya, a lowborn maiden who became the bride of the reigning prince after meeting him accidentally in the forest. Their wedding, interrupted by the Tartar invasion, was perforce concluded in the other world, the prince having fallen in battle and the city itself having been submerged in the waters of the lake Svetly Yar. Belsky's libretto is in itself a lofty work of art and combines with Rimsky-Korsakov's inspired music into one of the highest operatic achievements of all times.

Professor Ivan Lapshin, an idealistic philosopher and close friend of the Rimsky-Korsakov family, always held that the three highest pinnacles of Rimsky-Korsakov's art were *Snegurochka*, *Sadko*, and *Kitej*, and saw in them a kind of informal

[2] Alfred and Katherine Swan, *Reminiscences of Rachmaninov, Musical Quarterly*, New York, January and April 1944.
[3] My experience with this work was particularly vivid, as in 1913 the impresario Diaghilev commissioned me to do an English version with the unpractical idea of Chaliapin singing the role of Salieri in English for the London season of 1914.

trilogy.[4] He saw in *Kitej* the apotheosis of heroic, active love, but I would prefer to call it an apotheosis of nature in its divine aspect, as a reflection and mirror of the greatness of the Creator. Humility and righteousness on the part of Prince Yuri and the appeal of the people of Kitej to the Virgin effect a miraculous preservation from destruction and death.

The intonations and colours that Rimsky-Korsakov found here show him to us in a novel light and bring him extremely close to the Russian religious painters. It is especially Nesterov's *Youth of St Sergius* that comes to mind when listening to the Introduction which Rimsky-Korsakov (Belsky) called *Praise of the Desert*. By contrast to the meek and saintly Fevronya, the study portrays the abject villain-drunkard, ultimately a traitor, Grishka, whom the Maiden exhorts to pray to Mother Earth. In such pantheistic traits we sense Rimsky-Korsakov's true religious feeling. These pagan works seem much nearer to his heart than those he wrote for the Church during his service in the Imperial Chapel.

I remember the occasion of the *première* of the opera *Kitej* at the Imperial Opera Theatre in St Petersburg. It was 7 February 1907, the day of the elections of the Second Duma. The performance lasted till after midnight, and even though all the intentions of the composer were not immediately grasped, the impression was shattering. By that time Rimsky-Korsakov was already engrossed in his last opera *Coq d'or*, which he was destined not to see on the stage, as he was felled by a massive heart attack a little over a year later in 1908. The *Coq d'or*, truly a magnum opus, opens up wide horizons into the future and is the immediate forerunner of Stravinsky's *Firebird* and *Nightingale*. Suddenly then Rimsky-Korsakov was struck down when at the height of his fame, a tragic event which stirred the whole of Russia and, indeed, the rest of the world.

BALAKIREV

His friend, teacher and later his bitter enemy, Mili Balakirev did not end his days so actively or creatively. This great leader had long ceased to be involved in the main stream of Russian musical activities. When he withdrew in the seventies, he lost

[4] Ivan Lapshin, *Rimsky-Korsakov and Russian Music*, Prague, 1944.

any appreciable influence on others. But even so his own course was far from run. Laboriously and not without repeated minor setbacks, he brought to conclusion his symphonic poem *Tamara*. His pace was slow, so that the accomplishment required six years. As often happens with long-protracted works, the results were not commensurate with the time spent. The themes of *Tamara* in themselves are not sufficiently impressive

Example 26. *Symphony, No. 1*, Scherzo, 1898, Balakirev.

and the whole lacks the impetuous whirl of *Islamey* which must be considered a greater work. The years spent at the Imperial Chapel (1883-94) removed Balakirev even further from the St Petersburg musical scene.

But the gathering of strength began after his retirement, when at last the material that he had long contemplated for his symphony in D minor took shape, yielding a lively and attractive work, still uneven, but full of his old characteristics: folk-song intonations coupled with undertones of the chant, tremendously powerful sonorous accumulations (Example 26), and a supreme mastery of the orchestra. True, he did not

28. Anton Preobrajensky.

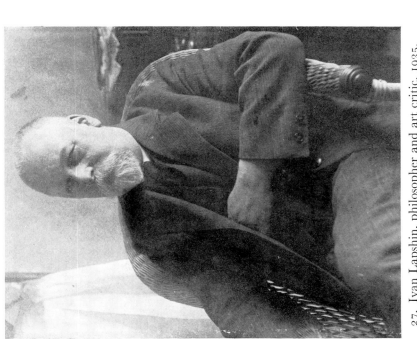

27. Ivan Lapshin, philosopher and art critic, 1935.

29. The first page of Rachmaninov's *Concert Spiritual*.

30. Glinka

31. Stravinsky at the Hôtel du Chatellard, 1913.

32. Musical gathering at the Lamm's, 1923.

33. Nicolas Medtner with wife Anna and Alfred Swan, 1948.

possess that gift of perpetual renovation that Rimsky-Korsakov showed in such abundance in *Kitej* and the *Coq d'or*, and this no doubt led critics like Assafiev, eminently aware of Balakirev's superb qualities, to speak of these late works as 'woven out of remembrances of the sixties'. Even so, one marvels at such a comeback after so many misspent years.

From the symphony, Balakirev moved back to folk-song settings and in 1898 issued an album of thirty songs from the Istomin and Dyutch collection which is richer than the one he brought out after his Volga expedition of 1858. Not content with stylization for voice and piano, he made another setting for piano four-hands which is one of his most lovable and

Example 27, *Vision*, 1903-4, Balakirev, words by Khomiakov.

felicitous efforts. Upon the folk-songs followed a set of ten art songs. The originality of this Russian genius, not unlike parallel pages in Moussorgsky and Borodin, is to be found in the three settings of Khomiakov, particularly in the one called *Vision*. Here poet and composer daringly portray the bizarre idea of an Orthodox service conducted in the Catholic Cathedral of Prague. Into the music for this service Balakirev wove the Orthodox motif of the risen Christ (Example 27). Finally, the B-flat minor piano sonata was completed. Intrinsically all these works contributed to what I have termed a Third Renaissance, which should have been hailed as such in Balakirev's lifetime. But, for his contemporaries, all his later achievements passed unnoticed and he enjoyed scarcely any recognition either in Russian musical circles or abroad. Only a handful of devoted friends—among them Serge Liapunov, himself a gifted composer—gathered around him to hear his final improvisations at the piano. His foreign friends, too, rallied around, spreading the word about him in their respective countries: Rosa Newmarch in England and M. D. Calvocoressi in France. Balakirev died on 16 May 1910.

GLAZUNOV

Glazunov's creative period extended barely beyond the turn of the century. From the moment he had found his bearings with the *First Symphony in E-major* in 1881, he forged ahead without deviating or slackening his course. Every new work, whether symphony, symphonic tableau, or string quartet, further consolidated his position, enhanced his prestige and earned lavish praise from Stassov and Belaieff and envy from Rimsky-Korsakov and Liadov. The high point of his creativity came in 1901-2 with two piano sonatas, one in B-flat minor and the other in E-major, and the *Seventh Symphony in F-minor*. But by then his career had already veered in another direction, for he joined the ranks of the Conservatoire professors. Day by day his involvement with the institution became more complete, his time for creative work correspondingly more limited.

From the outbreak of the Japanese War in January 1904, until after the civil war in 1921, the country was never free from periodic disturbances. Unrest among the student masses culminated in political assassinations of governors, ministers, and generals. Disasters in the Far East, sporadic peasant revolts —all disrupting the normal flow of life—occurred in the very midst of this great upsurge in the arts, literature, philosophy and science.   Wise reforms were needed, but these were shunned by a regime dedicated to the old autocracy and to the divine rights of the Czar. Finally in October 1905, a half-hearted constitution was wrested from the government leading to elections of the popular assembly, Duma. Many professors sided with the students, among them Rimsky-Korsakov, and the directors of the Imperial Russian Music Society, who headed the Conservatoire, insisted on their removal. A compromise was reached in the end by the election of Glazunov to the post of Director. From that post he never moved until his departure abroad in 1928, for the stormy situation required his incessant vigilance and eroded his creative powers. He finished his *Eighth Symphony in E-flat* in 1906. By this work, Stassov, who died in October of that year, was quite moved:

The Andante is something Glazunov had never done before. New, original into infinity. A great work!

Others, too, concurred in acclaiming the work, but the fact of the matter is that Glazunov had reached an impasse creatively speaking. The spontaneity and easy trend of the thematic spring had dried out. Unfortunately, he was not the man to turn to Lineva's collections or to Kastalsky's revival of the *znamenny* chant. What he wrote in the remaining years of the Empire was of sporadic and various nature: incidental music to the drama the *King of Judea* by the Grand Duke Constantine under the pseudonym K. R., and the *Masquerade* by Lermontev. Of the two concerti—one for violin (1904), one for piano (1912)—the first is much more convincing than the latter. His inspiration and creative force were fading away quickly.

Glazunov's musical talent was based on strong natural foundations, but was in no way nurtured by intellectual, literary, or philosophical pursuits and interests. Hence, he was bound to reach the limits of creative development sooner or later. Taneyev had gone on to the end because his intellect was steadily at work and because he combined mathematical with musical aims. Rimsky-Korsakov grew all the time because he drew sustenance from the very roots of Russian culture both philosophical and musical. His partnership with Vladimir Belsky,[5] the librettist of both *Czar Sultan* and *Kitej*, strengthened that side of him which drew from folk sources. Scriabin's visions were cosmic, his inspiration most inventive, even though his gifts were solely musical: throughout his life he did maintain creative momentum, though moving ever into narrower regions.

[5] V. I. Belsky was a graduate in both law and natural science. He became a great connoisseur of old Russian songs and legends and as a passionate lover of music, particularly Rimsky-Korsakov's, exerted a strong influence on him. Rimsky-Korsakov wrote of his tremendous knowledge masked behind a shy and modest manner.

On the other hand, Glazunov's mind had moved along a purely logical musical plan, which was exhausted by the Seventh and Eighth Symphonies.

If Belaieff's ideology had been insufficient to sustain Glazunov, it failed utterly with a whole army of lesser imitators who also partook of it. Conservatoire training had made them into competent musicians, but culturally and intellectually it gave them next to nothing. There was very little realization, even in these dedicated circles, of the general movement toward song and chant for inspiration: such manifestations as Lineva's travels paralleled by those of Listopadov, and the unique phenomenon of the Piatnitzky peasant chorus, were hardly taken in at all; and the art historians and icon-lovers—Grabar, Muratov, Kondakov—were engaged on their epoch-making labours behind closed walls. Tragically the Third Renaissance by-passed rank and file artists, whose eyes were opened only too late.

STRAVINSKY

Outside the Belaieff Circle, and removed from the Conservatoire conclave, there was the adventurous Igor Stravinsky, whose ideals, perhaps unconsciously, were very much in accord with the return to the sources, and closely akin to the world represented by Rimsky-Korsakov's last operas. His entry into Russian musical circles was even less spectacular than that of Scriabin. Born into the family of an enlightened singer and fine interpreter of bass roles at the Imperial Opera, he went through the normal Gymnasium schooling and later continued at the University as a student of law. It was at this point that he applied to Rimsky-Korsakov for private instruction and was accepted, more on the strength of his father's reputation than for his own achievement. In his *Autobiography*, he tells little of what happened during his sessions with his master, but it is clear that he was accepted into Rimsky-Korsakov's family, becoming a member of an intimate circle consisting of himself and another pupil, Maximilian Steinberg, who later became Rimsky-Korsakov's son-in-law. There were also Yastrebtsev, a 'Boswell', who recorded every detail of the master's daily doings; the critic Ossovsky; and the young doctor of philosophy, Ivan Lapshin. They met every Wednesday at the

Rimsky-Korsakovs' and tried to re-live the days of the Mighty Band. Thus it was that they inaugurated, one day in 1906, a revival of Moussorgsky's *Marriage*.[6]

Stravinsky's composing began seriously only after his graduation from the University. A few of his orchestral works were performed at the Symphony Concerts of Alexander Siloti, and, though little noticed at large, these impressed Serge Diaghilev, a personage who was to play an overwhelming part in Stravinsky's life. With his usual unfailing judgment, this impresario commissioned Stravinsky to compose the ballet *Oiseau de Feu* for his Paris season of 1910. For the young composer this was the turning-point; from a St Petersburg 'epigone' Stravinsky became, in a flash, the storm centre of the western world. Thus was he singled out by destiny from among a number of other composers such as N. Tcherepnin, V. Senilov and R. Merwolff, who had likewise turned away from the Belaievist line and shown some kinship with French Impressionist currents.

DIAGHILEV (1872-1929)

On the early life of Diaghilev far too little information is as yet available. He came from the province of Novgorod and was apparently exposed to powerful artistic impressions from childhood. For a while he was a government official with high connections in court circles, 'the spheres'. Of the arts, it was painting that attracted him first and foremost, and he became one of the founders of the movement '*Mir Iskusstva*'—a purely aesthetic counter-force to the realistic *peradvijniki*, or movable expositions. From painting he passed to décor, choreography, and finally to music. His vision was somehow bound up with the movement towards the sources and he moved with the wave of the future which drew its strength from restoration of the past. But, if anything, he overstressed the motto 'art for art's sake', and paid too little regard to ethnographical, religious, and philosophical aspects of the movement. He was supremely indifferent to any opposition or criticism, and pursued his way in a purely autocratic manner, which provoked innumerable incidents between him and the large number of

[6] A description of the Korsakov Wednesdays can be found in the July/August 1934 issue of the *Chesterian: Reminiscences of Rimsky-Korsakov* by A. Sandulenko, translated and arranged by Alfred J. Swan.

performers whom he directed. By dint of his Paris and London productions which had begun in 1907, he survived the Russian collapse and carried on with vigour during the ensuing emigration of White Russians. His circle epitomized the very best of Russian genius in the arts: in the ballet there were Karsavina, Nijinsky and Miassin; in stage décor and design Bakst, Benois, Korovin and Bilibin; and in music Stravinsky and Prokofiev. Gradually, Diaghilev was forced to enlarge his vision to take in western art—especially that of France and Spain—and as a consequence he outgrew his purely Russian mission. His role in the shaping of the various currents of Russian and western music and ballet attained gigantic proportions thereafter. Stravinsky's course after their meeting took a sharp westward turn. Thenceforward his creative work remained a kind of independent facet that never properly merged with musical activities in Russia. All his scores, after *The Rite of Spring*, were written in the West and, indeed, scarcely penetrated into his own country at all. Even now, his work is but partly known in the USSR and in official circles is still frowned upon.

MOSCOW

If in St Petersburg Belaieff's 'epigones' somewhat dimmed the brilliant atmosphere created by his leading composers, there was not a cloud on the Moscow horizon. Here the rays of the Renaissance movement shone in all directions, warming alike philosophers, poets, painters, and musicians. There are many testimonies to the intense spiritual life then developing, both openly and behind closed doors in the old capital. One of the most vivid pictures is that presented by the philosopher and literary critic, Feodor Stepun, in his book of reminiscences, *The Past and the Perennial*. Stepun, who stands in the centre of that searching, sombre world, describes some of the meetings in the salon of Margarita Morozova, already known to us as Scriabin's benefactor:

There are people who float in our memory as in a cinema reel and there are others who are condensed into a synthetically closed still picture. The latter are now rarer than ever. Margarita Kirillovna Morozova is definitely one of these. I shall always see her big, almost too heavy of figure, either standing in the middle of a room or sitting in an armchair somewhere along the wall. Her hands are usually calmly folded in her lap or sometimes playing with her long, massive chain of pearls. Unforgettable are her eyes: grey, steel-like, overshadowed, and at the same time intensified by dark eye-lashes. . . .[7]

She was the host and guiding spirit of the religious-philosophical society and published its mouthpiece, the journal *Put*. She was also an art collector, and rare icons hung in the dining-room of her house, built in the Palladian style. Stepun emphasizes how the atmosphere of art, beauty, spirituality and peace made one oblivious of the revolutionary concussions of those years.

SCRIABIN

The later life of Scriabin is projected against this background. At our last view, we saw him early in 1904 when, after a whole set of piano works, he turned again to symphonic writing and laid the plan for his *Divine Poem*. He was now in Switzerland and free to lead a purely creative existence. Not only musically, but in real life also, he modelled himself on Wagner. How powerfully they both attracted people is shown by the willingness of so many to come to their aid where practical difficulties were concerned. No sooner had he finished his *Divine Poem* and Third Symphony in C, than Mrs Morozova again stepped in and secured Nikisch for a performance of the new work in Paris in May 1905. On this occasion, the Russian ambassador is supposed to have spoken the following very true words: 'In actual life we Russians suffer defeat, but in art we are triumphant.'

Scriabin's growing fame, however, did not improve the desperate state of his finances. Belaieff's trustees had reduced his royalties, and Scriabin, in protest, made a foolhardy attempt to republish the works himself with the help of an unknown Paris agent. Since he was working with capital scores, like those of the Fifth Sonata and the *Poème d'Extase*, the project collapsed.

He now turned to Modest Altschuler, a former class-mate at the Conservatoire, who was at that time conducting a Russian-American orchestra in New York and often invited

[7] Feodor Stepun, *The Past and Perennial*, Vol. I, New York, 1956, p. 258.

Russian composers to send him their works. Altschuler invited him to perform, and Scriabin journeyed to the New World, played his piano concerto, and gave several recitals. But the tour was poorly organized and on his return to Paris he is said to have had but thirty francs in his pocket. Luckily he arrived there in May of 1907 just as Diaghilev's historic concerts of Russian music were in progress. In connection with these concerts the Russian world of music represented by Rimsky-Korsakov, Glazunov, and Rachmaninov were all assembled in Paris and, seeing Scriabin's plight, Rimsky-Korsakov interceded with the Belaieff firm to restore to Scriabin his outstanding royalties. But a decisive turn for the better came only when Kussevitzky appeared and, with a munificence comparable to that of King Ludwig II of Bavaria towards Wagner, threw open the doors of his new editorial enterprise to the harassed composer.

Kussevitzky was a fantastic individual who started life as a humble double-bass virtuoso and swiftly climbed to the top, thanks largely to his marriage to the heiress of the millions of the tea merchant, Ushkov. The money was of prime importance, but behind it lay taste, judgment and brilliantly organized musical gifts. After serving an apprenticeship with Nikisch in Leipzig and undertaking musical studies there, Kussevitzky founded a publishing firm of his own, learning from the practice and experience of Belaieff. But where the latter's method had been autocratic, Kussevitzky acted with tact and circumspection. He surrounded himself with an advisory council composed of musicians of the highest calibre. All decisions of this council he carried out without a murmur, even when he personally disagreed, as in the case of the council's rejection of the works of the young Prokofiev. Like Belaieff, Kussevitzky launched his own concerts, but he went further and, to ensure thorough rehearsing, assembled his own orchestra which he himself conducted. Kussevitzky's concerts in both capitals became the wonder of these last years before the First World War.

As if in answer to the Russian Restoration movement appeared the first issue of what he called *The Russian Musical Editions*, he and his wife being named as founders. The delightful cover design was done by the painter Ivan Bilibin, third and last of the great Russian religious painters in the tradition begun by Vassnetzov and Nesterov. The song-texts were translated anew into exemplary German and French versions and later into English. Scriabin was given a specially glamorous treatment, and the cover of his *Poem of Fire* was in itself sufficient to hypnotize those who saw it on the shelves of the Kussevitzky stores in St Petersburg and Moscow. A comparatively unknown figure, he had suddenly become one of the most talked-of composers of the day.

Meanwhile an energetic group of friends, headed by the selfsame Morozova, were steadily at work on conservative Moscow public opinion to welcome him home after his prolonged absence. In 1909 he was invited by the Imperial Music Society to hear performances of both his latest symphonic works—the *Divine Poem* and the *Poem of Ecstasy*, Op. 54. Scriabin came, heard, triumphed, and decided to return for good, promising to bring along his already begun *Poem of Fire* (*Prometheus*). The very anticipation of a new symphonic work by Scriabin[8] caused a period of enormous excitement. As Leonid Sabaneyev put it so eloquently:

The autumn of 1910 passed in our 'progressive' circles under the sign of 'waiting for Prometheus'. In the salon of Maria Luntz-Nemenova people assembled for whom moving in the moods of a Tchaikovsky and Rachmaninov cult was already a bit uncomfortable. This time we were invited to meet Scriabin and his wife. The conversation turned to philosophy, mystic philosophy, so dear to the composer. The subject of 'dematerialization' was raised, Scriabin quietly announcing that this dematerialization would occur at a certain moment in the contemplation of harmony. He said it in a tone in which one mentions something quite obvious, e.g., that the Volga flows into the Caspian Sea.[9]

He loved to play excerpts from as yet unfinished works and readily went to the piano to play the opening chord of *Prometheus*, which then sounded like the voice of eternal chaos but was later to send into raptures even people indifferent to him otherwise.

---

[8] Sabaneyev in his book *Reminiscences of Scriabin* recorded the last five years of the composer's life, 1910-15, in the same way that Goldenweiser had done with sections of Tolstoy's, and Ekkermann with his reminiscences of Goethe.

[9] Sabaneyev, *Reminiscences of Scriabin*, Moscow, 1925, pp. 40-1.

Scriabin's plans had nothing to do with Russian chant sources or with the folk-song. In fact, they were hardly concerned with Russia at all, and in all truth he, like the Parisian and later American Stravinsky, could scarcely be called a Russian composer at all. He looked towards India, the cradle of humanity, where, according to him, the human race would also perish after immersing itself in a work of art of colossal, cosmic proportions. The creation of that immense work—the *Mystery*—was what he considered himself called upon to accomplish. Absurd as it may sound, it was precisely this insane idea that actuated all the compositions of his last five years. So that he would not lose any of his purely musical inspiration, his more intimate friends tried to go along with him, even to encourage him, and were willing to listen to his fantasies and ravings. Meanwhile, the public at large remained ignorant, but flocked *en masse* to his recitals. These stand in my memory as vividly now as then. Such magic, I am certain, I have never experienced either before or after—a magic that emanated as much from his person as from the unearthly sounds he produced from the instrument. We were transported by the symphonic works such as *Prometheus* and the two poems—the *Divine* and the *Poem of Ecstasy*—as probably preceding generations had been transported by Beethoven, Wagner, or Brahms. But it was only when Scriabin himself had emerged from backstage in a small concert hall and found his bearings at the piano that the real magic began. I can see him now gazing off over the piano as if in a visionary trance, playing first haltingly and even inaccurately, but gradually coming into his own and gaining an increasing hold over the audience. Audience reaction mounted to near-hysteria as he played, in his unparalleled way, his works, from the early nocturnes to the last post-Prometheian works, his preludes, poems, masques, enigmas, and especially the late works *Ghirlandes* and *Flammes Sombres*, Op. 73. When the announced programme was over, the crowds rushed towards the platform, gesticulating, applauding, and shouting the names of the pieces they wanted repeated. He smilingly continued playing, virtually giving a second concert. Only by putting the lights out could the management force the people to go home.

When he was suddenly taken away from the world of music,

dying from blood-poisoning developed from a small carbuncle, his biographers recorded a life that seemed completely egocentric, even cruel. Judging from appearances, it seemed he had been bent upon only one thing—the satisfaction of creative impulses which overrode everything. But this view changed in 1925 when Sabaneyev's *Reminiscences* came out. Here is his résumé:

In the five years that I was destined to live with the Scriabin family in one kind of soul-life, all their interests were mine also— the whole spiritual world of Scriabin himself unfolded itself before us, not only in music, but in his dreams, beliefs, ideals. . . . And I came to love this winged soul, this boundless dreamer who knew how to dream without reservations, losing the sense of reality. Even his mistakes, his extravagances, were either touching or charming. He was not the man who was somehow called on to carry a logical or moral responsibility for his thoughts and actions; it was precisely such a winged soul that indulged in fancies, believed in them, and forcibly infected all around him.[10]

So viewed, all his high-flown, verbose programmes, discursions and fanciful epithets—in short, the substance of his whole eschatological vision—no longer appear frightening or affected. Like Sabaneyev, all of us who have been drawn into his orbit feel grateful for such a great and privileged experience.

RACHMANINOV

Scriabin's case may be seen as a familiar psychological occurrence. Often we perceive a touch of abnormality in the creative mind, which relates to a refusal to view life with sober mundanity, but Rachmaninov's attitude towards life presented an almost excessively normal state of mind. Curiously there is a total silence over his creative periods. This can be explained by the fact that his playing and conducting devoured a good deal of his inspiration, and all this was openly demonstrated in frequent public appearances. Thus, most of his composing falls into the summer months, in his beloved Ivanovka, an estate belonging to his relatives, the Satins, where he felt truly at home and relaxed from his winter activities. His most conscientious biographer, however, his cousin Sophie Satin, herself an

[10] *Reminiscences of Scriabin*, Moscow, 1925, p. 25.

inmate of Ivanovka, though she dwells on his pastimes 'in the hours free from work', does not mention anything about those 'hours'. Yet she says that it was there that he wrote his opera *Francesca da Rimini* (1904) and the *Fifteen Songs*, Op. 26, of 1906. Likewise, a little later he produced there the *Liturgy*, Op. 31, of 1911, and the *Fourteen Songs*, Op. 34, of 1912. To complete other important works, he fled from Moscow to Dresden: the *Isle of the Dead*, the *First piano sonata in D-minor*, and his most capital work, the *Second Symphony in E-minor*, Op. 27.

At that very time, when composers in general were pre-occupied with tone colours and their various orchestral refractions and were more fascinated with new harmonic combinations, and when melody conceived as a vital ingredient of composition was all but lost, Rachmaninov's genius manifested itself in the shaping of renewed melodic form. It would have been easy for him to adopt Tchaikovsky's way and continue the mournful moods of this Moscow idol; indeed for a while this is what he actually did, as may be seen in the *Trio*, Op. 9, in memory of Tchaikovsky, or in the opera *Aleko*. As usual there were those who were ready to label him an 'epigone' living in the shadow of Tchaikovsky. But soon it became clear that his art, though conservative, was not derivative. It reached beyond Tchaikovsky back into the aesthetic created by Glinka, and in his music we find what in essence is the old *pesennost* moulded anew by Rachmaninov into a personal idiom. His reformulation removed it from the sphere of folk-song as did Glinka's, yet somehow preserved a deeply Russian character. This quality the Petersburg composers failed to perceive, per-haps because they had been reared on the principles of Bala-kirev and Rimsky-Korsakov. But Medtner, whom we shall soon encounter, put it very simply when he said to me once during a walk on the falaises in Normandy: 'Rachmaninov is so profoundly Russian himself that he is in no need of folk-music'.

This 'Russianness' derives from the strong influence of the north-central plains which he had imbibed during the summers spent on his grandmother's Novgorod estate in 1884 and 1885, and it was quite a while before he could accustom himself to relish what Sophie Satin called 'the seeming monotony of the steppes and fields' of Ivanovka. But it was this vast expanse of

Novgorod in the north and Tambov in the south that became the home of Rachmaninov's 'valley-like' melodies, as Assafiev has so aptly described them. One finds examples in a whole set of slow movements: that of the *Second Symphony in E-minor*, the *Cello Sonata*, Op. 19, the *First Piano Sonata in D-minor*, the *Second Piano Concerto*. The same quality is to be found even in short pieces such as the exquisite *Prelude in E-flat major*, Op. 23. One is struck by the great, even, oneness of them all. The Petersburg critics, including Cui, who failed so miserably with the *First Symphony*, missed the true Rachmaninov, even while they were quibbling over his salon pieces and such minutiae as the gypsy element in some of his songs.

But in those days before Scriabin's return, Rachmaninov's career already seemed destined to land him at the very top of Russian music as its most versatile figure. An illustration of his many-faceted life-style in the first decade of the twentieth century was the conducting and performing in London and a concert tour of America during which he played for the first time his *Third Piano Concerto*, Op. 30, only to return to Ivanovka and tackle his first major work for the Church, the *Liturgy of St John Chrysostom*, Op. 31. And even while sustaining all this creative activity, he continued teaching and conducting the Private Opera in Moscow: somehow he managed not to slight any phase of his multi-faceted musical activity.

Rachmaninov entered the ranks of religious composers somewhat fearfully. Not content to make merely a casual token contribution as Tchaikovsky and Rimsky-Korsakov had done, he turned to Kastalsky, asking him a hundred questions about various liturgical and musical points. Though taking Kastalsky's replies fully into account, he steadfastly went his own creative way. Unsure of the authenticity of some of the traditional melodies, he wrote new ones in a liturgical style mainly his own; but the taste with which he tempered his own secular manner to suit the usage of the services is truly remarkable. Paradoxically, this highly sincere though not altogether mature work was not performed in the Church, where to this day it has probably never been heard, but rather was premièred on the concert stage by the famous Synodal Choir in Moscow. When it was performed in St Petersburg, Rachmaninov himself conducted the chorus of the Imperial Opera. Such continued neglect provides devastating testimony to the musical ignorance of Russian church choirs and their directors!

During precisely the same period in March of 1911, Scriabin's *Prometheus* also was premièred by Serge Kussevitzky. These two antipodal works reveal something of the scope of the Third Renaissance, and also demonstrate the preponderance of Moscow's role at that time. This piece—a work of super-proportions—required a huge orchestral apparatus with organ, solo piano, and chorus, as well as a curious keyboard with projector which cast into the hall an ever-changing rainbow of colours. Essentially, *Prometheus* is Scriabin's mystical vision of the final stages in the life of our race. In a sense it is an over-bearing arrogation, for he seems to be saying 'Let us be like gods'. Rachmaninov's *Liturgy* is the exact opposite, a work requiring but an *a cappella* choir, set mainly for the normal four or five parts in conformance with the oldest forms of musical worship as devised by St John Chrysostom in the fourth century, and sanctioned by the Fathers of the Church from that time forward. Even those who were aware of the gorgeous renaissance of all the arts of Russia in that decade overlooked the fact that these two works were by Russia's greatest geniuses and judged them as if they came from ordinary mortals. *Prometheus* did provoke an unusual sensation; the *Liturgy* was scarcely noticed. In our time the scales have tipped the other way, and one is much more aroused by the humble prayer before the cleaned and restored icons than by the demonstration of a world cataclysm.

The works which appeared between the *Liturgy* and its sequel, the *Vesper Service* of 1914, mark the mature autumnal phase of Rachmaninov's career. Its most sumptuous fruit is the symphonic cantata *The Bells*, a score which already shows touches of triteness and decay à la Strauss. There are also the last groups of songs (Op. 34 and 38) which because of over-elaborate, thick sonorities compare unfavourably with the simpler, more sincere cantilena style of the previous sets. But in the *Vespers*[11] a similar increase of sonority and harmonic

---

[11] The '*All Night Vigil*' (*Vsenoshchnoye Bdeniye*) is a combination and con-densation of services held in the monasteries between six p.m. on Saturdays and nine a.m. on Sundays. It is celebrated on the eve of Sundays and great holidays from seven to ten p.m.

elaboration has resulted in a gorgeously moving work, comparable to the *Sacred Symphonies* of Giovanni Gabrieli, or the *Motets* of Bach (Example 28). But Rachmaninov's late style, like the general aesthetic of the period in which he wrote, shows a touch of decay. One can but fall back upon the historic

Example 28. *Vespers*, opus 37, No. VII, Rachmaninov.

words of Tchaikovsky, as quoted earlier, concerning the need for a Messiah to destroy the old and find a new pathway back to musical antiquity which would lead to the resurrection of ancient chant in its proper tonal setting.

It is true that the 'ancient chant' referred to by Tchaikovsky becomes only a semblance of the old *znamenny* in Rachmaninov. Moreover its verisimilitude was still vastly handicapped by his own view of harmony. At best he arrived at only a sort of semi-modal conception, something like that which had been current in the West about the time of Bach. But who will argue this point in view of the main fact that Rachmaninov's liturgical pieces are the first true works of art in this domain? They are the individual expression by a great composer of musical substance scarcely touched on earlier in a style deliberately eschewed by all his precursors. Even had he been granted sufficient time and more propitious circumstances, he could not have accomplished the gigantic task referred to by Tchaikovsky single-handed. Yet his two massive works in the religious domain parallel Glinka's operas in the secular with their tentative attempt to link Russian music with its natural foundations in folk-song and chant.

The *Vespers* (with a very telling dedication to the memory of Smolensky) was first performed in March 1915 by the Synodal Choir under the direction of Danilin. 'The impression produced by this work', says Sophie Satin, 'was so great that by public demand it was done four times in the course of the same spring.' It could not then be undertaken by ordinary church choirs, and decades were to elapse before adequate concert performances could be achieved. Now, though, it is permanently preserved in a beautiful realization recorded by the State Academic Choir of Moscow under the direction of Sveshnikov (1966).

NICOLAS MEDTNER (1879-1951)

At this juncture Nicolas Medtner appeared on the scene. He was the new musical champion for his native city, Moscow, where he was to build a powerful and perspicuous musical establishment. Of German-Baltic stock, he was the son of the director of a lace factory, who evidently encouraged his musical talent quite early. He also entered the Conservatoire in Moscow when young, to become a star pupil of Safonov. According to his teacher's plan, he was to have gone on an extensive tour as a concert pianist upon completion of his studies, but he chose rather to go his own way. Announcing to Safonov that composing interested him more than playing, he alienated his teacher and yet as a composer found nothing of the success enjoyed by his slightly older contemporaries.

Nevertheless, Medtner made a formidable mark as a musician. He was out to conquer obstacles—unfortunately, these were mainly produced by his own temperament—and to forge a solid musical idiom. He had a singularly colourless mind and built his compositions from dense, refractory material, structuring them in huge blocks, with not an echo of folk-song or chant. He over-burdened his compositions with too many details, ornaments, and inner parts. What in Bach were known as 'doubles' or 'variations' with Medtner became a basic substance, to be subjected to further 'variations'. All this mass of sound he tried to fit into pianistic texture, or into songs with piano accompaniment, or, occasionally, into other small media, such as the duo for piano and violin. For the 'orchestral arithmetic', as he called it, he had very little use, nor did vocal ensembles attract him. Hence we find in him a sort of abnegation of everything that the Russian School had achieved with excellent results. In piano music, too, he forced upon his hearers a style that had nothing in common with that of Balakirev, Liadov, or the early Scriabin. Only a few of Glazunov's pages—his Second Sonata, for instance—may be cited as influential models. Medtner seems not to have been influenced by foreign masters, and the once-fashionable epithet of the 'Russian Brahms' actually carries no weight whatsoever. We stand before this monumental and solitary originality at a complete loss for comparisons or tidy labels.

Like Schumann, Medtner worked simultaneously as composer and critic. In the latter capacity, he made his début together with his elder brother Emil, under the pseudonym 'Wolfing'.[12] They unfurled their banner against modernism and called for a return to foundations. Their foundations, however, lay not in the melodic material of chant or folk-song, but rather in the harmonic root-chords and in the musical context practised by the classics. They preached a healthy, untarnished art, warned against an infatuation with virtuosity, and against its cultivation through child prodigies, and exposed the decadent tendencies of contemporary western figures, choosing Richard Strauss as a particular example. Their writings caused a furore of indignation, thus creating new obstacles for Medtner as a

[12] *Modernism and Music* was published in Emil Medtner's edition, *Musagat,* 1912.

composer. Yet such dedicated organizations as the Moscow 'House of Song' and its founders, the singer Olenina and her husband the Baron d'Alheim, took up the Medtners' cry and supported their theories. In gratitude Medtner inscribed to the 'House of Song' his second album of Goethe songs.

For a while Medtner's orientation was definitely Germanic. His ideal figures were Goethe and Kant, and after them the whole romantic coterie of Heine, Wagner, and Nietzsche whom he also extolled. But towards the end of the pre-war days, he began to turn to Russian poets in his work, and after three Goethe books (in all thirty songs) came the eminently beautiful collection of songs on texts by Tutchev, Foeth and Lermontoff, published by Kussevitzky from 1912 on. Thus Medtner not only emerges as a composer of piano music but is to be seen as a pre-eminent song-writer.

His songs—there are all told 110 of them—represent his greatest contribution not only to Russian but to all musical culture. Try as you may, you will not find anything like them in all song literature. Only the most sublime poetry seemed to stir his imagination—hence his preoccupation with Goethe and, later, Pushkin and Tutchev. With infallible instinct, he found the proper musical counterpart for their opening lines, then developed clearly delineated melodies from this germinal musical idea. In Medtner's thinking such a melody would definitely have entailed a sonata-like development, but the flow of the words prevented this. So the middle section of his songs usually brings an adumbration of the main theme through harmonies which are at times too involved, while the piano complicates the texture even further by dogged figuration. At last a halting-point is reached which seems a sort of musical impasse. The expected restatement depends on what turn the words take. The changing thought belies an exact restatement of thematic material, so he dispensed with it, writing those very characteristic endings on dissonant pedals.

It goes without saying that all this immensely complex construction, exaggerated by fluctuation of rhythm between the vocal and the piano parts, requires the most accomplished performers. Medtner used to demand from his singers an 'emersion' in the sense of the word, and only the highest intelligence would satisfy him. But intelligence and supreme vocal gifts are only very rarely found together, and this became the most serious obstacle to popularization of his art.

In those days Medtner appeared regularly in Moscow and Petersburg, nearly always playing only his own works. The public at large remained cold, and there were never such scenes as those which took place at Scriabin's and Rachmaninov's concerts. But gradually a Medtner circle grew up in Moscow, the Medtners themselves at the fiery centre. Around them there were philosophers such as Prince Trubetzkoy, Ivan Ilyin, and the poets Andrei Byely and Marietta Shaginian. But there were strangely few musicians. We know of no comments on his art by Taneyev, who at one time was his teacher. Scriabin brushed him off with the remark: 'Medtner has too many notes'. Kussevitzky published his works and occasionally engaged him as soloist, as for instance in a performance of Beethoven's Concerto No. 4. Only Rachmaninov praised him without reservations and listened attentively to his pronouncements. But Medtner resolutely refused to be drawn into the Rachmaninov circle.

Bulky works came from his pen, works that might have fared better as symphonies or oratorios. After the first sonata came eight more before 1917, among which the G-minor, Op. 22, and the violin sonata, Op. 21, stand out as compositions in which supreme loveliness alternates with new experiments with sonata form. In the violin sonata, the favourite Medtner scheme of *Canzona–Danza–Ditiranbo* is carried to its ultimate point of development. Smaller in bulk, though even here amounting to small sonatas, are the *Fairy Tales*, a generic type he was the first to introduce. Sometimes these fairy-tales attempt to tell us about elves and fairies (see Op. 14, No. 1, Op. 26, No. 1), but mostly their tale is about 'life's grim substance'. 'Have I not been threatened by life?' Medtner used to exclaim when asked about his frequent description—*minaccioso* (menacing).

With all his forbidding qualities, however, Medtner is not entirely detached from the sources. The undercurrent of *Winter Night*, Op. 13, by Pushkin (Example 29) or Tutchev's *Why, O Willow, are you bending* (Example 30) stands in the same relation to the folk-song as some of Tchaikovsky's haunting arias, such as Liza's in the last act of *Pique Dame*. But all this is far away from genuine folk-song and chant. Medtner's mission was to expound western culture for Russians. In carrying it forward he stopped at a musical crossroads between Russian and the West and from that time onward gradually began to wonder

Example 29. *Winter Night,* 1903, Medtner.

if the latter was really so superior. During this stage, he was profoundly moved by Pushkin and by the popular tales of Cinderella (*Zolushka*) and of Ivanushka the Fool. But the full impact of these struck only after he had emigrated and for a while tried life in the West, soon being filled with nostalgic longing for his homeland. During the war and throughout the desolation following upon it, his visions were profoundly tragic,

Example 30. *Why, O Willow, are you bending?* 1912, Medtner.

as may be seen in the *First Piano Concerto,* Op. 33, or the immense *Piano Sonata,* Op. 25, No. 2, which he dedicated to Rachmaninov. His most moving portrayal of the prevailing chaos—and in general one of the most abysmal sectors in all music—is the setting of Tutchev's poem *Sleeplessness (Bezsonnitza)*, so shatteringly sung by the singer Doluhanova in its first performance. Here one finds the essence of Medtner's whole philosophy, for it manifests not only his musical style, but his supreme, prophetic powers.

13

Beginnings of modernism

KARATYGIN AND THE EVENINGS OF CONTEMPORARY MUSIC

The first shoots of musical modernism in Russia are to be found in the early years of this century. Recalling his first encounter with it in *Muse and Fashion*,[1] Medtner vividly described a concert at which a new work was played which gave him the sensation that the fundamental basis of all music as he knew it was being shaken. He did not name the work that so horrified him, but intimated that it was one of the Strauss tone poems, perhaps one of the earlier works even less cacophonous than *Sinfonia Domestica*.

Something new had entered music at that time. It was not a new style that one might expect to find in the orderly periodic evolution of musical art, nor was it the underlying programmatic description of what the music meant which put him off. Of this sort of music the nineteenth century had provided an abundance. For Medtner it seemed something deeper—something akin to abuse or betrayal of the craft of the musician, something that seemed to offer shoddy goods for sale on the market. At first he realized that only specialists knew what was happening, the general audience being unaware. To him, it seemed like any counterfeit which, temporarily at least, might pass for the genuine thing among the commonality. Essentially, he felt that there was an abandonment of all strict criteria, an assumption that an inferior quality would do just as well, and that a basic dishonesty was involved in the difference between what had been before and was currently being presented.

[1] Nicolas Medtner, *Muse and Fashion*, Paris, 1935, translated by A. J. Swan and reprinted by Haverford College, 1952.

It is very important that this lowering of aesthetic quality be not confused with a daring quest for the new. Had not the new appeared before in immaculate guise as fashioned by the hands of Schumann, Fauré, or Grieg? Had not Balakirev, the arch-enemy of schools and academies, himself come forth with musical goods of the highest workmanship? And were there not available masterworks by Debussy and Scriabin, who were known for their flawless craft, who had founded something new on the older art? If novelty for its own sake be put before all else and made the primary criterion, he thought, even the keenest minds may be misled into confusing the 'good' with the 'less good', or even with the 'bad'.

This predicament was very like that in which the musicologist and scientist Viacheslav Karatygin found himself. He was one of the most conscientious of St Petersburg critics, and founder of the Evenings of Contemporary Music for presentation of the latest native and foreign musical trends. He was another of that pleiad of Russian intellectuals who, through sheer wealth of talents and interests, could not decide which road to follow. A gifted chemist and botanist, Karatygin was so strongly drawn towards music as to undertake formal studies with the Belaievist, N. Sokolov. He played various instruments and tried his hand at composing. But, above all else, he was preoccupied with writing on music. As a brilliant analyst, he was soon contributing to a whole series of newspapers, journals, and learned publications. Together with a few other encyclo-paedic thinkers, he decided in 1901 to acquaint the capital with various new aspects of music. For himself and his followers there was no banner around which they rallied. They were not folk-song enthusiasts, although they did not discount these entirely, nor was religious music their goal. Their main characteristic indeed was curiosity, and Karatygin's predictable reaction to some novelty or another was: 'This is rather interesting'. Being completely without financial support, they had to meet in dimly lit rooms, contenting themselves with meagre audiences. Nevertheless, they opened their series of 'contemporary' evenings in December 1901 and managed to carry them on for eleven years. During this time they specialized in contemporary French music, they welcomed Max Reger and propagandized effectively for Scriabin and the early Stravinsky.

They also made history in 1908 by sponsoring the first public appearance of the 17-year-old Prokofiev.

Much can be said for their dedicated efforts. But there was one disquieting factor about the venture. The minds of the leaders were too preoccupied with details, and these, precisely, were the 'interesting' details upon which Karatygin so frequently commented. These were frequently allowed to obscure the total picture, sometimes producing myopia which blinded them to the disintegrating, even pernicious quality of a given work. According to Medtner, Karatygin passed from Reger, who had undermined musical form and texture, to Schoenberg who annihilated harmony. Between them, Medtner felt that these two had ushered in that all-permissiveness that actually horrified him.

An evening with Karatygin, who was my musical mentor outside of the Conservatoire, comes to mind. He took me to a haunt of the *avant-garde* called the Basement of the Stray Dog in order to hear Schoenberg's *Second Quartet* with voice. The atmosphere was oppressively dense and unpleasant. Artists had nothing for their inspiration but scattered tables at which people sipped various liquids or smoked. I went home afterwards full of awe for Schoenberg; but my head literally spun. The whole affair was permeated by a hothouse atmosphere, somehow unhealthy. As for Medtner, he was convinced that no great things could grow from such beginnings, no matter how 'interesting' in detail or separate elements. It was precisely this quandary which trapped Karatygin and his circle through their own limitations.

However they did accept Prokofiev and were swept off their feet by the boundless energy and intoxicating current of new ideas generated by this youthful pianist and composer. Here the quest for novelty served well and, for once, the circle was not overly inquisitive about details or small points of interest.

PROKOFIEV (to 1920)

For an account of Prokofiev's youth and apprenticeship there are, of course, no better sources than his own autobiographical fragments. In these the bare facts of his life are greatly enlarged by excursions into his background, nature and society. Though neither of his literary efforts was completed,[2] both are worthy of being ranked with such classics of Russian autobiography as Serge Aksakov's *Family Chronicle*, Alexander Herzen's *My Past and Thoughts*, or Leo Tolstoy's *Childhood*. With a pen as if dipped in acid, Prokofiev has depicted many of the great figures of the Russian musical world. His observations on particular people are perhaps not so poetic as his portrayal of places— for instance, his native village Sontsovka or of events such as those fascinating excursions to the Crimea. Nevertheless, his special insights on personal characteristics, delineated by means of a few apt strokes, are truly astounding: Glazunov, Liadov, Taneyev, Rachmaninov, Medtner—all stand out in relief. Sometimes these men appear in a slightly comical light, but they are clearly recognizable.

As the only son of the production manager of one of the rich estates in the south of Russia, Prokofiev enjoyed a rare and happy childhood. Every opportunity was given him to develop his extraordinary, though at times wayward, musical gifts. Being so completely coddled gave him an overconfident belief in himself, and caused him at first to flaunt his originality to the point of undermining the healthy development of his faculties. Ignoring objections made by his teachers and over-riding all traditional and other impediments, he usually achieved his aim in an original fashion without much trouble. Allowed to perform his own piano concerto at graduation from the St Petersburg Conservatoire in 1914, he turned in a brilliant per-formance, even though he had not yet climbed the steps to Parnassus in any conventional way.

His early adventures as an artist were surrounded by a chorus of approving critics. We have already mentioned Karatygin. Assafiev and Miaskovsky wrote with similar enthusi-asm. Jurgenson published his examination piece, the *First Piano Concerto*, Op. 10, in time for the performance. Still more amazingly, the outbreak of the war failed to ruffle him. For his graduation his mother rewarded him with a journey abroad, and he later wrote that there was so much that inter-

[2] The first is entitled *Childhood* and was written in 1937-9, running to a little over a hundred pages. The second is shorter and is subdivided into: *Early Years*; *After Leaving the Conservatoire*; *Years Abroad* and *After the Return Home*.

ested him in London that he failed to notice the approaching European War and was terribly surprised when it began just a few days after he returned to St Petersburg.[3] Mobilization did not affect him, for in Russia, only sons were exempted from military service. Hence, despite the war—when Diaghilev, whom he met in London, commissioned a ballet—he was able to travel to Rome via Rumania and Bulgaria, amidst raging hostilities, to meet the famous impresario and discuss with him sketches for the ballet *Chout*. Soon even concert promoters like Siloti, who disapproved, had to yield, giving him opportunities to conduct his own works. Indeed it was at one of Siloti's concerts that Glazunov created a scandal by ostentatiously leaving the hall while Prokofiev's *Scythian Suite* was being played.

The result of all these and other successes and sensational events was that Prokofiev as a composer moved in many directions. But in spite of the pampering he remained steadily aware of his inner conflicts and problems, and therein lay his greatness. With finer precision than any other composer, he isolated those elements of music which provided his basic motivation; as he veered from one to another in rapid succession there appeared the classical, the innovating, the motor-like, and the lyrical. Rapid transitions from the deafening noises of the *Scythian Suite*, Op. 20, to the Haydnesque amiability of the *Classical Symphony*, Op. 25, from the acid dissonances of the *Ugly Duckling*, Op. 18, to the quiet, reassuring idiom of the *Tales of the Old Grandmother*, Op. 31, from the motor-like energy of the *Toccata*, Op. 11, to the melodious opening of the *First Violin Concerto*, Op. 19—all these fluctuations make an evaluation of Prokofiev's art incredibly difficult, at least during those long, formative years of his early life, a period which may be said to extend right up to his final return home in the nineteen thirties.

His search for novelty at times became totally disproportionate, misleading him into moments of all-permissiveness, during which familiar criteria fell by the wayside leaving the hearer with little more than a general feeling of protest. It was precisely for this reason, indeed, that Glazunov had left the hall, while others shouted and hissed. It took Prokofiev endless years to learn to control such excesses, and also to find how

[3] S. S. Prokofiev, *Materials, Documents, Reminiscences*, Moscow, 1961, p. 150.

to suppress yet a fifth aesthetic motivation which he himself mentions as an offshoot of the four named above—i.e. that which produced the musical grotesqueries. According to his own definition, 'jest, laughter, and derision' were his aesthetic objectives, and these established a line which culminated in his opera *Love for Three Oranges*. Similarly, the ballet *Chout* (the Buffoon), written for Diaghilev, also transcends aesthetic norms in the same direction. In fact, it becomes sheer caricature, as if Prokofiev were providing blasé western capitals—*Love for Three Oranges* was written for Chicago—with strong shocks which they especially needed to lift them out of their smug and satisfied complacency. At any rate, upon his return Prokofiev completely abandoned this line. It was at that time that the humanization of his art came about, a transformation which lent his works a radically new and very warm inner quality.

The domain of religious music, so far as I know, never interested him; but in the later works the impact of the folk-song became gradually stronger. I am tempted to trace the inception of this humanizing process at least partially to one of our meetings in New York early in 1920. I was at work on a collection of folk-music from many countries and was rounding up a few musicians then living in New York to persuade them to supply new harmonizations.[4] Struck by the beauty of some of the melodies collected by Istomin and Dyutch,[5] I was emboldened to send one to Rachmaninov and two to Prokofiev and, lo! I received them back with beautiful settings (Example 31). These very melodies Prokofiev elaborated much later in life, including them in his Op. 106, *Twelve Russian Folk-Songs*.

Prokofiev's departure from Russia took place almost immediately after the first performance of the *Classical Symphony*, just after he had given two piano recitals in Petrograd in April of 1918. Our paths crossed somewhat later, when I was stranded in Siberia for over a year and a half to take care of a number of children's colonies established there during the famine. He travelled in comparative comfort, reached Japan, and after

[4] Published by Enoch and Sons, London, 1923, as *Songs from Many Lands*. The thirty songs contained in it are but a fraction of the material that I had amassed at the behest of the Overseas Branch of the American YMCA.
[5] This is when I first got to know the Istomin and Dyutch collection of 1886.

giving concerts there crossed the Pacific to America. Having had to borrow money from some fellow-travellers, he landed in New York virtually without funds to give his first American piano recital in November 1918.

Letter from Sergei Prokofiev to the author. It reads: 'I have received your letter and the songs. As soon as I can tear myself away from the composition of the opera (*Love for Three Oranges*) I shall try to harmonize some of them.'

Example 31. *Lament,* harmonized by Prokofiev (1920).

14

War and revolution

THE WAR YEARS (1914-17)

The inroads made by the war and subsequent Revolution upon Russian music have already been alluded to, in so far as they affected the careers of Scriabin, Rachmaninov, Medtner and Prokofiev. But the first actual war casualty was Liadov, who actually collapsed after seeing his son depart for the front. Scriabin was rash enough to welcome the outbreak of the slaughter as a preamble to the end of the world he had mystically envisioned. Mercifully he himself died before having to face the unreality of his delusions. His death in April 1915 preceded only slightly the massive retreats of the Russian armies. Thus he did not experience the increased gloom that spread from then on over the whole of Russian life.

At Scriabin's funeral, Taneyev caught a chill from which he never recovered and died two months later, just as Brahms had done at the funeral of Clara Schumann. Such sudden losses seriously weakened the musical life of the country, already impaired by the curtailment of foreign artists due to the war. On the other hand, the temporary shutting out of western musical influences certainly spurred on native artists, whose activity increased prodigiously.

In the autumn of 1915 in Petrograd, St Petersburg as newly named for patriotic purposes, the *Musical Contemporary* began to appear. It was a periodical of great historical and artistic value and was directed by the best critical minds, including Andri Rimsky-Korsakov, son of the composer, Professor Ivan Lapshin, and one Igor Glebov, a newcomer to the scene. Under this pseudonym, Boris Assafiev, the finest Russian writer on music, made his début. Even the outward aspects of the new publication surpassed anything that had been known in Russia. The issues of that first year were focused on the above deceased composers, but also devoted much attention to Stassov, Balakirev, and Rimsky-Korsakov. These men determined the direction of the journal, giving it a strong bias for Russia's musical past and encouraging a very laudable excursion into the domain of church singing, as with Kastalsky and Preobrajensky. But along with this there was an almost complete exclusion of the present. No mention was made of Rachmaninov, Medtner, or Prokofiev, and Stravinsky was subjected to severe criticism.

The winter of 1915-16 witnessed the first serious transportational difficulties because of the massive movement of refugees from the occupied areas in Poland and western Russia. Many people were stranded, among them the Medtners who were on their way from Moscow to Petrograd in the company of the singer Olenina d'Alheim. While the Medtners found shelter upon arrival with some relatives, Madame Olenina was stranded for days at the station, unable to find a room anywhere.[1] The Siloti concerts continued. Medtner and Rachmaninov played, as before, and Chaliapin sang in opera and concert, but the note of anxiety was never absent. I remember the commotion at one of the Siloti occasions on the night when Rasputin was shot. It so happened that in the box next to me Dimitry Stassov was sitting—he was the brother of the more famous Vladimir Stassov who had died in 1906—a terrifying embodiment of the contrast between the quiet days of Glinka and Balakirev and the near-chaos of those times, for it was just a few short months until the old life would be swept away for ever.

MIASKOVSKY (1881-1950)

At these concerts a new figure was brought before the public in the person of Nicolas Miaskovsky. His development as a musician had been quite unusual. Destined for a military career, he was over twenty-five before any serious thought was given to a career as a composer. He succeeded finally in being accepted into the St Petersburg Conservatoire, but his teachers were none too encouraging. Thus, *apropos* of his first symphony, Glazunov expressed himself as follows:

[1] Reminiscences of Anna Medtner to Alfred Swan: *Das Leben Nicolai Medtner's, Music des Ostens*, Vol. IV, Barenreiter, Kassel.

How tenaciously he tries to attain clarity of form and does not realize that this is beside the point.[2]

And Liadov's opinion was even less kind:

I cannot understand how in Miaskovsky a sharp and lucid mind is united with his everlasting layers of creeping harmonies, a regular impenetrable network of them.[3]

They made the mistake of underestimating Miaskovsky's power of self-criticism and did not know how he would strive for perfection. Nature had not endowed him with such gifts as would make musical composition flow naturally or be inevitable. Less gifted in imagination than many and not possessed of the magic that would turn inspirations into unforgettable melodies, Miaskovsky was very strong, however, in reflection. Criticizing, scrutinizing and probing his own powers—these were his strongest capacities and always he performed on neutral, somehow uncharacteristic material; yet he never lapsed into triteness, a trait which he always criticized in Mahler.

What he applied to himself he demanded of others, and this explains his bent for musical criticism. With a clear view, seldom falling into exaggerations—except in regard to Scriabin whom he misunderstood as did most of us—he reviewed the musical phenomena of his time, writing extensive articles on Beethoven, Tchaikovsky, and Medtner. To comprehend Miaskovsky, we must read his writings, which seem to have served him as a guide from one creative stage to another. His observations on others he applied to himself. Looking upon music primarily as an activity of the human mind, along with mathematics, science, and history, he developed his musical thoughts mainly in the larger forms. He wrote twenty-seven symphonies, thirteen quartets, and nine piano sonatas. He seems to have had an aversion to dramatic and vocal music. Yet, with all its intellectuality, his music rarely seems abstract. Early influence, if any, came from Wagner and Scriabin, but later he invaded the sphere of folk-song and even studied liturgical chant, as may be seen in the final chorus of the *Sixth Symphony*, Op. 23. From the hyper-romantic chromaticism in

[2] *M. Moussorgsky*, B. V. Assafiev, Vol. I, Moscow, 1959, p. 13.
[3] Ibid.

his earlier works, he moved to clear, classical and rather care-free diatonic constructions in those of his mature period.

As a personality, Miaskovsky remains enigmatic. The only hint of characterization comes from the singer Konosova, wife of Vladimir Derjanovsky. In Moscow, the Derjanovskys had continued the 'Evenings of Contemporary Music' begun by Karatygin and his group in St Petersburg in 1913. The Derjanovskys, also responsible for the Moscow journal *Music*, watched over young Miaskovsky's first timid steps up to the time when with the outbreak of the war he was dispatched to the Austrian front. Conscientiously fulfilling his military duties, he seemed untouched by the convulsions of the entire Russian realm, unaware of the magnitude of the profound disturbances it was undergoing. His letters reveal that he was preoccupied only with musical concerns. Similarly, the revolution affected him only as an orderly and fully normal occurrence, which set him free to doff his uniform and to resume work on un-finished scores. The Derjanovskys lured him back to Moscow and their letters and memoranda invariably note: 'Among our regular visitors was Miaskovsky'.[4]

The nearest parallel case is that of Prokofiev, with whom he had enjoyed a close friendship since the days when they had studied at the Conservatoire together. Both men seem to have been oblivious to the world about them, totally unconcerned with events of those history-making times, and absorbed only in their music.

AFTER 1917

The revolution merely concluded the process of disintegration begun with the war. All life, in the old accepted sense, had now collapsed and for everyone there was but one thought: how to survive. Thousands perished from one cause or another—famine, cold, arrest, banishment—forgotten by the world around. Only the especially privileged could hope to escape. Among this class, strangely enough, musicians came first, as the authorities had little to fear from people who expressed themselves in music. But even they had to cope with cold and starvation, and woe unto him who did not have the ingenuity

[4] E. Kunin, *N. Miaskovsky*, Moscow, 1969, p. 91.

to join new cultural units such as the theatre or the cinema, or to enter with gusto into newly formed organizations of workers and soldiers, or to direct choruses, or instrumental ensembles. The conservatoires became rallying points for all musicians. The directors at Petrograd and Moscow, Glazunov and Ippolitov-Ivanov, continued in their respective posts although the institutions were taken over by the state. Most of the professors were retained on condition that they perform the *Internationale* from time to time. But those without official positions faced either voluntary exile or death. Among these was Rachmaninov, as we know from a note set down by Sophie Satin:

Near the end of November, 1917, at about six o'clock one evening Rachmaninov rode on a slow-moving street-car along the unlit streets of Moscow to the railway station. It was drizzling; somewhere in the distance one could hear isolated shots. Only two people accompanied him; a man from the piano firm of Diederichs, who had been sent to aid in the purchase of a ticket, helping him to find a place on the overcrowded train, and myself. . . .[5]

Having reached Petrograd, he got an exit permit and, together with his wife and his two daughters, left for Sweden.[6] The Medtners sustained one hard blow after another. When food supplies had given out completely in Moscow, they fled to the friendly household of Dr Troyanovsky in the country. Peasants were still able to supply victuals, especially when paid in the old money or in gold. There the Medtners had their hide-out for nearly two years and in 1921 were finally permitted to leave on a spurious Esthonian passport. Shortly before, the conductors Siloti and Kussevitsky, and a host of performers of the calibre of Chaliapin, Leopold Auer, Heifetz, and Elman, had also left their country.

Truly frightening was the fate of Lineva, of whose exile an account can be partially reconstructed from the known facts of the life of Charles R. Crane, the American philanthropist who helped her when she was in America:

[5] Sophie Satin, *Note on Rachmaninov, Recollections*, Moscow, 1967, Vol. I, p. 49.
[6] The departure of Prokofiev, which took place a few months later, has already been described in Chapter 13.

Immediately after the Revolution of 1917, Mr Crane travelled to Moscow as a member of President Wilson's special diplomatic commission. The Linieffs were in dire straits. Masses of songs were still unpublished. The publishers had their supplies of paper confiscated by the new government. Crane found himself frequently in the home of the Linieffs, discussing the disastrous situation. They were joined by Kastalsky, the famous liturgical composer and likewise a penetrating scholar of Russian folk-music. Mr Crane negotiated with Jurgenson, the publisher, and, as he says in his notes, 'one of the last things I did before leaving Russia was to get permission from the Government for Jurgenson to have the paper he needed'. But matters were already going headlong down the precipice and no more Linieff volumes appeared. Mr Crane was appointed American Minister to China and when he traversed Russia again in 1921, on his way home, he learned from Kastalsky that both Linieffs had died in 1919. It was obvious that Eugenie, who had always impressed Mr Crane as being a frail person, was a victim of the dreadful conditions of life in those years of cold and famine. The fate of her dossier (some 2000 songs) is as yet unknown.[7]

Kastalsky, likewise, had to undergo his share of hardships during the years of famine. But he did have the good sense to swim with the current, perhaps on conviction. He joined with popular activities at workers' clubs; he showed a lively interest in revolutionary literature; he scored and conducted the *Internationale*, and compiled projects to assist reform of the teaching system, which he submitted to the Ministry of Education. In general, he followed the political line, thus naturally finding himself among the privileged. With amazing ease, almost overnight, he relinquished his preoccupation with the old chant and switched over completely to a secular, unreligious point of view (see Chapter 10). The period in which the Bolshevik party relaxed for a while its grip on the populace saw the death of Kastalsky and of most of his collaborators in the liturgical field. Among these were the historians and liturgists: Metallov, successor of Smolensky at the Moscow Conservatoire and one of the finest connoisseurs of *znamenny* chant, though a somewhat confused writer; Findeisen, for nearly twenty-five years editor of the *Russian Musical Gazette* and the collections *Musical Antiquity*, whose capital work, *Sketches for the History of Russian Music*,

[7] Eugenie Linieff, *Folk Songs of The Ukraine*, Monticello College Press, Illinois, see preface by A. J. Swan, pp. iii, iv.

was published after his death in 1928; and Preobrajensky, an erudite musicologist of European stature and an excellent writer who upheld the theory of Byzantine origin for Russian chant. There are no detailed biographies of these men whose achievements are not clearly known; however, it is clear that their line did not die out with them. Liturgiology has continued to progress despite the incredible difficulties met by Church historians.

BRAJNIKOV (b. 1904)

The chief figure among them was Maxim Brajnikov, who is still living and very active as a scholar (see Appendix II). He graduated from the Leningrad Conservatoire as pianist and theoretician, but, under the influence of Preobrajensky who taught him, dedicated himself wholly to the study of the old chants. His expositions are as clear as those of his teacher, but he took the opposite view about the origin of *znamenny* chant. A penetrating student of the old Russian 'Alphabets' *Azubuki* of the fifteenth-sixteenth centuries, he pronounced them accurate and even eloquent as against Preobrajensky's assertion that they were totally undecipherable and confused. Just recently, he reiterated his theory that chant profoundly influenced Russian folk-songs. We have already spoken in Chapter 2 of his transcriptions of the canticles of Feodor the Christian, based on Malyshev's historic discovery in the north of Russia. N. Uspensky, a professor in Leningrad, where one of the few remaining ecclesiastical academies still continues, is the author of two books on the art of the old masters, filled with copious examples (see Appendix II). Curiously, all the transcriptions in Uspensky's books derive from the collections of Brajnikov, which shows the extreme rarity of specialists in the domain.[8]

For a while teaching in the conservatoires flowed along in the old channels. Glazunov stayed until 1928, when he requested a leave of absence and went abroad. Visiting various countries, among them the USA in 1930, he died in Paris in

[8] One of the greatest of them lives in Germany, having been brought up in the circles of the Old Believers in Moscow but thrown into emigration at an early age: Ivan Gardner, semi-cleric, semi-scholar, he studied in Belgrade, lived and officiated in Jerusalem, was deputy bishop in Berlin, and is now Professor at the University of Munich.

1936. His thoughts were always with his beloved institution and he frequently communicated from abroad with Maximilian Steinberg, son-in-law of Rimsky-Korsakov, whom he trusted above any other teacher at the Conservatoire. He was eager to sustain the old conservative traditions against the influx of modernism, but was in the course of time defeated by the official decrees against 'formalism'.

CATOIRE (1861-1926)

In Moscow the old teachers, G. Conus,[9] G. Catoire, and A. Goedicke, functioned as before. Catoire is one of the most elusive figures in the whole of Russian music. Originally with Tchaikovsky, who actually helped him with his first steps, he veered away from the Tchaikovsky path and developed a very subtle style of his own. Like Fauré in France, he was painfully shy and quite averse to ostentation; nevertheless he was always trying to find a new way to express something familiar. A man of intense sincerity and ardour, he reached real heights in the few works of his that are accessible: the *Poem* for violin and piano, the *Piano Quartet*, and one or two others that appeared in the Kussevitsky edition shortly before the war.

GOEDICKE (1877-1957)

Goedicke, essentially an academician, is a different figure. His style is generally dry, but there are a few inspired moments in his music as in that haunting *Prelude to the Blind* on a text by Maeterlinck. Even more surprisingly, this seemingly dry composer moved into the domain of the folk-song, leaving three books of settings with piano, violin, and cello—the very same combination that Beethoven used for some of the Lvov-Prach items. In commenting on Goedicke's work, Assafiev pointed to Tchaikovsky's famous *Andante Cantabile* from the first string quartet as another such precedent. Goedicke's melodies are taken from Filippov, Balakirev, Melgunov, and Rimsky-Korsakov (Appendix I).

[9] The family of the Conus (of French origin) included three prominent musicians: George, Julius and Leo. George was one of Scriabin's theory teachers, Julius, a violinist and composer of a concerto which Heifetz often performed, and Leo was a piano teacher.

15

The eclipse of modernism

The musical cultures of Russia and the West were destined to take widely different courses, although the parting of the ways did not come suddenly. During the first few years after the Civil War which ended in 1921, it looked as though Russian music had been drawn even nearer the West. Indeed Russians were generally eager to find out what had been happening in the rest of the world during the war years. Lively correspondences were carried on with all musical centres, and I remember myself sending communiques to the Moscow journal *Contemporary Music*[1] about concerts in New York, then increasingly dominated by extreme modernist groups. But as the twenties rolled on, there developed in Russia a revulsion against western trends, especially among organizers of mass educational activities. Sympathies with Parisian fashion were deprecated and writers urged, not without a good deal of coercion, to cater to indigenous needs and to follow the conservative line. Even the modernist spokesman Karatygin was deflected from his tendencies by living realities. His end was tragic, as his connection with the Conservatoire was only a recent one—he was made professor only in 1919—and he could not count on much concern there for his well-being. A. Ossovsky, another important musical writer, described him shortly before his death in 1925:

The revolution came and the soul of Karatygin responded a hundredfold to the call of life. He did not go to pieces. Mustering his last strength, he plunged into work. Many will remember how even in

[1] *Contemporary Music*, Moscow, April, 1924, p. 90.

the bitterest cold days of the devastation, Karatygin, in ragged attire, hungry, shrunk, ran from factory to factory, from one club or institution to another to deliver his numerous lectures, give concerts, attend meetings. . . .[2]

But the whole process of change was most eloquently demonstrated in two extraordinary musical careers: those of the critic, Assafiev, and the young composer, Shostakovich.

ASSAFIEV (1884-1949)

Assafiev's writings completely cover only the last two centuries of Russian music. Before that, he penetrated only sporadically, more with intuition than with certainty, preferring merely to indicate the musicologist's task rather than carry it out. His preoccupation with music goes back to his childhood, but he had little systematic training in music as he underwent normal schooling at the Kronstadt Gymnasium and later at St Petersburg University, where he attended the lectures of Platonov in history and Lossky in philosophy. He was prepared to go into life as an all-round educated and enlightened person and perhaps to occupy a government position. But the turning-point towards music came when he heard the music of Borodin, *Prince Igor* in particular. By a fortunate turn of events, Assafiev became acquainted with members of the Stassov circle shortly after hearing this opera. Hence he got to know Glazunov, Rimsky-Korsakov, and Liadov. Remembering those days, he wrote:

I was made to play a lot of Moussorgsky's music from *Boris* and *Khovanshchina*. While I was playing, Repin was busy at his current portrait of Stassov. . . .[3]

He had spent most of this early period listening and attuning his ear to the intonations of the Russian School. Through Repin, he also became acquainted with the domain of painting, while, following Gorky who also belonged to the Stassov circle, he developed and greatly refined his literary style. He entered musical life through an inconspicuous door—as concert master and accompanist for the ballet section of the Imperial Theatres. For a long time, even when his adopted name of

[2] A. Ossovsky, *Musical Annals*, Vol. III, Leningrad, 1925.
[3] B. Assafiev, *Russian Art, Thoughts and Contemplation*, Moscow, 1966, p. 11.

Igor Glebov had become familiar to readers of the musical journals, no one had the slightest idea that behind that *nom de plume* stood an unassuming functionary in the ballet.

Even in his earliest articles in Derjanovsky's Journal *Music* Assafiev showed an uncanny power of observation and an intellectual capacity for almost any problem connected with music. Whether it was some neglected work, or composer, or a poor production, or, again, an abstract question of musical philosophy and aesthetics, he always had something significant to say. The revolution opened up for him opportunities commensurate with his enormous gifts. Moreover, he was younger than Karatygin and could therefore adjust better to a new system and more easily surmount the hardships of the lean years. Following the general lines of Karatygin, but also vastly extending them with a tolerance unknown to the former, he sailed on the stormy sea of modern music. The culmination of that period came with his book on Stravinsky, a marvellously lucid and profound survey of this composer's career up to *Oedipus Rex* in 1928. In the eyes of Soviet officialdom this book proved a bone of contention, as at the time of its appearance a turning-point had been reached. The official attitude had changed from one allowing freedom of expression on musical matters to rigorous totalitarian surveillance.

It is difficult for us in the West to understand how such topics as Stravinsky, Prokofiev, or Shostakovich could become matters almost of life and death. Pronouncing open judgments, or even just speaking one's mind, often brought grave consequences. Assafiev, who by then had resumed use of his real name, passed through tortuous self-analysis and self-adjustment, for he was required to conform to the demands of the new social order and was far too honest to feign conformity with official requirements. Music for the people written in the old accepted language, somehow trite and stripped of its mystery, he could not accept. This legislated art may have been basically sound, yet it was pernicious, its slogans interfering with the artist's freedom of expression. Without rancour and without sacrificing any of his pithiness and acumen, he withdrew from his modernist position and devoted himself entirely to safe, time-honoured subjects such as the music of Glinka, Tchaikovsky, etc.

This retreat, forced also on others, eventually turned the whole field of Russian musical and artistic criticism into a perpetual assimilation and regurgitation of the recurring ideas on various unvarying stale topics. However, this wasteland aesthetic did not seem to affect Assafiev, who produced inspired essays in abundance. On the threshold of the thirties he came out with his best-known work, *Russian Music from the Beginning of the Nineteenth Century*.[4] This history, which stops just short of Shostakovich, is a mine of brilliant, penetrating characterizations and a landmark in music historiography not only by Russian, but by universal standards.

One of the strongest pleas made by Assafiev was for the restoration of the original manuscripts of Moussorgsky's *Boris Godunov* (see Chapter 6). A most delicate operation had to be performed to remove Rimsky-Korsakov's emendations and to salvage the version Moussorgsky had presented to the operatic committee early in 1870. Paul Lamm was chosen as musical surgeon, and he accomplished his difficult task to perfection, making possible the performance in 1928 of the original version as the world should have known it more than half a century earlier.

PAUL LAMM (1882-1951)

Musicology was then very new in Russia, as were principles of scholarly editing. Russian pioneers in this field had been critics mainly, as were Karatygin and Assafiev. Musicologists had been active in the liturgical domain, but acquisition of the tools of scientific research had been a slow process, as we know from the career of Preobrajensky. As a musicologist, Lamm was a new phenomenon even from a western viewpoint. He united the science of musicology with the practice and enjoyment of musical performance on a vast scale. The Lamm household was the scene of some of the most exciting musical gatherings in the twenties, when, for want of facilities for any kind of extended concert activity, music had to be cultivated in private homes. Piano performance was central, and arrangements from full score for four hands either with one or two

[4] Translated by A. J. Swan for the American Council of Learned Societies in 1946, published by J. W. Edwards, Ann Arbor, Michigan, 1953.

pianos were accomplished *a prima vista* on the spur of the moment. According to the testimony of his contemporaries, Lamm's skill in reading and reducing scores so that they be playable on keyboard instruments was quite uncanny. It was probably in this very activity that Lamm discovered and developed his own unique métier as musicologist-performer. As a musicologist, he developed a facility for meticulous study of modern works in manuscript form. As a performer, he translated his study into actual sound from the only concert platform then extant. His was an ideal and imaginative solution for a set of very difficult problems, and on these grounds we may term him a musicologist *par excellence*.

Lamm forms a bridge between the disappearing musicologist of the old school and the emerging new generation, as personified by Maxim Brajnikov—and, on another point, a link between the posthumous sketches of Findeisen and the first significant work of Brajnikov: *The Paths of Development of Znamenny Chant*, 1948. Musicology of the western type was of necessity brought to a stop with the ban on religious music and could not be resumed until this ban was relaxed, i.e., until after the Second World War. In Russia, theoretical and historical investigation were applied to a tradition of great music, and both pursuits are still being continued on in new works.

SHOSTAKOVICH (b. 1906)

Of the impressive possible results of such synthesis, no better demonstration can be found than the symphonies of Dimitry Shostakovich, who grew up during the dark days of the war and experienced the whole chaos of the revolution. At the age of thirteen in 1919, he entered the Petrograd Conservatoire and was brought under the attentive care of Glazunov, the director. Referring to his talents, Glazunov described him as:

A brilliant and very promising creative personality with tremendous imagination and inventiveness, as proved by a Prelude and a Scherzo. . . .[5]

The pieces referred to were student compositions which Shostakovich probably discarded later on and are no longer extant. His actual début as an important new member of the

[5] 'Glazunov' in *Musical Heritage* (Yankovsky), Vol. I, Leningrad, 1959.

composers' brotherhood was marked by a work that made a stir throughout the musical world—*The First Symphony in F-minor,* Op. 10.

A young musician reared on the traditions of the Russian classics and guided by a composer of Glazunov's orientation ought to manifest in his music some of the salient features of the Russian School. One would expect to find folk-song intonations, strong and persistent pedal effects, or a colour scheme akin to that of Rimsky-Korsakov (see Chapter 6). But nothing of this is to be found here. One can detect only a few echoes, and most unlikely ones as that of Elgar's *Falstaff,* or of the style of Richard Strauss, or, again, a touch of Mahler. Yet there is great maturity in the clever development of contrasted themes, and an inborn sense of the orchestra. Above it all there is a spring-like freshness.

After basking for a while in the success of his first major effort, Shostakovich was confronted with a dilemna: where next? At the Conservatoire they were telling him that all the new western experiments of Stravinsky, Hindemith, Schoenberg, Berg, Krenek and others could not be reckoned as serious music. But Igor Glebov wrote differently. There was also a certain Ivan Sollertinsky among his friends—philosopher, linguist, economist and a great enthusiast for the German 'expressionists'—and Shostakovich listened to him. He became involved in Gogol's story *The Nose* and produced an opera on it in three acts (1927-9). He likewise wrote a ballet in three acts called *The Age of Gold.* These were his extreme modernist thrusts, and even so they left him unsatisfied. Perhaps to counteract this current he ventured into 'programme' music, and, what was even worse, he became involved in political programme music. His second and third symphonies revolve around the October Revolution and the International May-day festival. For any artist it should have been clear from Beethoven's experience that such ventures into political topicality were undesirable in music. The political moment, even if there is abstract value in it, is essentially a fleeting one: what seems glorious today pales tomorrow. Can we not say this of Brahms' *Triumphlied,* written to glorify the Prussian victory of 1871? And even Tchaikovsky's *1812* is only acceptable in so far as it forgets political cause and effect and goes on its way as purely symphonic development.

Thus, neither of the directions taken by Shostakovich in the years following his first symphony was salutary from the point of view of future development. He passed through a tortuous decade, and not until his chamber music of the late thirties did he begin to reveal his stature as a really great master-builder. This, however, lies already beyond our present task, and we must leave Shostakovich at the crossroads and only conclude, with the knowledge that we now have, that he is to date the most recent of the Russian giants.

16

Conclusion

As this book began with a view of the sources of Russian music, it is appropriate that it should end in the same way. Chant and folk-song, the main currents in early music, have not lost their force. Though an increasing penchant for western manners caused various departures from folk-song and produced unwillingness to exploit the riches of liturgical chant, it would be vain to deny that even such firm believers in western culture as Glazunov and Medtner did not at times cast longing looks towards these native sources. As for their successors, Miaskovsky, Prokofiev and Shostakovich, their later works were to be incessantly replenished from the age-old intonations. Scriabin alone stood in complete isolation from the national heritage, and it is significant in this regard that he formed no school and had no actual following.

Folk-song collection and study did not cease with the transition from the old Russia to the new. There was scarcely a break in continuity, although many obstacles arose during troubled revolutionary times. Alexander Listopadov, a contemporary of Lineva, is typical of the modern folklorist in Russia. Having begun his studies early in the century, he carried on through the entire period of the war and revolution. His first journey into the Don Cossack regions took place in 1902, and his records list no less than ten subsequent journeys, some extended by prolonged stays in places of particular musical interest. He made his last collection in 1940 and, while collecting in the south of Russia, dispatched numerous expeditions, as before, to the north. Two volumes issued by the State Institute of the History of the Arts in 1927 form a regular encyclopaedia of the remnants of northern art in all its aspects, especially in peasant architecture, and were a preparation for the later expeditions into the Onega region, bringing about the restoration and preservation of such miraculous cases of the historic Russian art as the little Kiji island. In 1930 folklorists visited the Pinega areas, east of Archangel, and the result was a large edited volume of songs published in 1937.

After the Second World War the traditional Piatnitzky choir was set in motion anew by the composer Sakharov and the philologist Kazmin. Their efforts produced a most delightful collection in 1958. As all this material was collected and published, members of the Leningrad Institute of the Theatre, Music, and Cinema subjected it to a most minute study. One by one there appeared the books of Izaly Zemtzovsky, a collaborator of the Institute, whose most substantial work was that devoted to the Laments (*Protyajnaia*). It is impossible to mention here all numerous similar endeavours. The total picture shows incessant, at times even feverish, activity in the pursuit of various tasks necessary to the preservation of ancient Russian melodies and their texts.

The fate of liturgical melodies and texts, most of which were resting obscurely in various libraries and private collections, was far more unspectacular. Except for the Malyshev find of 1955, little of import can be recounted. Even for the inquisitive and patient Russian scholar the subject was too remote, the times too turbulent. Strictures on religious art also obstructed development. This was finally surmounted by Brajnikov, who opened up entirely new horizons for the study of the periods prior to the introduction of the Shaidurov marks. A parallel activity was that of Ivan Gardner in Munich. Now Professor Uspensky had become the third in this alliance, and between them these scholars may push the long-neglected study of the old chants and their notations into a new dimension.

From a practical point of view the utilization of *znamenny* melodies for new works of art has scarcely progressed at all since the early days of this century. Then their fate was in the hands of Rachmaninov, with the Moscow Synodal School providing a suitable background for development of their study. However, neither he nor the Moscow institution were able to consolidate their achievements after 1917. Religious composition is still dormant in Russia, and among émigrés I am, so far as I know, one of the very few who have used *znamenny* treasures in modern compositions, and even here these are only scattered through a few choral sections and chamber pieces.[1]

At the beginning of the book I described the collecting of fragments of the Gorodishche Wedding Rite and gave examples in Appendix III. I now remind the reader of these few but perfect examples by way of conclusion. My acquaintance with the music represented by these and indeed the line of enquiry that has guided my thinking over the past thirty-five years, began when I was shown the path I have since followed by Michel Ossorguine, precentor at St Sergius Monastery in Paris. He was a veritable prophet of *znamenny* chant, which he used almost exclusively in the daily round of services over which he presided, and his dedication and deep insights have provided constant inspiration in the years that have passed since first we met.

If I might have ended this book with fascinating descriptions of the manner in which a people's government had promoted and supported long-range programmes for rediscovering and utilizing the rich legacy left us by earlier Russians, how gratifying would have been my task in setting forth this study, not of the history of Russian music, but rather of the nature of Russian musical culture. However matters stand, there is no point in speculating on what might have been. I must end my narrative, reverently bowing my head in memory of Michel Ossorguine and of those who thought as he did.

---

[1] Of my settings, ten liturgical canticles of the Eastern Church were published by Boosey and Hawkes and six by the Orthodox Press of Berkeley, California. In a *Trio* for piano, flute, and oboe, the *Sixth String Quartet* published by Paxton, and an *Introduction and Allegro for String Orchestra*, I used *znamenny*, *heirmoi*, *akathistoi*, and *exposteilaria* which are special hymns to the Virgin or to particular saints.

Appendices

APPENDIX I

Russian folk-song collections from the beginning of the collection era:

Trutovsky	1776, 1778, 1779, 1795
Prach-Lvov	1806, 1815
Rupin (Rupini)	1831
Kashin	1833-4
Stakhovich	1851
Villebois	1860, texts edited by Appolen Grigoryev
Balakirev	1866
Prokunin	1872, edited by 'Professor' Tchaikovsky
Rubetz	1875, Ukrainian folk-songs
Rimsky-Korsakov	1877, 100 songs
Melgunov	1879, 1885, first collection listing *'podgoloski'*
Rimsky-Korsakov	1882, 40 songs, the Filippov collection
Palchikov	1888, listing of all *'podgoloski'*, no accompaniments
Lopatin-Prokunin	1889, with accompaniments
Istomin-Dyutch	1894, results of expedition of 1886 to the Russian North
Istomin-Liapunov	1899, results of expedition of 1894 to Vologda, Viatka, and Kostroma provinces
Balakirev	1901, harmonization of the Istomin-Dyutch expedition
Liadov	1898, 30 songs
	1901, 35 songs
	1901, 50 songs
	1901, 35 songs. In all, Liadov harmonized 150 songs

Lineva	1897-1900, 23 songs from Vladimir, Nizhni-Novgorod, and Voronezh provinces. The first songs to be collected with the aid of a phonograph
	1901, Novgorod songs
	1903, Ukrainian songs, published in English by Maria Safonov in 1958
Listopadov	1911, first volume of Don Cossack songs; four more appeared by 1948
Piatnitzky	1914, concerts with peasant singers
Swan	1936, published in 1939 by Belaieff in Leipzig
Gippius	1937, *Pesni Pinezhya*; 150 melodies of the extreme North
Kolotilova	1947, *Pesni Severa*
Mahler	1951, Pechory songs collected in 1937, 1938, and 1939
Sakharov-Kazmin	1958, 100 songs from the repertoire of the Piatnitzky chorus

APPENDIX II

Stages of clarification and readability of the old (*Kriuk*) notations.

(*a*) Fifteenth- and sixteenth-century Alphabets (*Azbuki*) explaining the various forms of the neumes, their combinations and abbreviations: the *thetai* (fifty) stenographic groups of signs.

(*b*) Appearance in the early part of the seventeenth century of the red-letter marks, invented by the Novgorod theoretician, Ivan Shaidur or Shaidurov.

There was a certain *didaskalos* or teacher of singing and his name was Ivan, son of Joachim, also called simply Shaidur; this Ivan, through great industry and much endeavour, invented some *znamenny* singing and delightful euphony. The Lord revealed to him the marks. . . .

(*The Tale of the Marks—Skazaniye o Pomyetakh*, seventeenth century)

This invention of Shaidur was accepted wholeheartedly and from about the middle of the seventeenth century nearly all manuscripts contain the red-letter marks, thanks to which both the pitch and the duration of the neumes are more clearly defined, permitting a more accurate transcription onto the stave.

(*c*) The commission of Alexander Mezenetz in 1668 was convened for the purpose of revising and further explaining the Shaidur marks. Mezenetz was an expert in the *znamenny* chant and advocated in the strongest terms the retention of the neumes as against the newly imported western stave. He tried to show that the former could render the meaning of the melodies much better than the 'lifeless' stave.

(*d*) But the convenience of the stave proved irresistible, and by the end of the seventeenth century Russian church singing was fully transferred to it. The first extensive transcriptions were made in the early years of the eighteenth century by Tikhon of Makarievsk, treasurer to the last patriarch Adrian (the Patriarchate was not restored until 1917). Thus, the line of the Russian theoreticians runs Shaidur–Mezenetz–Tikhon and gradually transfers us to modern musical notation.

(*e*) For the Byzantine neumes there were the Byzantine Alphabets (*Papadikai*), but no Shaidur appeared there to supply them with explanatory marks. So the tradition was lost, and only in the nineteenth century were the first efforts made to study the old musical manuscripts. Decisive progress was made only in the twentieth century, first by Oskar Fleischner, then by Egon Wellesz and the monks at the Grotta Ferrata Monastery near Rome.

(*f*) In 1909 the Russian scholar A. V. Preobrajensky drew attention to the fact that the Russian and Byzantine notations of the eleventh to twelfth centuries were exceedingly close, but since neither of them could be read at the time, it was only a *de visu* observation.

(*g*) In 1935 the series, known as *Monumenta Musicae Byzantinae*, began to appear in Copenhagen with transcriptions in bulk by Wellesz and Tillyard. In 1938 the Grotta Ferrata volume *L'Antica Melurgia Bizantina* appeared, and though the transcriptions in it by Dom Lorenzo Tardo did not entirely tally with the Wellesz transcriptions, it was now possible to gain some notion of the sound of the early Byzantine music. This sound was so radically different from that of the Russian manuscripts with the Shaidur marks of the seventeenth century, that it now became imperative to determine when the roads of the two chants, believed to be cognate, began to move apart. Two schools of thought immediately crystallized. One believed (with Preobrajensky) that the two chants had been for a while identical, or nearly so, and that it was mainly during the Mongol period (thirteenth to fifteenth century), when Russia was debarred from communication with the outer world, that the Russian chant went on its own, individual way. The other held (with most of the Russian scholars, and especially Smolensky who followed the study of Mezenetz) that the divergent ways were set almost immediately after the importation of the Byzantine chant into Russia in the tenth century. This school inclined to attribute the new sound of the Russian chant to the influence of folk-song.

(*h*) The Byzantine scholars, nevertheless, continued their studies of the early Russian manuscripts which the Russian scholars were wary of attacking, and applied to them the Wellesz transcribing technique. Here the line starts with Miloš Velimirovič, a Yugoslav scholar now working in America, and goes to Oliver Strunk of Grotta Ferrata and Kenneth Levy of Princeton, and finally to Constantine Floros of Hamburg. Some of the results of their combined efforts were demonstrated impressively at the Congress in Bratislava in 1964.

(*i*) The whole matter hinges on the postulate of Wellesz's mode of transcribing. The Russian scholars (severely handicapped by the long-imposed ban on the study of liturgical problems) have not accepted this postulate and prefer to build on the certainty of the Shaidur marks. This does not lead them beyond the seventeenth century. Vladimir Malyshev discovered in the extreme Russian North an anthology containing eleven Gospel canticles expressly marked as the work of Feodor the Christian (see genealogy in Chapter 2). Though Feodor lived in the pre-red-letter period, some thoughtful hand had inserted the Shaidur marks into these notations of Feodor. As a result of this, the Soviet musicologist Maxim Brajnikov was able to transcribe Feodor's work, introducing us thereby to the sound of Russian music of the sixteenth century—the age of Czar Ivan and his circle of master-singers in Moscow.

(*j*) Encouraged by this, Brajnikov and Uspensky, now in association, have studied and transcribed some works of Feodor's contemporaries and are, generally speaking, moving more rapidly into the mediaeval periods. It remains to be seen whether a meeting-point will be reached between the Russian and Byzantine procedures, but once the dam is broken, as it is now, endless possibilities arise in this adventurous century of ours. The next generation may be much more fully informed on the music of Russia and on the interconnections between folk-song, which is ageless, and liturgical chant. The chant still continues to puzzle us, hiding as it were behind a wall of a still unclear notation.

APPENDIX III

The wedding rite of the village Gorodishche, Pskov province.

After the marriage pact has been concluded preparations for the wedding begin. Meanwhile the bride's companions pursue both bride and bridegroom with incessant songs and choruses, such as these:

On the hill, the little hill, stood a small fir-tree
A fir-tree green with curly branches.
Under the fir-tree was a bed, a quilt of down,
A quilt of down and a blue pillow.
On the pillow lies a neat blanket;
Under the blanket lies the lovely maid,
The lovely maid, Katherine, Lavrentry's daughter.
She is weeping like a flowing river
And her tears are running like brooks.

White birch, green and curly,
Where are you bending?
Tell us, Laurentievna dear, where are you marrying?
I am marrying where my father gives me away,
Where my mother promised me.

For the groom

Before our turret stands a cloud with silver;
Behind our yard is a lake full of water.
There our hero gave his horse a drink,
Led him to the gate and tied him to the ring
Calling for Katherine.

In the garden grows a grapevine, green and juicy,
Our grape is Ivanushka, our grape is Vassilievich,
Our grape is Katerinushka, our grape is Lavrentievna.
All the people are admiring them, all the neighbors are astonished.
God give them love and counsel, it is good to live with counsel.

To the last couplet Lisa Ukatova (see plate 2) sang the following tune:

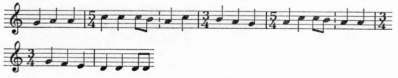

From the Mahler collection, 1951

After this the guests are invited by the bride in person. She walks in front, and behind her the companions carry her 'beauty' in the shape of a small pine-tree decorated with ribbons and sweetmeats. Its little trunk is thrust into a bottleneck which is wrapped in a paper blouse and apron. Having entered into a hut, the bride makes a low bow to the guests and utters the invitation.

A day or two before the wedding the companions assemble for the last time around the bride (the *devishnik*).

> I shall sit under the fair window on a bench of oak
> And shall ask you gently:
> What have you come for, my dear sisters?
> Why are you crowding in, my white swans?
> If it is for weaving—you bring no looms
> If it is for sewing—you bring no needles.
> You have gathered, O sisters, for the maidens' night.
> Help me pass the time till late.

The bride meanwhile sits covering her face with her hands and 'weeps out', in approximately the same words, her grief over her freedom which is now at an end. Towards the end of the evening the bridegroom arrives. He brings for his bride some gingerbread and a piece of soap for the wedding day. Finally, the companions leave the pair to themselves.

On the wedding day, songs are sung while the bridegroom is preparing to leave with his train of followers to meet the bride. There is a blessing first:

> The bright moon stood before the fair sun.
> The young prince stood before his own father.
> 'My beloved father, forgive me and bless me.
> Let me go on my way, supply me with bread and salt
> To appear before God's judgment—fearful thought
> To go up the steep steps—my swift feet will break
> To stand under the golden crown—my heart trembles.'

The preparations at the bride's include a final combing of her hair, the farewell to her maiden braids, the pride of maidenhood, for after the wedding they will be woven around her head and covered by a woman's headdress forever. In turn her father, mother, godparents and all the rest come up, scrape the comb through the hair, and drop some presents into the hem of her skirt. She herself sits with her face covered by her hands and laments. The girls sing:

'My own father, comb my head so very smooth.
I would comb it myself—but I cannot lift my arms
I cannot lift my arms, or bend my fingers.'

The bridegroom arrives. When he is admitted at last, the mother-in-law comes down from the porch and spreads a napkin in front of him. He opens his purse and places paper money on the four corners and in the middle of the napkin. His 'best men' meanwhile help themselves to wine. The girls sing:

The groundling writhes on the water.
The prince is wasting himself away by the gate

From the Swan collection, 1936

The mother-in-law picks up the napkin with money. The best man marches ahead, the bridegroom, led by his brothers, follows. 'Give way', shouts the best man and lashes his whip on the doors, as if there were those who blocked the way. However, the actual symbolism of this action is the sign of a cross. While he is crossing all doors through which he passes, the girls form up in a dense row, as if protecting their friend, and sing:

'Best man, do not begrudge us, open your purse of gold.
You will not get rich, or buy turquoise for your wife.
If you do, she will fail to wear it;
When she goes to church she will soil it;
When she comes from church she will lose it.'

From the Swan collection, 1936

After more preparations the best man leads the young couple to the table, to a seat of honour. All the guests sit down. Then grace is sung (*zastólitsa*):

'O Lord Christ, bless us,
To start the wedding game,
To set the tables, to spread the table cloths,
To bring bread and salt and the sweetmeats,
The sweetmeats and the mead from the cellar . . .'

Here, we have a clear instance of a pagan wedding game for which God's blessing is invoked:

From the Swan collection, 1936

Each guest, whether married or not, is honoured by a special song. If a guest pretends that he does not know what feast he is attending, the girls sing of the bride and groom:

> On the field the horses are let loose;
> They are tied by silken threads.
> They don't eat the green grass,
> They don't drink the cold water,
> They hear a distant procession;
> But it is not a king meeting another king;
> It is Ivan Vasilievich and his train
> Meeting the white swan, Katherine Lavrentievna.

From the Mahler collection, 1951

Now comes the time to sing 'The Beauty' (the little fir-tree):

> We have gathered your beauty in one spot.
> Stand away, dear people, allow us to come
> To the table with the fair maid.
> Greetings to you, dear Lavrentievna.

213

Is your beauty well adorned?
Take your beauty into your hands,
Press your beauty to your eager heart
And moisten your beauty with your bitter tears, etc.

From the Swan collection, 1936

The 'beauty' is taken away. Then one of the girls addresses the young couple with an incantation, proffering a plate on which they find a new headdress and a maiden's ribbon: the groom takes the headdress and places it behind his belt, while the ribbon is thrown into the crowd of girls:

So this is what Vanya has in mind—to take himself
a young mistress.

The gaiety continues with a song about the wedding pie (*pirog*):

Mother-in-law she did make a pie.
Four rubles' worth of salt she did buy,
Eight rubles' worth of sugar and rye,
Twelve rubles in all were spent for the pie.
Mother-in-law thought seven could be supped;
Young son-in-law all alone ate it up.
Mother-in-law she does pace up and down
And gently upon her son-in-law she does frown
'Heaven grant you split in two, my son-in-law'.
'Stiff and dry your tongue may wax, my mother-in-law.
One fine day you will come to visit me in carnival week,
Then I will soon make you obedient and meek
With four juicy rods of the birch neatly clipped,
All to order is made a whip.'

From the Swan collection, 1936

Various songs are sung about life in general; the following two are about the bath-house:

Appendix III

(a) Heat up, you steam bath-house!
  Flame up, you red brick house!
  Katherine fell to weeping
  About her lost freedom,

(b) About her smooth and blonde braids
  And her ribbons red.

From the Swan collection, 1936

Don't weary the girls, their feet are aching
And their shoes say they want a gold cover.

From the Swan collection, 1936

Then the wedding procession starts, accompanied on their journey through the village by many songs:

In Yaroslav city there stands a willow in gold.
Past that willow there lies a road wide.
On that road walked three maids, Katherine and her companions.
The first shook the willow, the second broke a branch;
Katherine herself tore out the roots,
Wound herself a golden wreath,
Put it on her head and went to morning service.

From the Swan collection, 1936

The best man leads the groom who, in his turn, leads the bride by the hand. Her head is covered by a kerchief. They get up on a bench trying to reach their seats behind the back of the guests.

The best man is noisily carrying on, but a glass of vodka helps to pacify him. The young couple have reached their places. The mother-in-law holds two glasses of vodka, the father removes the kerchief with a whip. The guests shout 'Hurrah'. The young couple cross themselves before the icons, click their glasses and, after a sip, splash out the rest over their heads against the wall. The girls sing:

> The berries have rolled together.
> The berries have met in the wood.
> The berries have ripened together.

At the end of the rite the following song is sung:

> In the garden the wide river flows.
> Who is riding a horse on the river?
> Ivanushka is on a horse, Vasilievich on the swift one,
> And who is at his feet but Katherine Lavrentievna.
> She hands him the whip and bows low,
> Gives him the Italian shawl and kisses it forty times.

From the Swan collection, 1936

Bibliography

In this abbreviated list are included works by Russian writers, or the composers themselves, that have been translated into English, and also works by western scholars, written in English, French, and German. A few of the works are obsolete, but all those listed have been consulted and found helpful to the author. Thus the listing is as personal as the book itself and excludes anything that goes beyond purely musical considerations.

Abraham, Gerald, *Studies in Russian Music*, New York, 1935; *On Russian Music: Critical and Historical Studies*, New York, 1939; *Rimsky-Korsakov*, London, 1945; Balakirev, Grove's *Dictionary*, 1954.

Arro, Elmar, 'Probleme der Provenienz des alt-russischen kirchlichen Gesanges', *Anfänge der Slavischen Musik*, Bratislava, 1966.

Assafiev, Boris, *Russkaya Muzyka ot Nachala 19 Veka*, trans. Alfred Swan, Ann Arbor, Mich., 1953.

Bowen, Catherine, *Free Artist: The Lives of Nicholas and Anton Rubinstein*, New York, 1939.

Bowers, Faubin, *Scriabin*, Tokya, 1969. Extensive translations from Sabaneyev's *Reminiscences of Scriabin*.

Brazhnikov, Maxim, 'Zur Terminologie der Alt-Russischen Vokalmusik', *Beiträge zur Musikwissenschaft*, Heft 3, 1968.

Calvocoressi, M. D., *Modest Moussorgsky: His Life and Works*, Rockliff, 1956.

Findeisen, N., *Ocherki po Istorii Muzyki v Rossii*, Leningrad and Moscow, 1928, 2 vols.

Flores, Konstantin, 'Die Entzifferung der Kondakarischen Notation', *Musik des Ostens*, Band 3-4, herausgegeben von Elmar Arro und Fritz Feldmann.

Russian music

Garden, Edward, *Balakirev*, Faber and Faber, London, 1966.

Gardner, Johann V., *Das Problem des Altrussischen Domestischen Kirchengesanges*, München, 1967; *Eine Alte Gesangsform des Credo in der Praxis der Russischen Kirche*, Kirchenmusikalische Jahrbücher, 1963; 'Diskographie des Russischen Kirchengesanges' 5.6.7. Folge. *Ostkirchliche Studien*.

Glinka, Michael, *Memoirs*, trans. Richard Mudge, Oklahoma, 1963.

Gretchaninov, Alexander, *My Life*, trans. Nicholas Slonimsky, New York, 1952.

Kastalsky, Alexander, 'My Musical Career and My Thoughts on Church Music', *Musical Quarterly* XI/2, April 1925.

Koschmieder, Erwin, *Die Ältesten Novgoroder Hirmologien-Fragmente*, 3 Folgen, die dritte mit Joh. v. Gardner, München, 1955-63.

Leonard, Richard, *History of Russian Music*, New York, 1956.

Levy, Kenneth, 'Die Slavische Kondakarien-Notation', *Anfänge der Slavischen Musik*, Bratislava, 1966.

Lineva, Eugenie, *Folk-songs of the Ukraine*, Godfrey, Ill., trans. Marie Safonov, preface A. J. Swan.

Mahler, Else, *Altrussische Volkslieder aus dem Pechoryland*, Basel, 1951.

Medtner, Nicolas, *Reminiscences of N. Medtner*, London, 1954.

Mooser, R. A., 'Annales de la Musique et des Musiciens en Russie au 18ème siècle', Geneva, 1948-51.

Newmarch, Rosa. Mili Balakirev, *Sammelbände der Internationalen Musikgesellschaft*, 1902-3.

Palikareva-Verdeil, 'La Musique Byzantine chez les Bulgares et les Russes', *Monumenta Musicae Byzantinae*, Subsidia, vol. III, Copenhagen, 1953.

Rachmaninov, Sergei, *Recollection as told to Oscar v. Riesemann*, London, 1934; 'Recollections by Alfred and Katherine Swan', *Musical Quarterly*, 1944, 1-2.

Rimsky-Korsakov, Nicholas, *My Musical Life*, New York, 1942; 'Recollections' by A. Sandulenko; *The Chesterian*, 1935, trans., Alfred Swan.

Sabaneyev, Leonid, *Modern Russian Composers*, New York, 1927.

Serov, Victor, *Shostakovich* (with materials provided by Nadezhda Galli-Shohat), New York, 1943.

Stassov, Vladimir, *Selected Essays in Music*, trans. Florence Jonas, Barrie and Rockliff, London, 1968.

Stravinsky, Igor, *An Autobiography*, New York, 1936.

Bibliography

Strunk, Oliver, 'The Antiphons of the Octoechos', *Journal of the American Musicological Society*, 1960; 'Zwei Chilandari Chorbücher', *Anfänge der Slavischen Musik*, Bratislava, 1966.

Swan, Alfred, 'The Znamenny Chant of the Russian Church', *Musical Quarterly*, 1940, 2-4; 'The Nature of the Russian Folksong', *Musical Quarterly*, 1943, 4; 'Harmonizations of the Russian Chant', *Journal of the American Musicological Society*, 1948; 'In Quest of the Sources of Russian Music', *Russian Orthodox Journal*, Feb. 1960; 'Russian Liturgical Music and its Relation to 20th Century Ideals', *Music and Letters*, July 1958; 'Die Russische Musik im 17 Jarhundert', *Geschichte Osteuropas*, 1964; *Notes on the Old Liturgical Chant of the Russian Church and the Folk-song*, Jordanville, N.Y., 1967; 'Das Leben Nikolai Medtners', *Musik des Ostens*, Band 4, 1966.

Tchaikovsky, Peter, *Diaries*, New York, 1946.

Tcherepnin, Alexander, *Anthology of Russian Music*, Belaieff, 1966 (English version by Alfred Swan).

Velimirovič, Miloš, 'Stand der Forschung über Kirchenslavische Musik', *Zeitschrift für Slavische Philologie*, 1962; 'Byzantine Elements in Russian Church Music', *Monumenta Musicae Byzantinae*, Subsidia, vol. IV.

Weinstock, Herbert, *Tchaikovsky*, New York, 1943.

Zemtzovsky, Izaly, *Die Folkloristik in der Russischen SFSR*, Leningrad, 1968.

Index

ADRIAN, Patriarch, 208
The Age of Gold (Shostakovich), 201
Aksakov, Serge, 184
Aleko (Rachmaninov), 149-50, 172
Alexander II, Czar, 23, 67, 73, 109
Alexeyevna, Katherine, 11
Alexis, Czar, 48, 50n
d'Alheim, Baron and Mme Olenina, 178, 189
Aliabiev, Alexander, 61
All-Night Vigil (Rachmaninov), 44, 174n
All-Night Vigil chant (Tchaikovsky), 119
Allegri, Gregorio, 45
Allegro Appassionato, Op. 4 (Scriabin), 152
Alphabets, old Russian, 32-3, 138, 194, 207
Altschuler, Modest, 167-8
Ambrose of Milan, St, 39
Andante Cantabile (Tchaikovsky), 195
Antar (Rimsky-Korsakov), 95, 126
L'Antica Melurgia Bizantina, 208
Apukhtin, 107 & n
Araja, Francesco, 52
Arensky, Anton S., 120n, 146n, 149
Assafiev, Boris (Igor Glebov), 16, 59, 68, 72, 96, 110n, 125, 146n, 161, 173, 184, 188, 195, 197-99, 201
Auer, Leopold, 192
Autobiography (Prokofiev), 183-4
Autobiography (Stravinsky), 164
Avdeyev, 142

BACH, Johann Sebastian, 26, 82, 91, 132, 133, 139, 175, 176, 177

Bakhmetev Ordinarium, 116, 117
Bakhturin, 67
Bakst, Lev Samoylovich, 166
Balakirev, Mili (and Circle), 70, 76-90, 91, 94, 98, 104, 113, 117, 125, 126, 127 & n, 130, 135, 138, 142, 155, 172, 177, 182, 189; relations with Cui, 79-80; and Stassov brothers, 79-80; his folksongs, 80-4, 107, 125, 132, 137, 161, 195, 206; Moussorgsky's opposing views, 84-5, 92-3; and Rimsky-Korsakov, 86-7, 95, 96, 97, 98, 125, 128; his dislike of academic discipline, 88; Serov's relations with, 88-90; withdraws from Circle, 103; Tchaikovsky and, 106, 107; influence on Borodin, 111; church music and, 119-120; clash between Belaieff and, 122; Glazunov and, 123-4; last years, 159-62
Ballet music, 109, 128, 147, 159, 165-6, 185, 186, 201
Basement of the Stray Dog (St Petersburg), 183
Beethoven, Ludwig van, 54, 56, 57, 66, 69, 82, 112, 113, 148, 170, 179, 190, 195, 201
Belaieff, M. P., 121-3, 124, 125, 142, 147, 150, 154, 155, 156, 162, 164, 166, 167, 207
Belinsky, V. G., 84, 135
The Bells (Rachmaninov), 174
Belsky, Vladimir, 158, 159, 163 & n
Benois, Alexander, 166
Berezovsky, Nikolai, 54, 63

Berg, Alban, 201
Berlioz, Hector, 66, 74, 78, 80, 111n
Besseler, Heinrich, 35n
Bezborodko family, 56
Bilibin, Ivan, 166, 168-9
Blumenfeld brothers, 123
Boris Godunov (Moussorgsky), 85, 92, 93, 94, 96, 99-103, 104, 105, 197, 199
Borodin, Alexander, 94, 97, 105, 122, 127n, 130, 197; Balakirev Circle and, 77, 90, 103; life and work, 110-13; chamber music of, 113-14; Belaieff publishes work of, 123; influence on Glazunov, 124; posthumous editing of his work, 125-6
Bortniansky, Dimitry, 54, 59, 63
Brahms, Johannes, 74, 82, 131, 170, 185, 201
Brajnikov, Maxim V., 11, 32, 38, 43-4, 45, 46n, 47, 194-5, 200, 204, 209
Bulgarian Chant, 35
Byely, Andrei, 179
Bylinas, byliny (historical songs), 22-23, 24, 156
Byron, Lord, 150
Byshkovsky, Stephen, 33-6
Byzantium, Byzantine music, 22, 30, 31-2, 34, 39, 42, 139, 140, 208-209

CACCINI, Giulio, 48
Calvocoressi, M. D., 162
Carols *(kolyada)*, 23-4
Catherine the Great, 28, 54, 57, 58, 66
Catoire, G., 195
Caucasian Prisoner (Pushkin), 78
Cavalli, Pietro Francesco, 48
Cello Sonata, Op. 19 (Rachmaninov), 153, 173
Chaliapin, Feodor Ivanovich, 153, 158n, 189, 193
Chant Nationaux Russes, One Hundred, Op. 24 (Rimsky-Korsakov coll.), 97n, 206

Cherubim Song, 11, 46n, 47, 50-1
Cherubim Song in C (Glinka), 67
Chicago World Fair (1893), 140
Childhood (Prokofiev), 184n
The Choir-Master's Companion, 36
Chopin, Frédéric, 68, 81n, 142, 145n 157; influence on Scriabin, 151-2, 154
Chout (The Buffoon: Prokofiev), 185, 186
Christmas Eve (Rimsky-Korsakov), 147
Christmas Kontakion (Kastalsky), 145
Chronicle of my Musical Life (Rimsky-Korsakov), 93, 94, 95, 156
Church music, *see* Liturgical chant; *Znamenny* chant
Les Cinq ('mighty little band'), 86 & n
Cinq Novelettes (Glazunov), 124
Classical Symphony, Op. 25 (Prokofiev), 185, 186
Concert Spiritual (Rachmaninov), 11, 150
Concerti, *see* Piano Concerti; Violin Concerti
Concerti Ecclesiastici (Viadana), 50
Concerts Spirituels, 63
Conservatoire, *see* Moscow; St Petersburg
Constantine, Grand Duke (pseudonym: K. R.), 163
Contemporary Music, 196
Conus, George, Julius and Leo, 195 & n
Coq d'Or (Golden Cockerel: Rimsky-Korsakov), 159, 161
Court Chant, 115-16, 117, 120
Coxe, Rev. William, 52, 55, 136
Crane, Charles, 19n, 140, 192-3
Crime and Punishment (Dostoyevsky), 73, 100
Cui, César, 77-8, 80, 82, 86, 95, 103, 113, 122, 127, 139, 153, 173
Czar Sultan (Rimsky-Korsakov), 158, 163
Czar's Bride (Rimsky-Korsakov), 158

Index

DA u LEBEDIA (folk-song), 28
Dahl, N. V., 153
Dance songs (*pylasovyia*), 22, 23, 137
Danilin, 176
Dargomyjsky, Alexander Sergeyevich, 70, 74-6, 78, 90, 93, 94, 95, 113, 158; death of, 111
Debussy, Claude, 69, 182
Decembrist uprising (1825), 66
The Defeat of Sennacherib (Moussorgsky), 94
Degree Book (*Stepennaya Kniga*), 31, 32, 36, 41
Dehn, Siegfried, 63, 65, 70, 74, 75, 87, 116
demestvenny chant, 31, 36, 40, 41, 42, 45
Demidov-San Donato, Count, 79
Derjanovsky, Vladimir and Mme Konosova, 191, 198
Diaghilev, Serge, 158n, 165-6, 168, 185, 186
Diletzky, Nicholas, 50, 51, 52
Dimitry Krasny, Prince, 40, 52
Dionysius, Bishop, 43
Divine Poem (Scriabin), 167, 169, 170
Doluhanova (singer), 180
Don Cossack Wedding Rite, 27-8, 207
Dostoyevsky, Fyodor, 73, 100, 109
Dove Book (*golubinaya kniga*), 22-3
Dvořák, Antonin, 82
Dyutch, G., 142; *see also* Istomin-Dyutch folk-song collection

EASTER OVERTURE (*Overture on Liturgical Themes*: Rimsky-Korsakov), 44, 120, 126-7
Egmont Overture (Beethoven), 69
Eight Russian Folk-Songs (Liadov), 142
1812 Overture (Tchaikovsky), 109, 130, 201
Elegy, *see protyajnaia*
Elgar, Edward, 62, 201
Elizabeth, Empress, 53-4, 57
Ellis, 134
Elman, Mischa, 192

Enchantress (Tchaikovsky), 128, 129, 130
Engel, Julius, 148n
Eugene Onegin (Tchaikovsky), 108n
Euphrosinius, 49, 51
Evenings of Contemporary Music, 182, 191
Examples of the Old Russian Art of Singing (Uspensky), 44 & n

FAIR OF SOROCHINTZY (Moussorgsky), 104
Fairy Tales (Medtner), 179
Falstaff (Elgar), 201
Family songs, 22
Fantasia on themes from Ivan Sussanin (Balakirev), 76
Fauré, Gabriel, 182, 195
Feodor, Czar, 29, 48, 50 & n, 51
Feodor the Christian, 24, 28, 38, 41, 42-3, 44, 51-2, 194, 209
Field, John, 62
Fifteen Songs, Op. 26 (Rachmaninov), 172
Fifty Songs of the Russian People (Liadov), 143
Filippov, Tertius (folk-song collection), 22, 98, 135-6, 137, 140, 195
Findeisen, Nicholas, 15-16, 40n, 55n, 57, 193-4, 200
Firebird (*Oiseau de Feu*: Stravinsky), 159, 165
Flammes Sombres, Op. 73 (Scriabin), 170
Fleischner, Oskar, 208
Floros, Constantine, 209
Folk-songs, 15, 16, 17, 19-29, 31, 38, 78, 135-46, 170, 190; grouping, 21-4; heterophony in, 25-6; lack of tonic, 27-8; and metrical construction, 28; close links between znamenny chant and, 38, 43-4, 46, 49; Teplov's song-book, 54-5; Trutovsky's albums, 55-6; Prach album, 56; N. A. Lvov, 56-7; serf orchestras, 58; Khandoshkin's *Variations* on, 58, 59; *pesennost* in, 60-1; Glinka's

Folk-songs—*contd.*
approach to, 65-6; and Odoyevsky, 71; Balakirev and, 80-5,
124, 161; Moussorgsky's use of,
84-5, 96, 102; and Tchaikovsky,
88, 107, 108, 109, 130; and
Rimsky-Korsakov, 96, 97-8, 99,
125, 141; Belaieff's indifference
to, 123; Taneyev's view of, 131-2;
and Filippov's enthusiasm, 135-6;
Melgunov collection, 136; Palchikov collection, 136; Istomin
and Dyutch collection, 136-7; and
Lineva, 140-1; and Liadov, 141-
143; Kastalsky's work on, 145-6;
Rachmaninov's use of, 151, 153,
172; early 20th century renaissance in, 156; Medtner's approach
to, 179-80; and Prokofiev, 186-7;
Goedicke's settings of, 195; modern folklorists, 203-4; list of collections (App. I), 206-7; Gorodishche Wedding rite (App. III),
210-16
Fortune-telling songs (*podbliudnyia*),
24
Forty Folk-songs (Filippov collection),
98n, 206
Foundations of Popular Polyphony (Kastalsky), 146
Fourteen Songs, Op. 34 (Rachmaninov), 172, 174
Francesca da Rimini (opera: Rachmaninov), 172
Francesca da Rimini (tone poem:
Tchaikovsky), 109
Free Music School, 93-4, 95, 97, 111
& n, 117

GABRIELI, Andrea and Giovanni,
50, 175
Gardner, Ivan A., 11, 194n, 204
also Gardner, Johann von, 36, 64
Gaze with attention (*Vaizay s prile-
janiem:* folk-song), 23
Gedeonov (Director of Imperial
Theatre), 127n
Genoveve (Schumann), 86

Gerke, 79
Ghirlandes (Scriabin), 170
Gippius folk-song collection, 207
Giraldus Cambrensis, 25
Glazunov, Alexander, 114, 127, 129,
168, 177, 184, 192, 197, 203;
Belaieff Circle and, 121, 122, 123-
124, 147; Borodin's work edited
by, 125-6; conducts Rachmaninov
symphony, 152, 153; slowing
down of creative process (1903-
1915), 162-4; protests against
Prokofiev's *Scythian Suite*, 185; and
criticism of Miaskovsky, 189-190;
last years, 194-5; Shostakovich
and, 200, 201
Glebov, Igor, *see* Assafiev
Glinka, Mikhail Ivanovich, 15, 24,
34, 53, 61, 62-72, 73, 78, 79, 82,
91, 106, 110, 126, 135, 136, 172,
176, 189, 198; early life and work,
62-3; *pesennost* of, 65-6, 142; operas
by, 66-9, 90; and Spanish overtures, 69; critics' view of, 70-2, 89;
relations with Dargomyjsky, 74-6;
and Balakirev, 76-7, 80-1; Rimsky-
Korsakov's admiration for, 95;
church music and, 116, 119
The God of the Fields (*Tausen:* folk-
song), 24
Goedicke, Alexander, 151, 195
Goethe, Johann Wolfgang von, 178
Gogol, Nicholas, 67, 84, 94, 104, 147,
201
Golitzyn family, 62
Golovina, Gavril, 35-6
Golubinaya kniga, see Dove Book
Goncharov, Ivan, 73
Gonzalez, 58
Gorky, Maxim, 197
Gorodishche Wedding Rite, 21, 205,
210-16 (App. III)
Gospel Stichera, see Stichera
Grabar, 164
Great Immovable Feasts, book of,
see Prazdniky
Greater Chant, 42-4
Greek Chant, 34, 35

Gregorian Chant, 37, 70, 140
Gregory I, 39
Gretchaninov, Alexander, 146n
Grieg, Edvard, 82, 139, 182
Grigoriev, Appollon, 81, 105
Grigory the Pretender, 22
Grotta Ferrata Monastery, 208, 209
Guido of Arezzo, 30
Guriliov, 61
Gutheil (music publisher), 149-50

HANDEL, George Frederick, 132
Haydn, Joseph, 113
Hebrew Melody (Balakirev), 84
Heifetz, Jascha, 192, 195n
Heine, Heinrich, 178
Heirmologian (Book I of *znamenny* canticles), 34
Helen Paulovna, Grand Duchess, 87
Henselt, 79, 147
Herzen, Alexander, 184
Heterophony, 25-6, 46, 136
Hindemith, Paul, 201
Historical songs, *see bylinas*
Hopak (Moussorgsky), 93
House of Song (Moscow), 178

ILYIN, Ivan, 179
Immortelles (Taneyev), 134
Imperial Choir, Chapel (St Petersburg), 53, 54, 59, 63, 67, 115-20, 122, 123, 125, 138, 145, 146n, 159, 160
Imperial Geography Society, 137, 140
Imperial Opera, Theatres (St Petersburg), 112, 127n, 141, 159, 164, 173, 197
Imperial Russian Music Society, 87, 97, 111n, 112, 162, 169; *see also* Saint Petersburg Conservatoire
In the field stood a little birch tree (folk-song), 109
In the Steppes of Central Asia (Borodin), 113, 126
In the village Pokrovskoye (folk-song), 57

Internationale, 192, 193
Ippolitov-Ivanov, Mikhail, 192
Ireland, John, 130
Islamey (Balakirev), 160
Isle of the Dead (Rachmaninov), 172
Istomin (Th.) and Dyutch (George) folk-song collections, 19-20, 23, 25, 38, 136-7, 140, 141, 142, 161, 186, 206
Istomin (Th.) and Liapunov (Serge), folk-song collection, 137, 141, 206
The Italian Capriccio (Tchaikovsky), 109
Ivan IV, Czar (the 'Terrible'), 22, 29, 31, 40 & n, 41, 42, 51, 52, 209
Ivan Sussain, see Life for the Czar
Ivanovka (Satin estate), 171-2, 173
Ivanushka the Fool (popular tale), 180

JENOUK, Serge, 11
Joseph II, Emperor (of Austria), 57
Josquin Després, 27, 133
Jota Aragonesa (Glinka), 69
Judith (Serov), 89
Jukovsky, 67
Jupiter Symphony (Mozart), 65
Jurgenson, Peter, 118, 145 & n, 150, 184, 193

KALLISTRAT (Moussorgsky), 94
Kamarinskaya (Glinka), 15, 69, 82
Kant, Immanuel, 178
Karamzin, Nicholas M., 101
Karatygin, Viacheslav, 182-3, 184, 196-7, 198, 199
Karmalina, 70
Karsavina, 166
Kashin, Daniel (folk-song collection), 61, 65, 81, 206
Kastalsky, Alexander, 26, 143-6, 163, 173, 189, 193
Kazmin, *see* Sakharov-Kazmin folk-song collection
Keldysh, Y., 58n
Khandoshkin, Ivan, 58, 59, 63
Khomiakov, Aleksey, 161
Khorovodnyia, see Roundelays

Khovanshchina (Moussorgsky), 92, 103, 104, 125, 197
Kiev chant, 35
King Lear (Balakirev), 82
King of Judea (Glazunov), 163
Kitej legends, *see Legend of the Invisible City Kitej*
Kliech (*Key*: Makarievsk), 33
Kolotilova folk-song collection, 207
Kolyada, see carols
Kompaneisky, Nicholas, 146n
Kondakov, 164
Kontratyev, 129
Korenev, Ivan, 49-50, 51, 52
Korff, Baron, 79
Korovin, 166
Koukouzeles, Master John, 39
Krenek, Ernst, 201
Kriuk notation, *see Neume*
Krylov, Ivan A., 127n
Kurbsky, Andrey M., 40n
Kussevitzky, Serge, 168-9, 174, 179, 192, 195

LAMENTS, *see Protyajnaia*
Lamm, Paul, 199-200
Lapshin, Prof. Ivan, 158-9, 164-5, 188
Laroche, Herman, 127
Legend of the Invisible City Kitej and the Maiden Fevronya (Rimsy-Korsakov) 120, 132, 158-9, 161, 163
Leningrad Institute of the Theatre, Music and Cinema, 204
Leo VI, Emperor of Byzantium ('the Wise'), 42
Leonova, 70
Lermontov, Mikhail, 84, 92, 163
Levy, Kenneth, 209
Lhevinne, Joseph, 148
Liadov, Z., 23, 24, 121, 122, 127, 137, 141-3, 147, 150, 162, 177, 184, 188, 190, 197, 206
Liapunov, Serge, 137, 141, 162
libri usuales, 29
A Life for the Czar (or *Ivan Sussanin:* Glinka), 63, 65, 66, 67, 71; Balakirev's Fantasia on themes from, 76

Lineva, Eugenie (folk-song collection), 19n, 26, 38, 140-1, 163, 164, 192-3, 203, 207
Listopadov folk-song collection, 27-28, 145, 164, 203, 207
Liszt, Franz, 69, 71, 74, 76, 78, 80, 87, 104, 110, 111n, 112
Liturgical music, chants, 15, 16, 28, 63, 70, 130, 143, 144, 161, 170, 190, 203; historical survey, 29-36; Smolensky's work, 32-3, 138-9, 144; nature of the *znamenny* melodies, 36-8, composers and performers, 39-45; Russian polyphony, 45-7; impact of new European music, 48-54; Moussorgsky's interest in, 84-5; Court Chant v. *znamenny chant*, 115-17; Tchaikovsky and, 118-19, 173; and Balakirev Circle, 119-20; Belaieff's exclusion of, 123; Rimsky's works, 126-7, 173; and Taneyev, 132, 133; and Rachmaninov, 150, 151, 153, 173-6; 20th century renaissance in, 156; effect of Russian Revolution on, 193-4, 200; modern research in, 203, 204-5; stages of clarification of Kriuk notation, 207-9; *see also znamenny* chant
Liturgy of St John Chrysostom, Op. 31 (Rachmaninov), 172, 173-4
Liturgy of St John Chrysostom (Tchaikovsky), 118, 119
Loggin the Cow (precentor of Troizk monastery), 43, 51, 52
Lomakin, Gabriel, 117
Lopatin-Prokunin folk-song collection, 206; *see also* Prokunin
Love for Three Oranges (Prokofiev), 186, 187
Love songs, *see Protyajnaia*
Lukoshka, Ivan, 41, 42, 51
Lullaby of Yeriomushka (Moussorgsky), 94
Luntz-Nemenova, Maria, 169
Lvov, Alexis, 63, 67, 116, 117, 120
Lvov family, 56
Lvov, Feodor, 63

Lvov, Nicolas and Prach, Johann-Gottfried (folk-song collection), 56-7, 58, 61, 71, 97, 195, 206

MAETERLINCK, Maurice, 195
Mahler, Elsa (folk-song collection), 21, 207, 210, 212
Mahler, Gustav, 190, 201
The Maid of Orleans (Tchaikovsky), 109
Maïd of Pskov (Rimsky-Korsakov), 107n
Makari, Metropolitan (of Moscow), 31
Makarievsky, 71
Malyshev, Vladimir, 38, 42, 43, 137, 194, 204, 209
Mamontov's private opera, 153, 173
Manfred Symphony (Tchaikovsky), 128
Manuel (singer of *znamenny* chant), 40
Markel the Beardless, 28, 41, 51-2
Marriage (Moussorgsky), 94, 165
Martini, Padre, 63
Maryinsky Theatre, 127n
Masquerade (Lermontev), 163
The May Night (Rimsky-Korsakov), 98, 99, 104
Mazeppa (Tchaikovsky), 130
Mazurkas (Scriabin), 152
Meck, Mme Nadejda von, 109, 118
Medtner, Emil, 177
Medtner, Nicolas, 133, 172, 184, 188, 189, 190, 203; life and work, 176-80; attitude to modernism, 181, 183; effect of Russian Revolution on, 192
Meier, Karl, 62
Meistersinger (Wagner), 69
Meletius, Deacon, 51
Melgunov folk-song collection, 26, 136, 195, 206
Memoirs of M. I. Glinka, 62, 63, 65, 68, 69-70
Mendelssohn Bartholdy, Felix, 74, 114, 145n
Merwolff, R., 165

Metallov, V. M., 39n, 40n, 193
Mey (Russian poet), 105, 107 & n
Mezenetz, Alexander, 32-3, 51, 61, 71, 138, 208, 209
Miaskovsky, Nicolas, 184, 189-91, 203
Miassin, 166
Mir Iskusstva, 165
Mlada (Tchaikovsky), 127, 128, 147
Moniuszko, Stanislaw, 77
Monteverdi, Claudio, 48, 50
Monumenta Musicae Byzantinae, 208
Morning Resurrection Hymns, *see Stichera*
Morozova, Margarita, 154, 166-7, 169
Moscow Conservatoire, 88, 106, 109, 115, 131, 133, 138, 144, 147, 148-149, 150, 154, 176, 177, 191, 192, 193; *see also* St Petersburg Conservatoire
Moscow Synodal School, Choir, 33, 120, 123n, 138, 144, 146 & n, 150, 173, 176, 204
Moskvitianin, 41, 136
Motets (Bach), 175
Moussorgsky, Modest P., 105, 106, 113, 122, 123, 127n, 130, 165, 197; relations between Balakirev and, 77, 78-9, 84-5, 86, 92-3; his view of Serov's *Judith*, 89; formative years, 91-3; songs (1864-8), 93-4, 103; Rimsky-Korsakov and, 95, 97, 98, 99; *Boris Godunov* by, 96, 99, 100-3, 199; decay and death of, 103-4, 109, 125
Movable exhibitions, *see peradvijniki*
Mozart, Wolfgang Amadeus, 65, 66, 76, 106, 139
Mozart and Salieri (Rimsky-Korsakov) 158
Mozartiana Suite (Tchaikovsky), 129
Muratov, 164
Murometz, Ilya, 22
Muse and Fashion (Medtner), 181
music, 191, 198
Musical Antiquity, 193
Musical Contemporary, 188-9

Musical Grammar (Diletzky), 50
Musikiya (Korenev), 50, 51
Mystery (Scriabin), 170

NAPOLEON III, Emperor, 70
Napravnik, Eduard, 97, 112
Narayshkin family, 56
'Native counterpoint' (Russian polyphony), 45-7, 48, 49, 139
Nesterov, Mikhail, 139, 159, 169
Netherland Fantasy (Taneyev), 132
Neume (Kriuk) notations, 30, 33, 35 & n, 36, 45, 64, 138; stages of clarification and readability of (App. II), 207-9
New Monumenta of the Znamenny Chant (Brajnikov), 44
Newmarch, Rosa, 162
Nicholas I, Czar, 73
Nietzsche, Friedrich, 178
Night in Madrid (Glinka), 69
Nightingale (Stravinsky), 159
Nijinsky, Vaslav, 166
Nikiforov, General, 148
Nikisch, 167, 168
Nikita, Archbishop of Novgorod, 41
Nikon, Patriarch, 51
The Nose (Shostakovich), 201
Noss, Ivan, 41, 42, 52
Not a Word, O My Friend (Pleshcheyev), 107
Not like thunder from Heaven (Moussorgsky), 78
Nouve Musiche, 48
Novgorod, 39-40, 41, 42
The Nursery (Moussorgsky), 103

OBIKHOD (Book IV of *znamenny* canticles), 34, 35, 36, 119, 143, 144
Oblomov (Goncharov), 73
Obrecht, Jacob, 27
Ocean Symphony (Rubinstein), 74
Ockeghem, Jean de, 27, 35n
Octoechos (Book II of *znamenny* canticles), 34
Odoyevsky, Prince Vladimir, 25, 34, 45, 46, 70, 71, 73, 115, 136

Oedipus Rex (Moussorgsky), 85
Oedipus Rex (Stravinsky), 198
Oiseau de Feu, see Firebird
Old Believers (*Raskolniki*), 30, 34-5 & n, 36, 51, 194n
On the porch, the little porch (*Po seyan, seniushkam:* folk-song), 27
Oprichnik (Tchaikovsky), 107
Oresteia (Taneyev), 123, 133
Orlando, 45
Orlev, 144, 150
Orphan (Moussorgsky), 94
Ossorguine, Michel, 146n, 205
Ossovsky (critic), 164-5, 196-7
Ostrovsky, Alexander N., 81, 99, 105
Overture on Liturgical Themes, see Easter Overture
Overture on Three Russian Themes (*Folk Songs*) (Balakirev), 80, 82
Overture to Schiller's Bride of Messina (Liadov), 142

PALCHIKOV folk-song collection, 26, 136, 206
Palestrina, Giovanni, 26, 27, 45, 48, 133, 134, 141
Pan Voyevoda (Rimsky-Korsakov), 157-8
The Past and the Perennial (Stepun), 166-7
The Paths of Development of Znamenny Chant (Brajnikov), 200
Paul, Czar, 58-9, 66
Peasant's Son (Moussorgsky), 85
Pechory (Pskov) monastery, 20, 207
Peculiarities of the Russian Popular System (Kastalsky), 26
Peradvijniki (wandering artists), 73, 139, 165
Pesennost, 24, 60-1, 65-6, 68-9, 76, 142, 172
Peter I (the Great), 23, 49, 51, 52, 53
Peter III, 55
Petite Suite (Borodin), 113
Petroshevsky Circle, 107n

Piano Concerto No. 4 (Beethoven), 179
Piano Concerto in D Minor (Brahms), 131
Piano Concerto (Glazunov), 163
Piano Concerto No. 1, Op. 33 (Medtner), 180
Piano Concerto No. 1, Op. 10 (Prokofiev), 184
Piano Concerto No. 2 (Rachmaninov), 152, 153, 173
Piano Concerto No. 3 (Rachmaninov), 173
Piano Concerto in one movement (Rimsky-Korsakov), 125
Piano Concerto (Rubinstein), 74
Piano Concerto (Scriabin), 150, 168
Piano Concerto No. 1 in B-flat Minor (Tchaikovsky), 107
Piano Sonatas in B-flat Minor and E Major (Glazunov), 162
Piano Sonata, Op. 25, No. 2 (Medtner), 180
Piano Sonatas (Miaskovsky), 190
Piano Sonata No. 1 in D Minor (Rachmaninov), 172, 173
Piatnitzky folk-song collection, 164, 207
Piatnitzky choir, 204, 207
Pictures at an Exhibition (Moussorgsky), 104
Pique Dame (Tchaikovsky), 129, 179
Platonov, Serge F., 73, 197
Platonova, 102
Pleshcheyev, 107 & n
Pobedonostzev, K. P., 138
Podbliudnyia, see Fortune-telling songs
Podgoloski (variant melodies), 26, 136, 206
Poem for Violin and Piano (Catoire), 195
Poem of Ecstasy (*Poème d'Extase:* Scriabin), 130, 167, 169, 170
Poem of Fire, see Prometheus
Poems, Op. 32 (Scriabin), 154
Poltoratzky, Mark, 54
Pomazansky, 142
Potemkin, Prince Grigoriy, 55
Potulov, 117

Prach, Johann-Gottfried, *see* Lvov and Prach folk-song collection
Praise of the Desert (Introduction to *Kitej:* Rimsky-Korsakov), 159
Prayer (Moussorgsky), 85
Prazdniky (Book III of *znamenny* canticles: Great Immovable Feasts), 34, 35, 36
Preface (to sacred music anthology, *c.* 1650), 32, 40-1, 51
Prelude in C-sharp Minor (Rachmaninov), 151
Prelude in E-flat Major (Rachmaninov), 173
Prelude to the Blind (Goedicke), 195
Preludes, Op. 11 (Scriabin), 148, 152
Preobrajensky, Anton, 51n, 189, 194, 199, 208
Prince Igor (Borodin), 112, 114, 123, 197; posthumous 'editing' of, 125-126
Prince Kholmsky (Glinka), 66, 69
Prison songs, 22
Prokofiev, Sergei, 166, 168, 183-7, 188, 189, 191, 198, 203
Prokunin folk-song collection, 26, 107, 108, 206
Prometheus (*Poem of Fire:* Scriabin), 169, 170, 174
Protopopov, Catherine (wife of Borodin), 111, 112, 114
Protyajnaia (elegies, love songs), 22, 24, 38, 204
Pskovityanka (Rimsky-Korsakov), 96, 97
Purcell, Henry, 62
Purgold, Alexandra, 95
Purgold, Nadejda (later: wife of Rimsky-Korsakov), 95
Pushkin, Alexander, 15, 67, 78, 84, 101, 108n, 158, 178, 179, 180
Put, 167
Pylasovyia, see Dance songs

QUARTET No. 1 in A Major (Borodin), 113-14
Quartet No. 2 in D Major (Borodin), 114

Russian music

Quartet No. 2 with voice (Schoenberg), 183
Quartet, Piano (Catoire), 195
Quartets (Miaskovsky), 190

RACHMANINOV, Serge, 11, 33, 44, 138, 155, 156, 158, 168, 169, 180, 184, 186, 188, 189, 204; early years, 148-50; difference in style between Scriabin and, 151-4; and later period (1903-15), 171-6; Medtner praised by, 179; leaves Russia for Sweden (1917), 192
Raimonda (Glazunov), 147
Raskolniki, see Old Believers
Rasputin, 189
Ravel, Maurice, 110
Razin, Stenka, 22
Razumovsky, Alexis, 45, 53-4, 138
Razumovsky, Dimitry, 115-16
Razumovsky Quartets, Op. 59 (Beethoven), 54, 56
Reger, Max, 182, 183
Religious art, 139, 140, 145, 159, 164, 169
Reminiscences of Scriabin (Sabaneyev), 169n, 171
Repin, Ilya, 104, 197
Reverie, Op. 24 (Scriabin), 152
Rimsky-Korsakov, Andri, 188
Rimsky-Korsakov, Nicholas, 44, 77, 105, 106, 110, 113, 114, 130, 132, 137, 139, 151, 155, 161, 162, 163, 168, 172, 189, 197, 201; relations with Balakirev, 86-7, 88, 95, 122, 128; his view of Serov's Rognyeda, 90; Moussorgsky and, 92, 93, 100, 101; formative years of, 94-7; folk-songs, 97-8, 107, 195, 206; and operas, 96, 98-9, 104, 107n, 127, 132, 136, 141, 147, 156-9; and church music, 119-20, 126-7, 173; relations with Belaieff, 122, 123; and Glazunov, 123-4; during 1880s, 125-8; editing of Borodin's work by, 125-6; last years of, 156-9; Wednesday evening gatherings of disciples at house of, 164-5

The Rite of Spring (Stravinsky), 166
Roeder, C. G., 122
Rognyeda (Servo), 90
Rogov, Savva and Vassili, 41, 42
Romeo and Juliet (Tchaikovsky), 88n
Roundelay (folk-song), 83
Roundelays (Khorovodnyia), 22, 23, 24, 137
Rubetz folk-song collection, 99, 107, 206
Rubinstein, Anton, 74, 87-8, 90, 93, 96, 106, 148
Rubinstein, Nicholas, 74, 87, 88, 105, 108, 115, 128, 131, 145n; death of, 109-10
Rupin, Ivan (Rupini), 61, 81, 206
Russalka (Dargomyjsky), 75-6, 89, 93
Russia (A Thousand Years: Balakirev), 82
Russian Civil War, 162, 196
Russian Music from the beginning of the nineteenth century (Assafiev), 16, 199
The Russian Musical Editions, 168-9
Russian Musical Gazette, 193
Russian Polyphony, see 'Native counterpoint'
Russian Revolution (1905), 162
Russian Revolution (1917), 16, 146, 166, 191-5, 200, 201
Russian soldier's song (Balakirev collection), 125
Russian Symphony Concerts, 121, 122, 165
Russlan and Ludmilla (Glinka), 66, 67-9, 71, 126
Russlan and the Russlanists (Serov), 72
Russo-Japanese War (1904), 162

SABANEYEV, Leonid, 105, 169 & n, 171
Sacred Symphonies (Gabrieli), 175
Sadko (Rimsky-Korsakov), 95, 97, 147, 156-7, 157, 158
Safonov, Maria, 148, 149, 150, 152, 154, 176
Saharov, I. P., 71

230

St Petersburg Concert Hall of the Nobility, 139

St Petersburg Conservatoire (formerly Imperial Russian Music Society), 87, 88, 95, 96-7, 106, 111, 124, 142, 153, 162-3, 164, 184, 189-90, 192, 194, 200

Sakharov-Kazmin folk-song collection, 204, 207

Salammbo music (Moussorgsky), 85

Sandulenko, A., 165n

Sartori, 58

Satin, Natalie (wife of Rachmaninov, 153

Satin, Sophie, 149n, 171-2, 176

Savishna (Moussorgsky), 94

Scheherezade (Rimsky-Korsakov), 126

Schoenberg, Arnold, 183, 201

School of the Reformed Churches (St Petersburg), 121

Schubert, Franz, 70, 128

Schumann, Clara, 188

Schumann, Robert, 63, 74, 80, 86, 106, 111 & n, 139, 142, 145n, 177, 182

Scriabin, Alexander, 33, 122, 130, 133, 156, 163, 164, 166, 173, 177, 179, 182, 190, 195n, 203; early years, 148-9, 150-1; differences in style between Rachmaninov and, 151-4; later years and death of, 167-71, 174, 188

Scythian Suite, Op. 20 (Prokofiev), 185

Selected Correspondence with Friends (Gogol), 84

Semenov, Ivan B., 11

Senilov, V., 165

Serenade for Strings (Tchaikovsky), 109

Serf orchestras, 58, 62

Serov, Alexander, 57n, 66, 70, 71-2, 74, 75, 77, 78, 93, 106, 136; opposition to Balakirev Circle, 88-90

Servilia (Rimsky-Korsakov), 157

Shaginian, Marietta, 179

Shaidur, Ivan (Shaidurov), 30n, 35, 49, 51, 64, 71, 204, 207-8, 209

Shchiglyov, Misha, 111

Shestakova, Mme Ludmilla, 70, 72, 75, 76, 77, 94, 95, 103, 122

Shostakovich, Dimitry, 197, 198, 199, 200-2, 203

Siloti, Alexander, 165, 185, 189, 192

Sinfonia Domestica (Strauss), 181

Sketches for the history of music in Russia (Findeisen), 15-16, 193

Sleep (Moussorgsky), 85

The Sleeping Beauty (Tchaikovsky), 128

Sleeplessness (Medtner), 180

Smolensky, Stephen, 11, 32-3, 45, 46, 138-9, 144, 146 & n, 176, 193, 209

Snegurochka (Rimsky-Korsakov), 96, 98-9, 105, 125, 158

So Quickly to Forget (Apukhtin), 107

So, you marriage brokers (*Da svaty moi*), 27

Sokolov, N., 182

Soldiers' songs, 22, 24, 125, 137

Sollertinsky, Ivan, 201

Solvetzky Library (Kazan), 138

Sonata No. 2 (Glazunov), 177

Sonata No. 3 in F-sharp Minor (Scriabin), 152

Sonata No. 4 (Scriabin), 154

Sonata No. 5 (Scriabin), 167

Sonatas (Medtner), 179, 180

Song of Georgia (Balakirev), 84

Song of Selim (Balakirev), 84

Song of the Golden Fish (Balakirev), 84

Song of the Volga Boatmen (folk-song), 82, 124n

Songs and Dances of Death (Moussorgsky), 104

Songs from Many Lands (Swan coll.), 186 & n

Songs of the Russian People (Istomin-Dyutch coll.), 20n

Souvenir of Hapsal (Tchaikovsky), 106

Spies, Maria, 21

The Spill (Loochina), 61

Spiritual Verses, 22, 23, 137

Spohr, Louis, 74

Spring Cantata (Rachmaninov), 153

Stahlin, Jacob von, 55
Stakhovich, Apollon (folk-song collection), 19, 25, 81, 97, 105, 107, 206
Stalin, Josef, 17
Stassov, Dimitry, 70, 77, 80, 189
Stassov, Vladimir, 68, 71-2, 74, 77, 79-80, 82, 85n, 88, 89, 92, 93, 94, 95, 97, 101, 103-4, 106, 111, 112, 114, 121, 122, 123, 139, 162, 163, 189, 197
State Academic Choir, Moscow, 176
Steinberg, Maximilian, 164-5, 195
Stenka Razin (Glazunov), 124n
Stepennaya Kniga, see Degree Book
Stephen the Pauper, 41, 42
Stepun, Feodor, 166-7
Stichera, Gospel (Morning Resurrection Hymns), 40, 40, 42-3
The Stone Guest (Dargomyjsky), 90, 93, 158
Strauss, Johann, 114
Strauss, Richard, 177, 181, 201
Stravinsky, Igor, 159, 164-5, 170, 182, 189, 198, 201
Stroganov family, 41 & n, 51
Strunk, Oliver, 209
Suite No. 1 in D Major (Tchaikovsky), 109, 118, 130
Suite No. 2 (Tchaikovsky), 129
Sunless (Moussorgsky song-cycle), 104
Svetik Savishna (Moussorgsky), 93
Swan, Ekaterina, 21n
Swan folk-song collection, 20-1, 207, 210-16
Swan Lake (Tchaikovsky), 109
Symphony No. 1 in D Minor (Balakirev), 127n, 160-1
Symphony No. 1 in E-flat Major (Borodin), 90, 111-12
Symphony No. 2 in B Minor (Borodin), 112
Symphony No. 3 in A Minor (Borodin), 114
Symphony No. 1 in E Major (Glazunov, 121, 162
Symphony No. 6 (Glazunov), 147

Symphony No. 7 in F Minor (Glazunov), 162, 164
Symphony No. 1 (Miaskovsky), 189-190
Symphony No. 6 (Miaskovsky), 190
Symphony No. 1 in D Minor (Rachmaninov), 152-3, 173
Symphony No. 2 in E Minor, Op. 27 (Rachmaninov), 172, 173
Symphony No. 1 in E Minor (Rimsky-Korsakov), 95
Symphony No. 2 (*Antar:* Rimsky-Korsakov), 95, 126
Symphony No. 1 in E Major (Scriabin), 154
Symphony No. 2 in C Minor (Scriabin), 154
Symphony No. 3 in C (Scriabin), 167
Symphony No. 1 in F Minor, Op. 10 (Shostakovich), 201
Symphony No. 2 (Shostakovich), 201
Symphony No. 3 (Shostakovich), 201
Symphony No. 1 in G Minor (Tchaikovsky), 106-7
Symphony No. 2 in C Minor (Tchaikovsky), 107
Symphony No. 4 in F Minor (Tchaikovsky), 109, 118, 130
Symphony No. 5 in E Minor (Tchaikovsky), 128, 129
Symphony No. 6 in B Minor (*Pathétique:* Tchaikovsky), 129, 130
Symphonies, *see also Classical, Jupiter, Manfred, Ocean* and *Sacred Symphonies*

TALE OF IGOR'S HOST (Borodin), 112
Tales of the Old Grandmother, Op. 31 (Prokofiev), 185
Tamara (Balakirev), 126, 160
Taneyev, Serge I., 123, 124, 130, 131-134, 148, 149, 156, 163, 179, 184, 188
Tardo, Dom Lorenzo, 208
Tchaikovsky, Peter, 15, 69, 77, 86, 112, 113, 127, 145n, 154, 155, 156,

169, 175, 176, 179, 190, 195, 198, 201; his approach to folk-music, 87-8; Moscow life up to 1881, 105-110; church music and, 118-19, 120, 173; influence on Glazunov of, 124; last years, 128-31; influence on Taneyev, 131; Rachmaninov and, 172
Tcherepnin, N., 165
Tcherevickhi (Tchaikovsky), 130
Tchernyshevsky, Nicholas, 135
Tchesnokov, Paul, 146 & n
Ten Preludes for Piano, Op. 23 (Rachmaninov), 153
Ten Settings from the Obikhod (Liadov), 143, 144
Teplov, Grigory (song collection), 54-5
Theatrical music, 58-9
Theotokia-Dogmatic, 146n
There Races on the Gallant Troika (Rupin), 61
Thirty-Five Songs of the Russian People, 23, 24
A Thousand Years, see Russia
Tikhon of Makarievsk, 33, 51, 208
Tillyard, 208
Titov, Vassili, 51, 52
Toccata, Op. 11 (Prokofiev), 185
Tolstoy, Leo, 73, 100, 153, 184
Tolstoy, Th. M., 62
Tragic and Satanic Poems (Scriabin), 154
Trio, Op. 9 (Rachmaninov), 172
Trio in A Minor (Tchaikovsky), 109-110, 128
Triodion (Book V of *znamenny* canticles), 35, 37, 41, 42
Triumphlied (Brahms), 201
Troyanovsky, Dr, 192
Trubetzkoy, Prince, 179
Trutovsky folk-song collection, 55-6, 57, 61, 206
Turgenev, Ivan, 94
Tutchev, 178, 179, 180
Tvorimir, Jacob, 50
Twelve Russian Folk-Songs (Prokofiev), 186

UGLY DUCKLING, Op. 18 (Prokofiev), 185
Ulybyshev, 70, 76
Upon the Reading of a Psalm (Taneyev), 132
Uspensky, N., 44 & n, 45-6, 194, 204

VANLIARSKY, Feodor, 78
Variations on Folk-Songs (Khandoshkin), 58, 59
Varlamov, 61, 71
Vassili II, Czar, 29, 42
Vassnetzov, Viktor M., 139, 169
Vaughan Williams, Ralph, 46, 82
Velimirovic, Milos, 209
Vespers (Rachmaninov), 174-6
Viadana, Lodovico Grosso da, 50
Villebois folk-song collection, 81, 107, 206
Villoing, 87
Violin Concerto (Glazunov), 163
Violin Concerto No. 1, Op. 19 (Prokofiev), 185
Violin Concerto (Tchaikovsky), 109
Violin Sonata, Op. 21 (Medtner), 179
Vision (Balakirev), 161
Volga Expedition (Balakirev's), 81-2, 161
Voskressensky chronicle, 40

WAGNER, Richard, 69, 71, 74, 78, 89, 90, 105, 124, 127, 145n, 152, 154, 167, 168, 170, 178
War and Peace (Tolstoy), 73, 100
Weber, Carl Maria, 98
Wedding songs, rites, 22, 27-8; Gorodishche, 21, 205, 210-16
Wedel, 54
Wellesz, Egon, 208, 209
White fluffy snow (Sneshki belye, pushisty: folk-song), 25
Why (Mey), 107
Why, O Willow, are you bending (Medtner), 179, 180
William Ratcliffe (Cui), 86
Winter Night, Op. 13 (Medtner), 179, 180

World War I, 156, 184-5, 188-191
World War II, 200, 204

YASTREBSTEV, 164-5
Youth of St Sergius (Nesterov), 159

ZABELIN, Ivan, 49
Zaitsev, Karil (Archimandrate Constantine), 110n
Zemtzovsky, Izaly J., 11, 24n, 204
Zimmerman, Prof. Franklin, 11
Znamenny chant, 31-44, 60, 65, 71, 78, 99, 102, 118, 127, 143, 175, 193, 194; origins, 31-3; and preservation of, 33-6; melodic nature of, 36-8; close link between folk-songs and, 38; makers of, 39-42; Gospel *Stichera*, 42-4; Russian Polyphony, 45-6; Golden Age of, 48-9; attacks against, 49-50; impact of new European music on, 50-4; 19th-century Court Chant and, 115-17; Liadov's use of, 143, 144; and Kastalsky's revival of, 144-5, 163; Tchesnokov and Kompaneisky, 146 & n; use in modern music of, 204-5; clarification and readability of Kriuk notation, 207-9
Zverev (Nicholas) Pension, Moscow, 147-8